HUAREO
Story of a Jamaican Cacique

Fred Kennedy worked as a teacher and principal for over thirty years, in both Jamaica and Canada. He has devoted much of his retirement to writing historical fiction: the well-acclaimed *Daddy Sharpe* (2008), his present novel, *Huareo* (2015) and soon-to-be completed, *Where the Pineapple Could Not Grow: Memoirs of a Maroon Chief*. He and his wife Georgianne share their time between his native Jamaica and adopted Canada, where their three daughters and families reside.

Dear Nicole,

HUAREO
Story of a Jamaican Cacique

with best wishes.

A Novel by
Fred W. Kennedy

Fred

IAN RANDLE PUBLISHERS
Kingston • Miami

First published in Jamaica, 2015 by
Ian Randle Publishers
11 Cunningham Avenue
Box 686
Kingston 6
www.ianrandlepublishers.com

NATIONAL LIBRARY OF JAMAICA
CATALOGUING-IN-PUBLICATION DATA

Kennedy, Fred W.
    Huareo : Story of a Jamaican cacique / Fred W. Kennedy

    pages : illustrations, maps; cm.

 ISBN 978-976-637-859-2 (pbk)

1. Historical fiction, Jamaican   2. Jamaican fiction
I. Title

813   dc 23

Cover image Portrait of Huareo, Taíno Cacique
by Lloyd George Rodney © Fred W. Kennedy
Cover and Book Design by Ian Randle Publishers
Printed and bound in the United States

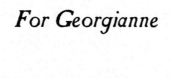

For Georgianne

Those who remain alive after my death will enjoy their dominion for but a brief time because a clothed people will come to their land who will overcome them and kill them, and they will die of hunger.

Cacibaquel, Cacique of Haití

Jamaica,

it is the fairest island that eyes have beheld:

mountainous, and the land seems to touch the sky.

Christopher Columbus

But did his vision
fashion as he watched the shore
the slaughter that his soldiers

furthered here? Pike
point & musket butt
hot splintered courage. Bones

cracked with bullet shot
tipped black boot in my belly. The
whips uncurled desire?

From "Colombe" by Kamau Brathwaite

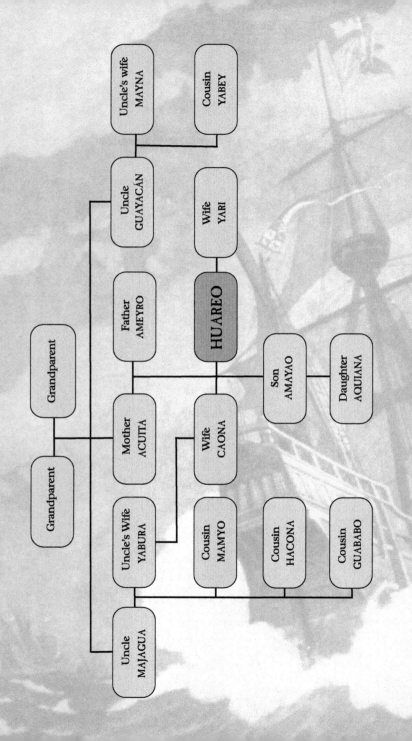

Contents

He is in heaven and is immortal, and no one can see Him, and He has a mother. But He has no beginning. His name is Yocajú Bagua Maórocoti.

Fray Ramón Pané

Part One
The Chiefdom of Majagua
1490–98

They cried so long, "Toa, Toa."
The children were changed into little animals.
They were changed into tona.

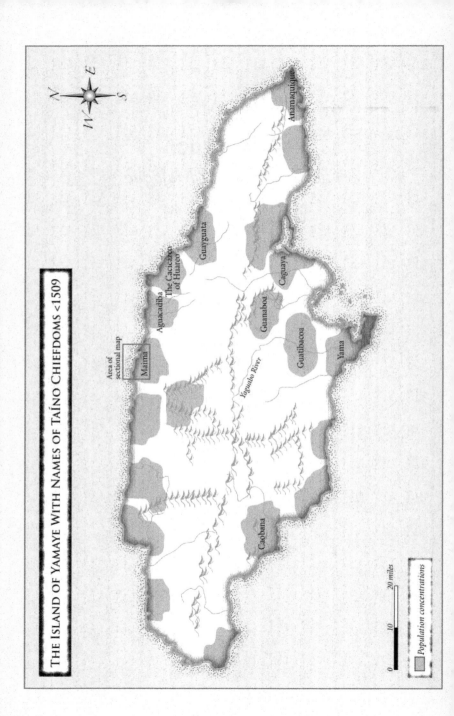

THE ISLAND OF YAMAYE WITH NAMES OF TAÍNO CHIEFDOMS <1509

Maima

Aguacadiba

The Cacicazca of Huareo

Guaguata

Caguaya

Guanaboa

Guatibacoa

Caobana

Yama

Anamaquique

Yaguatho River

Area of sectional map

N
W — E
S

0   10   20 miles

Population concentrations

Introduction

Most Sacred, Catholic Majesty of the Holy Roman Empire,

Your Majesty, Holy Roman Emporor and King of Spain, I, a humble servant of the most Holy Catholic Church, do kiss your feet in supplication, hoping that you receive these words I write with the understanding that I do all in the name of our Saviour, Jesus Christ.

I humbly submit with this letter the following account of the life of Cacique Huareo and the sojourn in Jamaica of my dear friend, Fray Antonio Diaz del Castillo, as I knew them to be. I pray that in reading the narrative, your Majesty will understand and appreciate the ways in which our people lived before and after the arrival of the Spaniards to Jamaica.

I begin the narrative in the year of our Lord, 1490.

> *Your humble servant,*
> *Diego del Castillo,*
>
> *Santo Domingo*
> *Anno Domini, 1535.*

Chapter One

To fight the trembling in his legs, Huareo planted his feet flat on the dirt floor in the house of his uncle, Cacique Majagua, paramount chief of the island of Yamaye.

"Sit here, young Huareo." Majagua's voice thundered in the boy's ears as he pointed to the *dujo*, the special seat of power reserved for the cacique and his guests of honour.

Huareo obeyed. He squatted low like a frog, placing his thin legs on either side of the shiny dark seat, made of *guayacán*, the hardest wood of Yamaye. His bare buttocks rested low to the ground, supported by the short legs of the *cemí*, the spirit of Majagua's ancestors.

What did his uncle mean by placing him in this seat? Huareo was still young, not yet into manhood. He was not married, he was not a chief or a person of wealth or importance.

"I have called for you to leave your parents' land for a special purpose. You will remain here in my village for a long time to come." His uncle's voice was deep and his words rumbled. "It is a time of sadness for the Taíno, Huareo. The rains have not come and the crops have not sprouted."

Huareo shifted nervously, his skin cold against the high back of the *dujo*.

"You have the expression of the dead on your face, Huareo. Be brave of heart, for you are a *nitaíno*, a noble one, eldest son of my sister. You are now a boy, but one day you will inherit this *cacicazgo*." His uncle stood like the *caoba*, the mahogany tree, his long arms swaying above the boy's face as he spoke.

Huareo wanted to be home with his mother and father, who lived in a faraway place, a walking distance of more than two days. His family had told him he would be going to live with his uncle, but no one said it would be for a long time. No one said that he would be chosen from such a young age to be the nephew to inherit the *cacicazgo* of Majagua. He wanted to crawl like a crab into its *bohío*, the home where he could hide.

"Today I will teach you to hear the words of your ancestors," Majagua said.

Huareo knew that the cacique and his special priest, the *bejique*, were the only ones who communed in this way with the spirits of those who came before.

"Our people are troubled because the Great One is angry. Our bread of life, the *yuca*, withers in the ground."

Three men carrying intricately woven baskets entered Majagua's house. They were followed by a dark, bent over figure whom Huareo recognized to be Macú, the *bejique* of the village, the man the cacique trusted the most. He was the one who brought the sick back to health and told the secrets of the spirit world. His skin was scabby, falling loosely from his face, arms and legs. One eye was closed shut and the other bulged out, fixing the unblinking stare of the iguana on Huareo.

The boy leaned forward on the seat to cover his body and grabbed the face of the *cemí*, burying his fingers deep within the sockets of its golden eyes. He held himself there until the large hands of Majagua pulled him backwards.

"Welcome, Macú. Today I grant you the privilege to divine the words of Yocajú. I trust you have fasted for six days as I asked you. I am not seated on the *dujo* today." Majagua patted the boy on his head. "Huareo is in the seat of power. He will hear your words when you speak in the tongues of the spirit."

The *bejique* did not utter a sound. He motioned to the three men to place their baskets on the ground next to him. They first removed a wooden seat with a rough surface, not decorated or finely carved like Majagua's, and placed it in front of Huareo. Macú lowered himself on the *dujo*, so close that his stale and rotten breath sickened Huareo. His face was fat like the *jutía,* the hefty rodent, with coarse hairs growing from his chin. The top of his head was dressed in the bright red feathers of the macaw and his entire body painted black with dye from the seeds of the fruit tree, *jagua.* Around his neck he wore the image of the dog, the Guardian of the Dead, whose single eye stared bright and whose mouth widened with clenched teeth. He was clothed with straps bound just below his knees, armbands above his elbows and a cotton belt worn about his waist bearing the image of a *Caribe*, his enemy slain in battle.

His assistants prepared a special powder for Macú. They ladled the *cojoba* seeds from a clay vessel and placed them on a wooden stand made for the cacique in the image of Boinayel, the Spirit of the rain. They crushed the black seeds until they turned to powder, which they then mixed with finely cut leaves of green tobacco and pieces of crunched shell.

Macú reached for the *tobacú*, an inhaler carved from a small hollowed branch, and placed one end directly into the *cojoba,* and the other two pieces, at the other end, into his nostrils. He held his head back, making loud sniffing noises as he inhaled the grey powder in quick, successive snuffs. He held the top of his head with both hands as it jerked and twisted violently. He bent low, and after a short pause, grabbed the *tobacú* again, this time inhaling the *cojoba* more rapidly. His arms flailed wildly and his upper body twisted like a snake as he circled the centre pole of the house. The mad *bejique* paused in front of Huareo and again pushed his ugly face near to the boy's. Spittle rolled uncontrollably from Macú's mouth and black-greenish mucus dripped from his nose. Huareo retched from the ugliness and stench of the man who frothed at the mouth.

One of the men passed Macú a maraca, which the *bejique* beat forcefully against his hand. As the rhythm quickened and the sound of the ball within the maraca clamoured, the *bejique* fell into a trance. Huareo knew that Macú was then travelling to a different place. His soul was leaving his body and ascending to the blinding light of the sun, to the abode of the divine where he could communicate directly with his spirit guides. As he came back down from this height, his mind's eye would regain its sight and see the world and its chambers turned upside down.

Majagua signalled to the assistants. "We must have our guest partake of the *cojoba*."

One of the men removed the inhaler from the *bejique's* grasp and, with his other hand, pressed hard on Huareo's head. He inserted the ends of the *tobacú* into the boy's nostrils. Huareo jerked backwards to free himself from the burning sensation of the powders in his nose, but the man steadied him with such force that he could not move. He slowly inhaled the holy substance. The snuff seeped within him until he could no longer feel the heaviness of his limbs. His body became so light he floated upwards from the seat, his thoughts whirling around like the wind. Then all was blank, blue as a cloudless sky.

The *bejique's* words sounded loud. "The Creator tells us that there lives among us someone who pollutes the village. One whom we least expect brings shame to Majagua's *cacicazgo* and places the cacique in disfavour with the *cemí*. The cacique shows no respect to the Spirit of Spirits by allowing this person to dwell in his midst. So, Yaya punishes Majagua by starving his people. He who brings this poison must be banished from the land before the Great One will restore prosperity to Majagua's people."

"How do I bring dishonour to my people if I do not know this person?" his uncle asked. He approached Macú, lifting his hands as if to hurt him.

"I know nothing more than what I tell you." The man's eye darted madly about.

"What else does Yocajú tell you so that our people may understand their suffering?"

Macú raised himself from the seat, and with arms and legs spread wide, he spoke in a quivering voice, "The powerful Breath of the Yuca, Yocajú Bagua Maórocoti, says that he has spoken to Cacibaquel, father of Guarionex, leader of a principal *cacicazgo* of Haití. He says Majagua must seek knowledge of these revelations. Those of his people who will remain in the land of the Taíno will enjoy the fruits of a good life, but for a short period only." His body shuddered and his tears splattered on the floor.

"You have said enough. You must take your trappings, and with your assistants, be gone from my house until I call for you again. Be sure that you show respect and honour to Huareo while he resides here in our *cacicazgo*. Go now, as I wish to speak with him alone."

Rays of sunlight streaked through the open entrance. Huareo saw the main supports made from trunks of the red mangrove. The walls were sealed with thick layers of mud and the roof was laden with woven thatch. Dark roots with knotted patterns and pieces of whitened tree bark decorated the interior.

Next to the *cojoba* stand of Boinayel was another image of the rain spirit. This one stood half the height of a man, fully naked. He was made from black polished wood with inlays of shell. Tears streamed down his cheeks, his shiny belly was distended, and his arms tucked back, wrapped about his lower hips above his groin.

Above these wooden carvings, hung two tapestries of red and yellow cotton, woven by the many wives of the cacique. Opposite to these were strung several *jamaca*, where Majagua and his family slept, and above, the skulls of enemies whom the cacique had slain in battle.

Huareo noticed the finely wrought *guanín*, yellow and round like the sun, hanging low on Majagua's breast. This was the mark of his authority as cacique. "You now know why I have brought you here from your mother's village." He looked down from his soaring height to Huareo seated on the floor. His uncle was the most powerful cacique in Yamaye, and some said, the largest man ever seen.

Huareo found the courage to speak. "People in my mother's land told me I would visit my uncle for a short time."

"You are blessed by the Great One, Huareo. You have been chosen to inherit my *cacicazgo* as the eldest son of my sister. I will teach your spirit to be powerful by the strength of the *cemí*, but your stay will not be short. You have much to learn before you become cacique."

Huareo tightened his arms and legs to stop the trembling he felt creeping through his body. "I will do as you command, uncle." Huareo wondered how he would ever be as mighty as Majagua. Would his voice sound like the thunder when he was cacique? Would he grow to be as strong and brave?

He watched his uncle reach his hand into a clay vessel and with two long fingers, Majagua marked Huareo's face in patterns of red and black paste.

"You will be brave and the spirits will guard you. Opiyelguobirán, the Guardian of the Dead, will not find you. He will not capture you when he roams the forests by night." His uncle paused. His expression saddened like Boinayel, the *cemí* whose tears bring the rain. "If strangers ever come to Yamaye, I will be too old to fight them, but you will be strong, capable of leading your people." He held the *guanín*, pressed it hard against his chest and spoke again. "I have word that a cacique and his son, Hatuey, are coming from the land of *Haití*, the birth place of our ancestors."

"Have you been to this place, uncle?"

"Yes, it is a land much bigger than ours, the mother earth where we were born and to which we return, the place where there is gold in plenty in the mountain, *Cauta*, which has two caves. You will gain knowledge of our ancestors from these noble ones who live across the sea."

"I want to know these places, uncle."

"You are to stay in the house of my brother, Guayacán. He and his son Yabey and my son Guababo will welcome you to your new home. Ask, and the villagers will tell you where he lives."

Huareo was eager to explore the village and wanted to free himself from the confinement of the cacique's house, to be welcomed by the open air and bright sunshine.

Huareo considered how much the village was like that of his parents. The chief's house, called the *caney*, was located in the centre. It measured ten paces by twenty, strongly built with thick posts cut from the red mangrove of the swamp. The roof was covered with branches of the bull thatch palm and the walls were made from cane tied securely with vines. It faced the *batey*, a ceremonial ground, which was a stretch of levelled land longer than it was wide. Here, his uncle held meetings, ball games and dances. Around the edge of the open ground were the *bohío*, the homes of the leaders and noble ones of the village. Close by but further from the open ground stood another set of rounded houses inhabited by *naboría*, those in the community who looked after the daily chores of fishing, hunting and planting.

His uncle was the chief of chiefs, the principal cacique of five *yucayeque*, villages that were similar to his own, each containing twenty or more *bohío*. They were built on small hilltops away from the flat, wet ground, but near enough to the shore so the cacique would always have sight of strangers who might come from other lands. The chiefdom overlooked a bay lined with white sand beaches and an island close to shore.

The grounds beyond the village were cultivated with crops of *yuca*, sweet potato, cocoyam and arrowroot that normally would have been ready for reaping before the first rains. But with the drought lingering over many seasons, the plants withered and their growth was stunted. Women farmers were downtrodden, unable to till the hard ground with their digging sticks.

Huareo approached a group of women and children who sat in a circle not far from the cacique's house. They were singing as they plucked and cleaned a sizeable catch of white-crowned pigeons.

"You must be Huareo looking for the house of Guayacán. You are standing directly in front of it," one of the women blurted. "We welcome you, Huareo to our home. My name is Mayna, wife of Guayacán, and these are some of his family and *naboría*."

Macú suddenly appeared through the opening of the *bohío*. He approached the boy with outstretched arms. "The people of Majagua welcome you, Huareo. Please come in." His voice rattled in his throat.

"Thank you." He moved back from Macú to avoid touching him.

"Yes, this is the home of your uncle, Guayacán. He wants you to enter." Macú clenched his teeth like Opiyelguobirán, the Guardian of the Dead.

Huareo sidestepped the *bejique* to enter his uncle's *bohío*. The opening, even though small compared to the height of the cane walls, allowed streams of light to flow inside. He felt immediately at home, for he smelled smoke and ash and the aroma of a cooked meal. On the floor were two flat clay pots and a *guayo*, a grater used to scrape the *yuca*, a mortar and pestle, and four painted earthen vessels, intricately decorated with red and white circles. He turned to the entrance, comforted to find that Macú had vanished.

His uncle and a boy about Huareo's age sat on the ground near the hearth. Guayacán was older than his brother, Majagua, his body already bent and his arms and legs worn with age. His eyes were dark and his face was lined with wrinkles, but his spirit was kind, his countenance smiling and welcoming. He reached for one of the painted vessels, from which he poured a hot stew into a bowl.

"Welcome to my home, Huareo. This is my son, Yabey." The boy smiled, his eyes bright with a kindness of spirit like his father's. "My brother has told me you will be living with us."

In one hand he held a peeled pineapple, and with the other, he skilfully carved out the eyes of the fruit with the sharpened end of the *buyón*, a small knife made of stone. He looked at Huareo, fixing his eyes on the boy's physical appearance. "You are growing into a man, Huareo, just like my son, ready to learn the ways of your elders."

Huareo accepted a slice of the fresh pineapple, fully ripened with a bright yellow colour. The succulent *yayama* was his favourite fruit. He loved the sweetness and coolness of the juice as he bit into it. "Thank you. I am happy to be here." He sensed a peacefulness sitting with his uncle and cousin, eating pineapple and drinking *ajiaco,* the pepperpot stew. Majagua had not welcomed him in this way.

As he sat with his elderly uncle, he felt the vigour of his own youth, in contrast. Huareo was bigger than most boys his age, the muscles on his arms and legs already developing. His flattened forehead had become wider and his straight black hair, longer. His skin had darkened from a golden hue to reddish brown, a sign he was maturing into manhood. He looked at Yabey and thought that he too was leaving his boyhood behind; his chest was lean and strong, his brow and chin prominent as if someone had chiselled them.

Behind his uncle, he noticed a display of unfinished stone carvings resting on planks of wood. "May I look at these, uncle?"

"Yes." Guayacán turned to face the sculptures. "Many of them are not complete. I do not work as quickly as I used to."

Huareo ran his fingers over the stone sculptures, and as he rubbed them, he sensed the spirit of each speaking to him. He felt the rough shapes of a turtle, of a dog with its head still not carved, and the teeth of the *manatí* laid in a stone with three points. He touched the bones of fishes carved into belts and picked up carvings of the *inrirí*, the woodpecker, and of the frog made in the form of amulets.

"They must speak to you, uncle, when you shape them with your chisel." His body heated as if a spirit were entering him.

"They spoke to me more when I was younger."

Huareo noticed Yabey had moved to a corner of the *bohío.* He was sharpening three pointed celts used for fastening to the ends of spears.

"Why is that, uncle?"

"My spirit has weakened. They are asking for a new spirit, Huareo."

"But yours is not ended."

"I am tired. This is why I will teach you the divine art, so the *cemí* may breathe life." His eyes brightened.

"But I have never held a chisel." Huareo looked at the bone and flint instruments that rested on the boards next to the sculptures.

Guayacán stood and placed one of the chisels in the boy's hand. It shone bright green, smooth like a river stone, but sharpened at both ends. "I will teach you the wondrous art."

"Have you also taught your son?"

"Yes, he works with me. He loves to make spears and clubs. He will be a brave one, a *guaribo,* some day."

Two shadows appeared in the opening of the *bohío.* The dark image of Macú was unmistakable, spreading its crooked shape across the floor. Also shifting in the light was a smaller reflection, which moved with the other.

Guayacán turned sharply, startled by his visitors. "Welcome, Macú, and to you, son of Majagua."

As they moved further inside the *bohío,* the images were clearer. Macú's back was hunched, and he bobbed his head as he walked. The boy also had a nervous gait. He was smaller in stature than Huareo, at least one head shorter, with a plump, rounded face.

"My uncle is the greatest sculptor in Yamaye." Majagua's son approached Huareo, grabbed the chisel from his hand and threw it to the ground.

Surprised by his cousin's abrupt action, Huareo looked to his uncle for reassurance, but he gave none. "Yes, he was showing me his art."

"Huareo, this is Guababo, who will be your friend while you visit with us." His uncle placed his hand first on his cousin's head and then on Huareo's.

"It will be good to be your friend." Huareo searched for his cousin's eyes but Guababo did not look at him.

"And I trust Yabey will also be your friend, Huareo." Guayacán raised his voice for his son to hear but Yabey, who was preoccupied with his work, did not respond. "You should go now with your cousin through the village. Guababo, show Huarero your father's *canoa* at the mouth of the river, and make arrangements to go to sea with the fishermen." He motioned for them to leave.

Macú's voice cut like the *buyón* through the air. "Guayacán, they must know that the Great One, Yocajú, is not only the giver of *yuca* but is master of the sea, and He is the one who is displeased."

"We will disappoint him more if we stop our work, if we do not dig the land and fish the sea." Guayacán waved his hands for the *bejique* to leave with the boys.

As they left their uncle's *bohío*, Guababo whispered in his ear, "I will be your friend, cousin. I have a secret to tell you, but you must promise not to tell anyone."

Chapter Two

On the night Huareo ventured out with the fishermen, the sky was bright with shining lights, far too many for him to count. He often wondered where this splendour came from. His father told him once that long ago fishermen were stolen by *güey*, the sun, and scattered through the night sky. He strained his neck to look, amazed that the twinkling lights spread out from one end of the sea to the next.

Huareo and the fishermen rowed with wooden *naje* to push the *canoa* forward, beyond the coral reef. Many moons had passed with no catch, but that night they hoped it would be different.

The *canoa* was a large *caimán*, a crocodile, asleep in the water, tired from its long swim. The jaws rested quietly for now, waiting patiently for the first sight of prey. The *canoa* was Majagua's finest and most powerful, the front and sides painted in red and black lines that curled like waves.

His cousin, Guababo, was next to him at the back of the *canoa*, and three experienced fishermen sat in the middle, each holding a fishing rod. In the bottom of the boat were neatly folded fishing nets for use in shallower waters, and long wooden spears for piercing fish like the barracuda.

Huareo twisted his body and held tight the handle of the *naje*, which he raised just above the surface of the water. He looked deep into the ocean, clear from the brightness of the stars. Nothing.

"Not one fish tonight." His cousin Guababo broke the silence. "We should turn the *canoa* around and go home," he shouted.

The fishermen jerked their heads like pigeons, startled by the sound of the boy's sudden outburst. Huareo put down his oar and grabbed Guababo about the neck, pulling his head back strongly. "Hush! You fool!"

"There is no catch," Guababo whined. "I want to go back home." He banged the side of the *canoa* with a *naje*. "Tell the men to paddle to shore."

Huareo grabbed the oar with both hands and pushed it against his cousin's neck, forcing him backwards over the side of the *canoa*. He leaned over Guababo, pushing even harder, more than once, so that his cousin's head touched the water. Guababo raised his hands in surrender and wrested himself back into the boat, without saying a word.

"We do not return until we get a catch," Huareo silenced his cousin. He turned to the fishermen. "Let us draw up the lines to see if we need fresh bait."

Huareo and Guababo assisted the men.

"These lines are not dark enough. Bring out some fresh ones and make sure they are darkened," Huareo said.

The boys stretched the new lines the full length of the boat and the fishermen split thin young roots of the mangrove, which they had stored in a dry spot. They rubbed the white cotton lines through the slits of the wood until they soaked in the dark brown dye.

"Yes, this will also strengthen them," Huareo said.

The stars changed their positions in the long night. One group, a set of small suns resembling a one-legged man, shimmered with brilliance that time of year. Huareo remembered the story of his ancestor, Guahayona, who tricked his brother-in-law by throwing him over the side of the *canoa*. The one-legged man he saw in the sky was that unfortunate one who was drowned by Guahayona. His name was Anacacuya, who rose that night as bright as Huareo had ever seen, shining directly over his head.

Huareo looked at the fishermen whose eyelids drooped and heads bobbed with the gentle rocking of the boat. A cold breeze had descended from the Blue Mountains, creating waves that lapped against the sides of the *canoa*, the coolness teasing out bumps to crawl on Huareo's arms and legs. Nothing yet. Not even the freshening of the lines seemed to have worked. Maybe his cousin was right. Huareo looked at Guababo's sullen face, wondering what secret he held hidden in his heart.

"Let us move nearer the coral." Huareo's voice awakened the men. "We have drifted too far; our lines are too short to reach the depths. Let us pull them up." He pointed to the reef where pelicans circled and dived in a broad, calm stretch of water. "Over there! The *aruna* are calling us."

Faint streaks of morning light played on the horizon. Huareo steered the *canoa* until it came to rest in the shallower water inside the coral reefs. He looked across the still expanse of blue. There was the beginning of life. Fishes of every colour and size were coming out of their homes to feed: the silver *guaymen* with yellow stripes, the blue and green *buyón*, and the red mouthed *cachicata*, bunched together, their eyes staring up at him as if they knew they were trapped.

The fishermen unfolded two nets, making sure the stone sinkers hung free. The man on the left side of the boat lifted his net first, securing it around his wrist with a loop at the end of the cord. With his other hand, he eased the net up so he gathered it in sections, and when he held two halves, one in each hand, he leaned over the side of the *canoa* and hurled the net so it spread the full length of the boat, and at a distance of many hands. The fish scattered to try to escape, but as the net slowly sank with the weight of the stones, they rushed in to feed on the crabmeat that the other fishermen threw into the water.

Baba Güey rose out of the sea, calming the night breezes and shedding a white light over the ocean. The men took turns casting their nets, each time hauling so much fish that their full strength was scarcely enough to raise the catch into the boat. They filled the *canoa* with the bounty of the sea.

As they folded the nets, the reef shark, unmistakable with its grey fin slicing the water, began to circle them. The man in front hoisted his spear. Its base was heavy and unbreakable, made solid from the tough wood of the *guayacán*. At the tip, a sharpened celt was fastened for piercing the gills of the large fish.

"Wait! Our boat is full; we can hold no more," Guababo shouted.

"If the *tiburón* has come to feed, let us kill him. It is Yocajú who has sent him as a blessing. If we can hold no more, we will tell the men on shore to cast larger nets so the whole village may be fed."

Huareo signalled to the fisherman to cast his spear.

"The corrals are full of fish," Guayacán announced to the cacique.

Huareo was seated with his cousin Guababo and two uncles on the floor of the *caney*. One of Majagua's daughters stood opposite with her mother. She was of medium height, the same age as Huareo. Her thick black hair fell over her shoulders down to her waist. She was adorned with cotton bands about her arms and legs and a string of beads tied below the navel.

"Huareo, you have brought goodness from the land of my sister. We will send word to the *cacicazgo* of Anamaquique." Majagua rubbed the golden eyes of the dujo then twisted Huareo's shoulders so the boy faced him. "You must know that with this gift comes a burden, to follow in the footsteps of the noble ones who came before us."

"I am still a boy, uncle."

Guababo was restless, shifting his legs and drawing circles on the floor.

"Yes, but you need to learn the ways of a man," Majagua replied.

Huareo watched as Majagua's daughter held one end of a band of woven cotton, the width and shape of a man's belt. Her mother showed her how to use a wooden needle, weaving threads of cotton to form red and black patterns. On the ground were sets of black seeds and pieces of pink conch shells that they used to decorate their art. Huareo thought perhaps they were making a belt for the cacique or a visiting dignitary. The girl noticed him staring. Her eyes smiled, just for a fleeting moment. They were kind, and as strong as the spirit that sings in the wind.

The *bejique* appeared at the entrance. "Guayacán called me here to join you," said Macú.

"Sit with us. We are joyful for the abundance of fish, but we do not know why the *yuca* does not grow." The cacique pulled Huareo closer to make room for Macú.

"I told you a polluter lives among us."

"Do not speak in riddles, Macú. Tell us what secrets you know." Majagua raised his voice.

"I speak only the words that were told to me," the *bejique* replied. "Did not your father teach you to be the all knowing cacique?"

"I will have you removed from my house." Majagua puffed out his chest.

"The rains have not come because the spirit of Yocajú is not with us," Guayacán interjected.

"What did you say?" Majagua leaned one ear towards him.

"The *cemí* of Yocajú is absent from the fields," Guayacán shouted.

Huareo understood the danger of which his uncle spoke. At the beginning of each growing season, Huareo would walk the fields with Ameyro, his father, and there within the *conuco*, the mounds of earth used for planting, they would ceremoniously unearth and rebury the *cemí* of Yocajú. Its male spirit was strong and wilful, sprouting from the middle of the sculpture. Its mouth was greedy, a gaping hole eager to swallow the richness of the soil, which made the *yuca* grow.

"How do you know this Guayacán?" Majagua asked.

"Because the ground is empty where I buried him."

"Did you know this, Macú?"

"This is why the *yuca* has withered, Cacique," the *bejique* replied.

The earth trembled as Majagua stomped on the ground. "The polluter will be found and so will the stone that was lifted from the fields. Macú, be gone from my house. You are a speaker of riddles."

He motioned for his visitors to leave the *caney*.

Huareo left the home of the cacique without meeting his girl cousin. Even though they had not spoken, he felt a closeness of spirit and a burning desire he could not contain.

"Your sister is beautiful," he told Guababo.

"Of course, for we are the children of Majagua." Guababo led the way down the hillside.

Huareo balanced himself carefully on the stones that his cousin loosened with his feet. Guababo's spirit was unsettled and spiteful, as if he wanted Huareo to trip.

"She is golden like the sun." Huareo was out of breath as he reached the shore.

"That is why she is called, Caona." Guababo ran to dive into the crashing waves.

At the far end of the beach, five men talked and laughed under the shade of the *guayabón* trees, laden with bunches of purple grapes. Above their chatter, he heard the hacking sound of the *manaya*, axes of stone, used to hollow the burned trunk of the sacred *ceiba*, the silk cotton tree. One day when he would be cacique, he wanted a *canoa* to be made especially for him and his family. It would be magnificent, painted and carved as the sacred *cemí* of Huareo.

"Why do you not swim with me? Are you afraid of the rough waves, Huareo?" his cousin mocked him. "If you are to be cacique, you need to be more courageous than this." Guababo pulled himself from the water and scooped fistfuls of sand to throw at Huareo.

"Your spirit is restless, Guababo. You need to tell me what is wrong."

"Nothing is wrong." He then sat by Huareo.

"Do you think your father will find the *cemí*?" Huareo wondered aloud.

"Why do you ask me this? Are you not supposed to know the answers to all questions?" Guababo threw another fistful of sand at Huareo.

"You are hiding the truth from me."

Guababo drew up his legs and grabbed his knees.

"Why are you sad?" Huareo asked.

"Can you keep a secret?"

"It depends."

Guababo straightened, and wiped tears from his eyes. "The *bejique*."

"What about Macú?"

"Do you like him?"

"I do not think he could be my friend." Huareo laughed. "He is not as pretty as your sister."

They both laughed but Guababo's expression soon changed. "He took me into the fields to show me where the *cemí* was buried." He spat into the sand.

"Why did he take you there? Do the villagers not know where the *cemí* was buried?"

"Yes, but I did not know." He looked at Huareo with pleading eyes. "Will you be my friend, cousin?"

"I will be your friend, Guababo."

"How can I trust you?"

"You have my word and promise of friendship."

Guababo paused, then blurted out, "I did something the Great One would not like."

"What did you do, cousin?" Huareo asked quietly.

"I cannot tell you."

"But you must. The secret is too heavy for you to carry."

After a long pause, his cousin sighed. "I went one night late when the *opía* were about, and ever since then the spirits of our ancestors haunt me in my sleep."

"Where did you go?"

"I went to the place where the *cemí* was buried and I removed him from the earth."

"Why did you do that, Guababo?"

"I did not want to do it." His legs shifted back and forth in the sand.

"You must tell your father what you have done."

"I cannot tell him, Huareo. He will kill me."

"The truth will be known, cousin, even if you do not tell it."

Guababo reached over and punched his cousin in the arm. "I knew I could not trust you." He wrestled Huareo by pushing him backwards on the sand, but his spirit weakened, and he cried. "Huareo, I am a fool. I do not know what to do."

"The punishment will be harsher if you do not tell him. Yaya will punish you more than your father will. Why did you do it, Guababo?"

"He is a wicked man."

"Who is wicked?"

"Macú. He is a trickster, he deceived me."

"How did he trick you?"

"It does not matter. I was the one who removed it."

Huareo extended his hand to his cousin to help him up. "Remember what I said. You must tell your father, or else I will not be your friend."

Chapter Three

The *bejique* of the village stood in the ceremonial ground. Green feathers dressed his head and black and red dyes masked his face. He held his mouth to the pink conch shell, blowing out low, deep tones in short and long vibrations. The crowds moved nearer to fill the four edges of the *batey*.

Drummers formed a line to the left of the cacique's house. Each crouched over the top of the *mayohuacán*, which lay flat on the ground before them. In unison, they beat the sides of the hollowed drums with their wooden sticks, and from the mouths of the sacred carvings played music in loud, rhythmic sounds.

Majagua processed out of his home with his family, nobles and attendants. He had a stern look on his face, but he was magnificently dressed, crowned with green and white feathers. The *guanín* glittered about his neck on a string of pearls, and golden rings decorated his ears and nostrils. With one hand, he supported the *yuke*, the heavy stone belt, carved in the image of the fish with no head.

Accompanying him were his principal wife, Yabura, other wives and ten of his children, including his eldest daughter, Caona. She had yellow flowers in her hair, bands of red cloth on her arms and legs and a string of beads of black stone about her waist. Guababo cowered with his shoulders bent under the heavy weight of his father's hand. A few paces back followed four noblemen and two assistants who carried the sacred *dujo*, the images of the Rain Spirit, Boinayel, and of Baibrama, the *cemí* who helped the *yuca* to grow.

Huareo stood with his uncle Guayacán and his family to the side of the *batey* in full view of the cacique's family. He felt a pain as if the sharp blade of the *buyón* were stabbing his heart. His cousin Guababo looked to him with beseeching eyes. Huareo wondered if he had told his father the secret of his wrongdoing.

Majagua rose, a giant bird from his seat. He outstretched his arms like wings, the green and white feathers of his head gleaming in the sunlight. His voice reached out in long, sad tones:

> Someone in the house of Majagua
> has defiled the land of Yamaye.
>
> We pray to Atabey,
> Mother of the supreme Yocajú
>
> *Busicá guakia para yucubia*
> *Yukiyú jan, maboya uá,*
> *Bibi Atabey,*
> *Busicá guakia para, yucubia.*
>
> Give us rain for the *yuca*
> Good spirit, yes, trickster spirit, no,
> Mother Atabey,
> Give us rain for the *yuca*.
>
> My people will be the judge.
> Twenty of our strongest men
> will combat in the *batey*.
> They will decide the fate
> of the one who wronged Yocajú.

The drummers struck the sacred wood of the *ceiba*, the voices of the *mayohuacán* reaching far across the *cacicazgo*. Huareo danced in time with the vibrations, his feet tapping to the beat of the drums.

Two *naboría* wrestled Guababo to the ground. The boy groaned and jerked violently, writhing like a frenzied snake. Huareo wanted to help him, but he dared not, for fear of Majagua's wrath. The men stomped harder on his cousin's back.

Macú stepped forward at the cacique's request. He began a prayer to Bibi Atabey. His voice creaked like a dead limb of the *ceiba*, his body contorted and his eye rolled back, he flailed his arms and legs, and twisted his belly. He howled with a ferocious sound as if the *maboya*, the bad spirit had entered his body.

The cacique signalled for four assistants to remove the *bejique* and his son, Guababo, from the *batey*.

Huareo hung his head in shame as he watched his cousin being dragged through the dust.

"You have awakened early," Huareo said. He stood by the river, shallower than usual because of the drought. The horizon was beginning to lighten, the air still cool from the mountain breeze.

"We often come here to bathe." Caona splashed water on her arms and breasts.

Two of Caona's younger sisters stood behind her. One lifted her hair off her back, and the other used a calabash to pour water over her shoulders. Her small breasts showed, golden and round like the *mamey* fruit.

"My name is Huareo."

"I am glad to meet you, Huareo. You must know, of course, that the whole village knows your name." She crouched so the water reached just below her shoulders. "My name is Caona."

"Your brother, Guababo, told me your name the first day I saw you. It is beautiful." He squatted to taste the water and then splashed it on his face. "The water is cold."

"It will soon be warmed by *güey*, the sun, for it is not deep. Do not be shy, come down into the river."

"I will wait until you are finished bathing."

Caona's sisters giggled, slapping the water nervously. Huareo wondered if they were laughing at him. He felt boyish and foolish, not the man he wanted to be.

"I will climb the rocks with you to visit the fast waters." He stood from his crouched position, feeling exposed before her. "I have not been up into the river."

"It is not dangerous. From the waterfall, we will see the villages of Majagua's *cacicazgo*, beaches and the island beyond."

Her eyes smiled just as kindly as the first time he had seen her. She stood so the water reached just below her navel.

"Will you wait for me here?" she asked her sisters. "We must return home together."

Huareo jumped into the river. His feet felt the smooth touch of the *tibes*, the rounded pebbles shining white from the growing sunlight. He reached for his cousin's hand.

The first climb was not even the height of two men. The rock face had its own steps as if someone had carved them there, making it easy for his toes to grip the ledges. He steadied himself with one hand by holding the rock above him, and with the other, he gently pulled her with little effort. The cascading water chilled the front of their bodies.

"Yeooooooooooow," they shouted with joy, but their screams were lost in the crashing sounds of the water.

The river widened and deepened up in the hills where the water formed pools. She let go of his hand and dived into one of the holes. Her body shimmered through the water, faster than the *dajao*, the mullet of the mountains.

He chased her but could not catch her.

She came up for a breath, resting against a boulder by the embankment. "I thought you would be a fast swimmer."

"Yes, I am, but you are faster than the fish."

"My brothers taught me to dive for conch."

"You learned well." He waded over to her.

"We cannot stay long. My sisters are waiting for me."

He wanted the time with her never to end.

"We can return through the forest. It will be easier." She pointed to the trees and thick brush close by.

He climbed out, reaching for her hand to help her step over the boulders.

"I should be the one helping you," she said.

"Why is that?"

"I know the rivers and land better than you."

"You can show me," he said.

"Majagua has a big land." She leaned against the sacred *ceiba* that filled the woodland by the river.

"Yes, the *cacicazgo* is huge." He looked below him to admire the view. The five villages of Majagua's chiefdom with its hundreds of *bohío* spread out over the rolling hills. In the distance the vast blue of Bagua, the sea, lay calm with the small island snuggled close to shore. Would he lead this *cacicazgo* one day? And would the lovely Caona be his wife?, he wonered.

She glanced away and shook her head. "I am worried, Huareo."

"Why are you worried?"

"It is Guababo. Majagua does not let him leave the *caney*."

"Has your father harmed him?"

"No, but I am afraid for my brother. He does not sleep or eat. The *bejique* has tried to cure him but Macú is of no use. Guababo acts as if the *maboya* possesses him."

"You know what the people will do if they discover the *maboya* lives within him?" He raised his middle finger to his eyes and then touched his groin.

"Yes." Her breath quickened, and she covered her face.

"They will use the *manaya*."

"Do not say it." She pushed him, her fingers caressing the middle of his chest.

His body warmed from her touch. "You are lovely, Caona." His words burst from him in a fit of boyish passion. He held out his arms to her.

"We are too young, Huareo. Majagua has not given his blessing."

"Yes, we are, but that should not stop us."

"You must wait," she said.

His passions made him feel embarrassed, foolish to think she would love him.

"The villagers say you have special powers, Huareo."

"I am not powerful. I have no wives, no *cemí*, no *cacicazgo*."

"They say you are favoured by the Great One. Bagua gives you fish to feed the villages."

"I do not understand these gifts but, yes, I am blessed." He sat on the ground with his back leaning against the rough bark of the tree.

"If you are blessed, you can help my brother." She sat by his side.

"What do you want me to do?"

"Do you know why my father is punishing Guababo?"

He did not answer her.

"You know something, Huareo." Her eyes pierced him deeply.

"Has your brother told you anything?" He asked.

"No."

"Then, I cannot say, Caona."

"So you know. My brother says you will help him because you are his friend."

She rose suddenly and walked a distance from the tree to hide in the brush. "Catch me if you can, Huareo." Faster than an arrow, she flew through the thickness of the *jiba*.

He dragged behind, his body bigger than hers. She arrived first at the pool where her sisters waited. The three girls took their leave, moving quickly along the path to the village, not turning even once to bid him farewell.

Chapter Four

Thousands gathered by the *batey*. Two teams of twenty men assembled on either side of the court, one led by Hacona, son of Majagua, and the other by Hatuey, son of the visiting cacique from Haití. The warriors were painted in patterns of black and red, and wore cotton bands about their arms and legs. Both leaders walked back and forth in front of their men, proudly displaying the *yuke*, stone belts that adorned their waists. Hacona carried his father's *cemí*, carved by Guayacán in honour of the Great One, Yaya. On its sides, it had etchings of fish scales and the figure of the frog, and in the middle, hanging just below the warrior's waist, the pointed shape of a serpent with no head. Hatuey's belt was wider, the colour more of sand than grey stone, with carvings also of a headless snake, resting above the combatant's groin. The *yuke* were the *cemí*, spirits who gave the warriors strength in the battle of the *batey*.

In front of his house, Majagua sat on the *dujo*, surrounded by his wives and children, noblemen and *naboría*, Hatuey's father from Haití, and visiting caciques of Yamaye including his eldest son, Mamyo, Cacique of Maima. Majagua looked magnificent, with white feathers and a crown of green and red stones resting on his head, rings of gold in his ears and nose, and a jewel of coral covering his forehead. On one side, his brother, Guayacán, sat in place of the *bejique*, and on the other, the prisoner, his son Guababo, with his hands tied. Directly behind them, Huareo sat between his parents, who had come especially for the occasion from the chiefdom of Anamaquique.

His mother's comforting smell, the sweetness of pimento, beckoned him home. She wrapped her arms through his, holding him tight. "You have grown bigger in the short time you have been away, Huareo."

"I missed you, Bibi."

"He will soon be a man, Acuita," said his father, Ameyro, Cacique of Anamaquique. "I hope you will return soon to your parents' home, my son." He had red hawkish eyes with a deep penetrating gaze.

Huareo wanted to tell his father he would not be going home, that the Great Spirit willed for him to be in the *cacicazgo* of Majagua, but he said nothing. He feared those eyes. He wanted to tell his father he was the one who had sent him to Majagua, that he should have known his son would not be returning home any time soon.

Guayacán, the new *bejique* of the chiefdom, stood to signal the start of the ceremony with the blowing of the horn of the *guamó*. The drummers, who had gathered at one side, beat out the sound of the *mayohuacán*. The warriors, holding each other's arms, lifted their feet in time with the drums and followed the steps of their leader, who danced in front of them. Guayacán shouted above the song and dance so he could be heard far and wide:

> Yaya, the Spirit of Spirits,
> be praised by all our people,
> you have spoken to us.
> Your *guaribono*
> will bring honour to you,
> in combat with each other.
> The wager will be made,
> Guababo, son of the cacique,
> the one who has done wrong,
> will be punished.

Before the game was called, Hacona and Hatuey met in the centre of the court. As a sign of friendship, they greeted by touching each other's foreheads with both hands. They decided on the wager for the *batey* and negotiated the rules, including the number of faults to be allowed in the game. Both leaders returned to their team of warriors, the expectation of glory on their faces.

The *guaribo* from Haití, even though younger than Hacona, was taller and more muscular. His hair was pulled back, which showed the strength of his chiselled jaw and thick neck. His eyes had a fierceness Huareo had never seen in a man so young.

The men squatted like frogs, their leg muscles tense and ready for the start. Hatuey served the ball first, forcing it downward, hard, so the *batú* played low to the ground. Hacona, the nearest player on the other side, reached down and placed his right hand on the earth to gain his balance. In a quick turn, his rump raised high, he returned the *batú* with a strong push of the hip.

Huareo bent forward to whisper in his cousin's ear, "You must be brave, whatever the outcome."

Guababo leaned back to him. "I am afraid."

"Your father will be merciful."

"You were wrong." Guababo sobbed.

"About what?"

"I should not have told him."

Majagua reached over and pulled his son's hair to force his chin up.

The game played on until the *güey* travelled high in the sky. The warriors were heated, their movements becoming faster and more skilful. A wind picked up to blow dust from the *batey* into their faces, but this did not stop their determination. Both sides pushed harder, equally matched as the fiercest of Taíno *guaribono* in combat.

But then the ball from Hacona's team flew high over the end of the *batey*. The leader of the drums signalled for the play to stop. He gave the count, and the *batú* was given to Hatuey. The game resumed just as quickly as it had stopped. Hacona spread his legs apart, bent his upper body and stomped his feet, his tense muscles ready to attack his opponent. Majagua's team was losing the game.

The *batú* was in play. Hacona shot it high and hard. Hatuey jumped to reach above the ball, and returned it with a powerful slam, which forced it to the ground. Hacona dived to save it, but the ball was too fast and too low. He tumbled, rolled over twice, his face scraping in the dirt. It was the losing point.

Hacona raised himself from the floor of the *batey* in a cloud of dust. "Yaaaooo," he howled. His men stepped back to give him space. He lunged with his powerful legs, flying through the air to land on top of Hatuey. The two *guaribono* wrestled, the visiting warrior's face bloody from the beating Hacona gave him.

With a signal from the cacique, the main drummer played the *mayohuacán*. Men from both teams pulled the fighting warriors apart. The son of the cacique raged, flailing his arms even as his team of warriors pried him away.

The two leaders stood before Majagua.

The cacique raised the arms of the victor in celebration. "Yaya has willed it thus. The visitors from Haití have won the *batey*," Majagua announced. "Hacona, you have fought for the *cacicazgo* of Majagua and lost. In times past, our ancestors would have punished you."

Hacona remained brave, not shrinking before his father. "I am at your command, Cacique Majagua."

Guababo dropped to the ground, whimpering, but he was quickly pulled up and held by two attendants.

"You have won the wager, Hatuey. What punishment do you wish for my son, Guababo? He deserves death for the wrong he has committed."

"My wager was for his banishment," Hatuey said.

"Then Yaya has willed it so. My son will be banished from Yamaye." Majagua shoved Guababo and signalled to the attendants for him to be removed.

"The son of Majagua, like Yayael, the son of Yaya, is banished from his father's land." He looked up to see black clouds gathering on the hills. "The son of Boina will soon bring us rain."

Huareo's heart was pierced, wounded by the blame of betrayal in his cousin's eyes. Guababo, an injured *jutía*, squealed as the warriors dragged him across the *batey*.

Chapter Five

Macú remained isolated in his *bohío* for many moons. The villagers shunned his presence because the *maboya*, the trickster spirit, possessed his body.

Huareo was curious about the one-eyed man. What did he do hidden away in his house by himself? Was he meaner and uglier? People warned Huareo not to visit Macú because the *maboya* would capture his spirit, but he was not afraid. He wanted to punish the lunatic for bringing harm to Guababo.

"Macú," Huareo called.

The house stank of decayed fruit and fish. It was dark, and empty except for a single *jamaca* in which the man lay; there were no *cemí* or jewellery, baskets or pottery, no fishing rods or *coa* for planting, no axes or spears, nothing that Huareo could see.

"Macú." Huareo rocked the bed.

The sick man opened his eye and reached to grab Huareo, but he was too quick to be caught by Macú's bony hands. The *jamaca* shook violently, emitting a putrid smell.

"*Tuyra*, you are a dirty man." Huareo pushed his head near to Macú's face. "*Tuyra, tuyra,* I am not afraid of you," he taunted him.

Macú grabbed Huareo's head and pulled his face down into his lap.

Huareo freed himself and wiped the man's stench from his body. "*Buibá maboya*, go away from me, you trickster spirit." Huareo swung the bed so hard that Macú rolled about, cursing and screaming.

"Be gone, Huareo. You are a fool. You know nothing," he rasped, and scooped spittle into his hand.

"You are not a Taíno," said Huareo. "You are a man who deceives others. You caused my cousin to be banished. I know what you did and I will tell my uncle."

"You know nothing. Your uncle Majagua is an imposter."

"You are the fool, for you entrapped Guababo with your lies. The people of the village will crush your seed with the *manaya*."

Macú leaned forward and slapped spittle on Huareo's belly.

"You are ugly and nasty." Huareo wiped away the man's slime and kicked the *jamaca* with such force Macú fell out of the bed. He left him motionless on the floor.

In the morning, Macú was missing. Word spread through the chiefdom that brave Huareo must have killed the mad man and disposed of his body. Huareo tried to quell the rumour, but to no avail. The people of Majagua believed the future cacique to be stronger than the *maboya*.

On that same morning, the *cemí* of Yocajú Bagua Maórocoti mysteriously appeared at the *bohío* of Guayacán. No one could explain how it got there. They thought it was the Great Spirit made manifest through Huareo.

Huareo followed his uncle to the fields where they re-buried the *cemí* within the *conuco*, committing him once again to the earth, his proper resting place. They dug the hard ground with the *coa*, and placed the *cemí* in a mound of earth, which stood at the centre of a fresh clearing in the forest.

Majagua asked Guayacán and Huareo to remove his most prized possessions from the *caney*, to take them to the sacred place of prayer. They carried the *cemí* of Baibrama and the twin brothers, Boinayel and Márohu to the shrine within the cave carved into the face of the mountains on the edges of the *cacicazgo* of Aguacadiba.

The image of the guardian of the underworld, Macocael, was etched into the rock at the cave entrance. The opening cast light inside, revealing shapes of white and green stone as thick and round as the *ceiba*. The ceiling was painted with images of birds, frogs, fishes and turtles, stained in black, the dark juice of the *jagua*. Bending low on his knees, Guayacán carefully untied the *cemí*, placing them in a secure spot deep inside the temple, the sacred portal to the underworld from which the Taíno people were born.

The golden discs of Baibrama's eyes glared at Huareo. The *cemí's* arms stretched to grasp his knees, his ears filled the sides of his head, and white teeth spread menacingly across his face. The male sex was broad and erect, waiting to feed the crops after the rains drenched the land and the new shoots of the *yuca* sprouted from the black ashes of the fields. The *cemí* waited for Guayacán to bathe him in *naiboa*, the poisonous juice of the *yuca*, which gave him the power to make nutritious roots grow thick and deep within the earth.

Next to Baibrama, Guayacán placed the stone image of the twins, joined as one, Boinayel and Márohu, whom the Taíno of Haití had given to Cacique Majagua. In their land, they honoured the spirits in the cave of Iguanaboina, from which the sun and moon were born and whence life began. Majagua revered the brothers because, when his people offered prayers, *the cemí* gave the weather of rain and sun, both of which the *yuca* needed in order to grow. Boinayel was the son of the Grey Serpent who created the dark clouds, and Márohu, the spirit without clouds, who brought light.

Accompanying Guayacán and Huareo to the cave were
Yabey and two *naboría*. His son was growing to be a strong
warrior and had developed a passion like his father for
communing with the *cemí*. The *bejique* squatted, his head
bowed in reverence.

> Boinayel,
> Son of the Grey Serpent,
> Giver and Spirit of the rain,
> servants we are
> of the Great Spirit,
> whose mother,
> Mother of the Waters,
> Attabeira,
> has forgiven us our wrongs.
> We beseech you,
> *Busicá guakia para yucubia*,
> give us the rain for the *yuca*,
> bring us the dark clouds
> and with your brother,
> Márohu,
> create the rain and sun
> so our people may have food.

Yabey passed Huareo a small bundle of the leaves of the
manaca, the royal palm of Yamaye. He unwrapped two *casabe*
for Huareo to place in the bowl on the head of Baibrama.
They fed the *cemí* the flat rounded bread and rubbed his
body with the *naiboa*. Baibrama would no longer punish the
Taíno, no longer bring them sickness and hunger; the spirit
of the Yuca would now make the plants sprout and bear
fruit.

As they left the cave, Huareo prayed for Guababo's
protection. Guayacán had taught him to make offerings,
to feed the *cemí* so the rains would come, but Huareo did

not know how to commune with the spirits to make his cousin safe. The spirits seemed far away. He wondered if the cacique had instructed Hatuey to punish his son, to kill him by throwing him overboard. If he had arrived safely in Haití, was someone caring for him in his banishment? Who would look after him in a strange place with no father, mother or relatives?

Chapter Six

Before long, Boinayel, Son of the Dark Serpent, brought the black clouds. He filled rivers that overflowed into nearby fields to make them ready for planting. Mountain mullets ran wild and plentiful, swooped down by the force of waterfalls to the mouths of rivers where villagers stood ready to trap them. The people of Majagua rejoiced and gave thanks to the *cemí* for the bounty.

The caciques met in assembly to assign men to prepare the land for planting. They abandoned old fields that had remained fallow for the duration of the drought and chose new ground in a plateau above the main village. The men would clear a common area for growing food, and in addition, portion out a set of *conuco* for each family.

The farmers carried *manaya*, sharpened stone axes, to cut and hollow trees, which they then set on fire. Before they felled the *ceiba*, Guayacán and *bejique* of other regions held chants, reciting names of the spirits of Yamaye, to seek permission for sacrifice from each of the *cemí* that dwelled within the trees. They asked the masters for their favour and promised them their wishes would be granted.

Women carried food for the men and strung *jamaca* between the trees for rest time. The *naboría* laboured all day, hauling away burnt trunks to be used again for making *canoa*, in accordance with the wishes of the *cemí*. They dug the ash into the soft earth with the *coa*, mixing it with human waste and refuse. With the earth enriched, they prepared the *conuco* by piling mounds of earth to form raised gardens, as wide as twelve feet and as tall as a man. They spaced the rounded knolls three to four feet apart and, in each of these, they placed five or six cuttings of the *yuca*.

They also planted other root crops interspersed with the cassava: sweet potato, cocoyam and arrowroot. Majagua bartered with neighbouring chiefdoms to supply farmers with tubers and green stalks of the *yuca*. In exchange, he offered turtle, barracuda, and the sacred, pink conch.

After a few moons had passed, Majagua called for a meeting of Huareo, Guayacán and his son, Hacona. They sat in a circle inside the *caney*.

"Justice has been done with the banishment of Guababo." Majagua beamed, and quickly turning his attention to Hacona, he said, "I have met in council with the judges of the *batey*. They ruled that you and the *guaribono* fought valiantly in the contest with Hatuey and his men from Haití. You will receive no punishment from your father."

"I serve you with respect and honour, Baba." Hacona showed no emotion.

"I know I have a devoted son in you, Hacona." He leaned back in the *dujo* and looked at Guayacán. "And do you, *bejique*, have words of prophecy to share with us?" Majagua chuckled.

"Yes, Cacique," Guayacán replied.

"What do you know?"

"I have fasted, Majagua, and cleansed my body of impurities."

"What do you wish to tell us?"

"It is a dreadful revelation, told by Yaya to our ancestors."

"Let us hear what Yaya says." Majagua fiddled with the *guanín*.

"Yocajú Bagua Maórocoti revealed truths to two ancient caciques of Haití, Cacibaquel, father of Guarionex, and Guamanacoel," Guayacán spoke firmly.

"And what did The Great One tell them?" Majagua asked.

"He told them that the Taíno, who remained alive after them, would *enjoy their dominion for but a brief time because a clothed people would come to their land who would overcome them and kill them, and they would die of hunger.*"

Majagua tensed the muscles in his arms and legs. "Is this not the prophecy that Macú spoke?"

"Yes, Cacique, except he did not tell us about the clothed people."

"But the man was mad and not to be trusted."

"I divined the words to be true, Cacique."

"This was a long time ago, Guayacán, and we have seen no enemy, no clothed people," Majagua insisted.

"I know, but the Great Spirit always tells the truth."

"Perhaps he means the *Caribe* will invade us."

"Even if this is so, Baba, we must prepare our men to be warriors," Hacona shouted.

"We will wait. Maybe you have heard the prophecy wrong, Guayacán. Our people must not know of this, for now they celebrate the harvest. Yocajú has brought us prosperity."

"But your son speaks wisely, Majagua. If our elders have warned us about an enemy, then it would be wise to make preparations," Guayacán challenged the cacique.

"We will speak no more of this. No harm will come our way," Majagua said.

With the approach of the third rainy season after Boinayel had sent his blessing, the crops were ready for harvest. From the fields, women hauled *yuca* bigger than the Taíno had ever known, as long and as fat as a child, free of rot and disease.

In a clearing outside the village, Huareo and other young men joined the women to make *casabe*, the bread of the *yuca*.

"Would you like me to show you?" Caona reached to take the clamshell from Huareo's hands. She squatted on the ground to place the root of the *yuca* between her legs. She moved the sharpened edge of the *caguará* up the rough sides of the tuber so thin slices of husk fell off to show the white flesh beneath.

Huareo watched her hands scrape the *yuca* in even strokes. "I have a *buyón*," he told her.

"Yes, you can use the flint in the same way to peel the skin."

He reached for a pile of tubers from hundreds that lay in the wide circle of villagers.

"You will be busy now that the harvest is here," Huareo said.

"Yes, and you men will rest." Her eyes smiled. "I think you prefer play to work." Sweat beaded on her face as she scraped faster.

"I work hard, Caona."

"That is good. So when you are married, you will be busy making gifts for your wives." She laughed openly.

"I will be busy, for I will want many wives when I am a man."

"As cacique, I am sure you will enjoy many."

"But only one will be special." He yearned for her to look at him.

"And how will you know who that is, Huareo?"

"I already know."

She turned, her face flushed and red.

Caona's mother, Yabura, entered the circle with four *naboría* who handed wooden graters to each of the women.

Huareo steadied a plate under the *guayo* to catch the white pulp. Between her legs, Caona held a grater, about the length of a man's foot, its surface covered with inlays of pointed chips of flint, whose sharp edges shredded the peeled root into bits.

"Yocajú Bagua Maórocoti has sent this gift to us." Huareo watched the white fibres falling from the *guayo* to fill the plate.

"You must hold the plate steady," she scolded him.

Huareo and Caona filled forty plates with the white pulp. He knew not to taste the forbidden juice for it was poisonous when raw and uncooked.

"Come with me," she said, as she stood. Her lips were full and red, her waist decorated with a cord of pink and white shells.

They wandered not far from the *batey*, into a grove of *majó* trees that sheltered the area between the houses and the fields.

"Hold this while I press the *yuca* inside of it." She handed him a sieve made of woven cotton, which extended the length of three feet, reaching from the top of his chest to below his waist. She pushed the pulp down the *sibucán*, and when the sieve could hold no more, the poisonous juices seeped through the sides of the woven mesh. Droplets spilled out on to his chest and belly.

"Do not worry; I will not make you drink the juice." She laughed. "Hold the *sibucán* away from you so it does not drip on you."

"I would not, unless you drink it with me as do the widows of the cacique who bury themselves alive in the tomb."

"Do not speak like that. It frightens me." She grasped her throat as if she had swallowed the *naiboa*.

They took turns filling each *sibucán*. They hung them on tree branches low to the ground. They tied a stick to the bottom of each sack, and then twisted them for the juice to drip into containers below.

"We must wash." Caona led him through the forest to the river Majó that curled snake-like over the hilly ground. She crawled into a shallow pool.

He followed her into the river and gently splashed water on her back.

"You may wash me," she said.

He cupped the river water and poured it over her shoulders and back.

"Huareo, did you mean what you said?" She turned to him.

"What did I say?"

"When you are cacique, you will take me as your wife."

"Yes, if your father gives his blessing."

"And if the cacique does not?"

"Then we will escape to a faraway place, the two of us."

"I know my mother will approve." She drew nearer to him.

She ignited a fire in him. He pressed against her and kissed her lips.

She pushed at his chest, moving back as if to tease him, and caressed his mouth with her finger.

Her sweetness reminded him of the night jasmine. He placed his arms about her waist and she folded in his tight embrace.

"You will be a mighty cacique, Huareo."

"How do you know this?"

"I know because Majagua's people already love you."

"And I love them too, but I have a deeper love for someone special."

"And who might that be?"

"Well, of course, she is Caona, the golden one, the daughter of the cacique."

Chapter Seven

"We have seen strange wonders never before known by our ancestors." The man took short breaths. "We first saw the lights on the line where Bagua meets the sky. They twinkled like stars, but they were different, for they moved along the horizon. We thought we were in a dream. The sea was calm, so we could see clearly. The lights came closer and I became alarmed. I sent a signal for the men of the village to gather on the beach." The man inhaled smoke from the *túbano,* a cigar of rolled tobacco leaves, which Majagua shared with him. His eyes reddened and widened as if he had seen Guayaba, the Spirit of the Dead.

Huareo sat in the home of the cacique with Majagua, Guayacán and ten nobles of the highest rank. These included Hacona and Yabey, and a man named Cuayaoya, a friend of Guayacán's family. The messenger had arrived earlier that morning in a *canoa* with four other men from the big island of Caobana at a time when the winds and rain were coldest.

"What is your name?" Majagua asked.

"My name is Guamá. I thank you for welcoming me to Yamaye." The man stood and then knelt to kiss the feet of the cacique.

"Where are you from?"

"I was born in the island of Guanahaní in the Lucayos."

"Are you warning us of danger to come?"

"I do not know."

"You have come from a faraway place to speak with us, and you do not know what message you bring."

"I come to tell you that we have seen peculiar creatures, Cacique."

"What creatures are these, Guamá? Are they from the

sky? Are they from the sea? Where did they come from?" The cacique cawed like the crow and his nobles mimicked his laughter.

Huareo remained quiet for he saw no reason to laugh. He wanted to hear the man's story.

"They are taller than any man we know, and their faces as white as the flesh of the barracuda. They have bushy hair, not only on their heads, but also on their faces. They wear clothes that cover the entire body."

"Are you saying they were clothed?" Majagua suddenly coughed on the *túbano*.

"Yes, Cacique."

"Well, did you see them drop from the sky?" Majagua mocked his guest.

"They came from across the sea, Guami Majagua, in boats they call *navíos*. The boats are mountains floating on the water, the size of twenty *manatí*." He spread his arms as wide as they could reach.

"This man is mad. Take him from here," the cacique said.

"It is wise to listen to him, Majagua. His story does not harm us," Guayacán pleaded with the cacique.

Majagua nodded for the visitor to continue.

"Their boats made noises louder than thunder and spurted balls of fire as bright as the *güey*. They had white cloths of cotton, tied to poles that reached the sky, and when the wind blew, the cloths filled with air and pushed their boats through the water." His hands twitched as he told his story.

"Did these people have a cacique?" Majagua asked.

"Yes, he was a man taller than the rest and he showed kindness to our people. He gestured to his men not to harm us and gave us strange gifts from his distant home. Our Taíno people loved him and called him *Guamikeni*. When they realized he was not their enemy, they swam out to the *navíos* to be with the *arijuana*, strangers."

"So, did this *guamikeni* tell you where his home was? I suppose he said Yaya sent him to visit you," Majagua said.

"We do not think they are *cemí* for they smell of rotten fish. If they were sent by Yaya…"

"And when did you first have dreams and visions of these creatures?" Majagua interrupted him.

"I did not see them through dreams, Cacique, but with my own eyes."

"And where are these hairy creatures now?"

"I escaped from them in the *cacicazgo* of Sagua in the island of Caobana."

"These kind creatures made you their prisoner?"

"Yes, they captured seven of us and said they wanted us to be with them."

"Why did they capture you?" Guayacán asked the visitor.

"They wanted us to be their guides, to show them the place where the *guanín* came from. They brought us in their *navíos* from our home in Lucayos to Caobana. We offered them gifts of cotton, we gave them water, the iguana and *casabe*, but they were not satisfied. They wanted the *guanín*. They desired it so much they asked to take it from our ears and noses. We told them we did not make it, that it came from another land, but they seemed not to understand or believe us."

"The man speaks with a false tongue, Guayacán. We must listen no more." Majagua stood, placing his feet on either side of the *dujo*.

"Cacique, I tell you only the truth," he said. "I escaped, but my brother, Guaicán, is still with them. The stranger *cacique* treated him kindly, and loved him so much he gave him the name of his own son, Diego Colón."

Majagua gestured to Hacona with a jerk of his head. His son wrestled Guamá from behind, bending both his arms backwards.

"Please free me, Cacique Majagua. I mean no harm. I will show you what they gave us."

Hacona released Guamá. The visitor pulled two small discs from a basket and held them up for Majagua to see. "They gave us these, they call them *blancas*. The *arijuana* are real, Cacique. I did not dream them. They came to Lucayos, took us to Caobana in their boats, and now they are with our people in Haití."

Majagua rubbed the strange objects with his fingertips. "What do you want from us, Guamá?"

"I come to tell you a stranger people have come among us," the visitor said.

Guayacán leaned towards the man. "You know, Guamá, that if we discover you are lying, you will not return home. You will be our prisoner, and your eyes will be removed from your head."

"What do I gain from speaking lies? Why would I put my life in danger to come so far from home?" He spoke in a high pitch. "The stranger people told us they planned to return home to tell their rulers of the wonders they have seen, but promised us they would visit us again. They were so happy when they arrived at Guanahaní that they cried, they kissed the ground and sang praises of thanks to their spirits."

"Take this man away," Majagua commanded his son. "Let us think no more of these tales. Make sure he leaves tonight with his friends and that their *canoa* are well stocked for a safe return."

Hacona dragged the man away.

The cacique turned to Huareo, "I want you to forget what he has said. Our people need to be provided for. In addition to the supply of fish and *yuca*, we must increase the hunt.

Hacona and Huareo sat beside an outside fire, which they built at the rear of the *caney*. Each held a green calabash between their crossed legs. Imitating Hacona, Huareo scraped the white pulp from the shell of the *jiguero*.

"How many do we use, cousin?" Huareo asked.

"The hunters will bring their own carved gourds, but they will also have those that the women have cleaned." The black fringe of his cousin's hair hung low, covering his flattened forehead.

"When do we go? It will be dark soon." His mother had always warned him about the *opía*, spirits of the dead that roamed the forest by night.

"Just as the light is ending is the best time to hunt." Hacona laid the gourd on the ground.

"Watch what I do," he commanded. He picked up the cleaned calabash shell and placed it over his head. He marked two spots with his fingers on the outside, opposite to where his eyes were hidden. He removed the calabash, and, with the *buyón*, cut two holes in the exact shape of his eyes.

"The inside smells like urine." Huareo held his nose.

"We will wash them clean."

Huareo carved his own and fitted it to his head. When he peered through the slits, his cousin's face loomed large before him. His vision was sharp; the holes were in the perfect spots.

"The men will soon be here. We need to scrape a few more before they come, but we will not carve holes in these."

"Hacona?"

He ignored Huareo and continued cleaning the calabash.

"Your father is preparing me to inherit his *cacicazgo*," Huareo said.

"Yes, we know this is why you are here."

"When I am cacique, I will want you to serve as my *nitaíno*."

"I will do whatever Cacique Majagua commands of me." Silence fell between them.

Eventually, Hacona spoke. "I saw you with my sister."

"What do you mean?"

"In the forest." Hacona averted his eyes.

"Did you follow us there?"

Hacona stood and gathered his weapons, the *macana*, a thick wooden club, and the spear, which he proudly carried as a sign that he was a *guaribo* of Majagua's chiefdom. "The men are here for the hunt."

Yabey and his friend, Cuayaoya, approached with twenty *naboría* carrying torches, and nets filled with gourds.

The horizon flashed red as if painted with annatto, but the colour soon faded. With the deepening dusk, bats escaped the ancestral caves and filled the darkness. They squeaked in a frenzied search for the *guayaba* fruit.

Huareo showed no fear. The Great Spirit was present to give him courage. If the *opía* greeted him, he would forbid them to touch him because they were spirits of the dead, creatures without navels who lived in the house of Mauquetaurie Guayaba, the one with no flesh. His *goiesa*, the spirit of the living, was stronger than their desires, brave enough to frighten them off.

The men trekked in a single line through the thick forest, the *naboría* in front lighting the way to the marshes where the *yaguasa* lived, the brown-coloured duck that whistled in the wind. The men, painted in black, were dressed with cords of sisal about the waist and they carried spears with points of sharpened flint.

As Huareo pushed his way through the overgrown paths, branches dampened his face and chest with drops of the early dew. The trees warned him of the dangers of the *opía* who wanted to take him to the underworld, but the spirits of the forest smiled and protected him from the dead.

Shadows cast white shapes in the dark. They hurried beside him as if they were travelling with him, darting about but making no sound. They resembled clouds of mist, but Huareo knew them to be spirits of the dead in the shape of living persons. He quickened his pace to follow the men in front.

One shape looked different from the rest. It moved like the other shadows but it had a distinctive face. It had long white hair and its eyes were wide and hollow. It ran naked in the bush with no protection, too fast for Huareo to tell if it had a navel, which was the scar of the living.

The pond formed a clearing in the marshes adjacent to the sea. The moon rose from the cave of Mautiatibuel, son of the dawn, with a smile that stretched from one end of her face to the other. Baba used to say the moon often hid from the sun because she was sad not to be with her brother, but that night she was happy. Her light was bright, shining white on the shimmering waters of the lagoon.

The bobbing *yaguasa* swam over the entire marsh, feeding, unaware of the dangers to come. Their bills reflected the white of the moonlight. In contrast, their necks were dark brown, and their striped wings, tucked to their sides, darker yet, almost black.

Hacona instructed Huareo to remove the uncarved gourds from the nets, the ones that had no slits.

Huareo floated twelve *guataca* one at a time, allowing the gentle breeze to carry them across the pond to mingle with the *yaguasa*. The men waited in silence to see if the birds would be disturbed. Not one took flight.

Each man fitted himself with his own mask. Huareo followed Hacona into the water. He slid into the lagoon, surrendering himself to the cool darkness of Attabeira. Huareo remained calm, but inside he burst with excitement, in anticipation of the hunt.

Huareo looked through the slits of the *guataca* that covered his head. The empty gourds floated, drifting in and out among the oblivious *yaguasa*. He waded silently in the water towards a bird that had moved away from the flock. Its eyes darted about when it sensed the danger, but Huareo was quick to reach under the *yaguasa* and grasp its legs with both hands. With a sudden pull, he dragged the bird deep under the water and in a final act, freed one hand and wrung the bird's neck. The animal went limp. He tied the feet of the dead bird to the sisal cord about his waist and then looked around to search for his next victim. All else was quiet on the lagoon. He had done it just as Hacona had instructed him.

One after another, the *yaguasa* fell prey to the hunters; they drowned in their own feeding waters until only a few remained.

"I will tell my father."

"What will you tell him, Hacona?"

"I will tell him the future cacique is a hunter. I will tell him Attabeira, the Spirit of the waters, welcomed you to the feeding ground of the *yaguasa*."

"And I will tell him that you are a natural teacher."

The *naboría* plucked and cleaned the birds and the women later preserved them in a mixture of pimento, nutmeg and *ají*, the red hot pepper of Yamaye. The whole chiefdom gave thanks to Yaya, the Spirit of Spirits, for Huareo and his hunters.

Chapter Eight

Three or four moons had passed since the visit of the man from Lucayos. The villages were prosperous and the Taíno at peace. Huareo had earned the respect of his uncle, Majagua, so it would not be long before he would ask the cacique for his daughter's hand in marriage. He was ready to take a woman as his wife.

"I will teach you to be a sculptor." Guayacán smiled, the wrinkles in his face disappearing for a moment. "You will learn to paint and carve images and to create *cemí* from wood and stone."

Next to Huareo on the floor of his uncle's house was the unfinished wooden figure of Opiyelguobirán.

With the sharpened end of the *buyón*, Guayacán cut deep gouges into the face of the dog to create sockets for his eyes. "This is the guardian that watches over the spirits of the dead. Here, hold this." He handed Huareo the knife. "The *caoba* is good for carving. The *buyón* will penetrate the wood but you must be careful not to crack it."

"Where do I cut?"

"I marked the place for his mouth. Cut a sharp edge, smooth and even, along this line."

Huareo slid the knife along the lower jaw, making an incision the full width of the dog's face.

"Repeat the cut, but this time, dig much deeper. Gouge into the wood because his bottom lip is fat." His uncle rubbed his finger across the smooth mahogany.

Huareo pressed the knife into the wood, curved the blade and sank it deep to form the rounded lips of Opiyelguobirán.

"Uncle?"

"What is it Huareo?"

"Do you ever become angry?" Huareo continued carving.

"We all do at times, Huareo. Why do you ask?"

"I never see you upset."

"Maybe as I have grown older, I have come to understand my dark sides and how to leave them behind." His uncle smiled.

"I feel my angry spirit a lot, Uncle."

"When have you been angry?

"Once, I almost killed my cousin." Huareo carved deeper with the knife.

"I am sure he must have wronged you in some way."

"He was a fool but I should have spoken to him, not fought him."

"It is good to tell me this, Huareo. *The true warrior is the one who goes into the dark places within himself to find the truth.* Just as the Great Spirit guides your hand today, He will give you wisdom to know yourself."

"Is it true He has no name, uncle?"

"Our ancestors tell us He is Yaya, Spirit of Spirits. No one knows his real name. His son is Yayael, whom He banished for four moons."

"Why did He banish him?"

"Banishment is a curse worse than death. It is the fate of your cousin, Guababo. Yaya banished his son because Yayael wanted to kill his own father."

"But Guababo did not want to kill Majagua."

"The cacique believes he did. And if his son returns, Majagua will kill him. Yaya killed his own son and put his bones in a gourd to hang from the roof of his *bohío*."

Huareo remembered the story his father told him. "And from this gourd came the fishes of the sea."

"Yes, and it came to pass that one day Yaya wanted to see his son, and this made his wife happy, but as she took down the *guataca*, she spilled her son's bones. Many fish, big and small, gushed forth and fell on the ground and filled the seas."

"Did they eat the fishes, uncle?"

"Yes, they ate some of them. Yaya gave us the fishes of the sea as food to nourish our bodies. He is the Great Spirit, Huareo. He is born of a mother, but has no father. *He is in heaven and he is immortal and no one can see him.*"

"He is also Cemí of the Yuca, uncle."

"And master of the sea." Guayacán admired the carving, rubbing the deep impressions of the dog's mouth. "You must finish your work." He showed his nephew the outlines of the nose and ears.

Huareo cut into the wood. "Uncle, do you think Macú will return?"

"People say you killed him." Guayacán laughed.

"No, this is not true. He disappeared by himself."

"If he returns, I know the villagers will kill him."

"I think he is still alive, uncle. I see him in my dreams and in the night when I go hunting. His *maboya* will hurt me if I do not kill him."

"If he is alive, then the time will come for us to punish him."

Huareo shaped the nostrils. "Uncle, do you think the man from Lucayos told the truth about the bearded men?"

"You ask me so many questions, Huareo." Guayacán patted him on the head. "I do not think he was mad."

"So why did Majagua tell me to forget what the man said?"

"Maybe he was worried the prophecy might come true."

"Then do you think the *arijuana* will come to Yamaye?"

His uncle fidgeted with his hands. "We must soon withdraw to the forest for seven days and seven nights."

He looked away.

"Why is that?"

"To purify the body and to drink the juice of *digo*, the sacred herb. I will teach you everything I know. You will learn that every tree has its own spirit and I will show you how to commune with them. You need to control this power to make it your own, and then you will be able to teach others. Otherwise, the forces of the forest will harm you, the *cemí* will be hostile and lead your people to sickness and death."

"You are a good teacher, uncle."

"As cacique, you will be the most valued member of the *cacicazgo*, the one who knows the *areíto*, the narratives and songs of our ancestors. Through this knowledge, you will dominate the forces of nature. The people will watch you and judge you. They will say, yes, this is the one chosen to lead us. You will know how to make tools, to use herbs and paints. You will make *cemí*, who remind us of who we are, and from whom we gain power and strength."

"I am ready to learn all that you teach me."

"You will be your own *bejique* one day. As you learn to master the arts, you will come to possess powers, to commune with the supernatural and to have control over the *cemí*."

"I am barely a man."

"This is good, for you have the vigour of youth."

"Look, uncle. It still needs work, but it is taking shape." Huareo admired the dog's long front legs and its ears as large as crocodile eggs. He peered into its eye sockets and imagined shiny discs of *guanín* inserted in the holes.

"The workmanship of a true artisan."

"Thank you, uncle, but I am merely finishing what you started."

"When you are finished, we will smooth the wood, rub and shine it with river stones blackened from the coal fires." His uncle frowned and leaned over to hold his hand.

"What is wrong?"

"It is the prophecy. If it tells us an enemy is coming, then we need to prepare just as Hacona has said."

"Even if they come we have the protection of the *cemí*."

"Our people have never before heard such a prophecy so ominous," Guayacán said.

Chapter Nine

Hatuey returned from Haití early one morning in a *canoa* with twenty men. The warrior was greeted by hundreds of Majagua's villagers and carried by *naboría* on a litter up from the beach to visit the cacique.

Majagua held council under the branches of the sacred *ceiba* that spread its shade over the roof of his house.

"The stranger cacique returned to his land and left forty men to build homes in Haití." Hatuey twisted his mouth. "And when he returned he found not one of them alive."

Majagua turned to ask Guayacán, "Are these the *arijuana* of whom the madman of Lucayos spoke?"

"Did you have a visitor from Lucayos?" Hatuey asked.

The cacique snickered. "Yes, he told us wonders of men with hairy faces and clothes that covered their bodies."

"These same creatures came to Haití in big boats from Lucayos and Caobana, ten or twelve moons past."

"How did the forty men die?" The cacique inhaled tobacco smoke and passed the *túbano* to his guest.

"Cacique Caonabó sent his warriors to burn their homes."

"I know you to be an honourable man who would not lie to me, Hatuey."

"Every word I speak is true, Majagua. I come from Haití out of respect for you and your people." The visitor offered the cigar to Huareo.

Smoke rushed into Huareo's throat and nostrils, which caused him to cough and spit.

Hatuey laughed. "Is this your first time? Pull the smoke in slowly. Hold your breath and then exhale," Hatuey said.

"Did Caonabó kill all the strangers left in Haití?" Majagua asked the visitor.

"Yes. I would have pierced them through with my own spear. They forced themselves on our women and destroyed our *bohío*." With a stick, he poked the *guatú*, the fire, which flared and reddened his face.

"Where is the cacique of the *arijuana* now?" Majagua asked.

"He prepares his boats to return to Caobana. He also wants to visit Yamaye which he heard about from the people of Lucayos," Hatuey replied.

"Why does he want to come here?"

"He wants to find gold. He believes you dig gold from the rivers of Yamaye to make jewellery."

"These *aijuana* are fools. The jewellery we have is *guanín* from the Yucatán. Let them come and see for themselves."

"You do not want them here, Cacique. They are dangerous."

"What do the cacique of Haití say?"

"They want them to leave, Majagua. Hundreds of the bearded ones have arrived to settle and build their own village."

"Have any cacique made friends with the strangers?"

"They are divided. Guacanagarí is their friend, but others do not trust them."

"The Great Spirit will guide us, Hatuey." Majagua shifted his weight in the *dujo* and beckoned to Huareo.

"You must stand united against them, Cacique Majagua. Do not let them build *yucayeque* in Yamaye. They are not our friends. One day I will gather an army to defeat these invaders."

"I thank you for the warning and for the goodwill you bring from your homeland. I believe you come in the spirit of friendship. My nephew wishes to offer you a gift."

Hatuey exhaled smoke that rose into the branches of the sacred ceiba. "You have given enough by listening, Guami Majagua."

The cacique stood and pointed to the royal *dujo*. "Here, please sit. This is reserved for you."

Huareo removed a collection of body stamps from a *macuto*, a deep basket made from vines. They were made of stone, intricately carved with etchings of *tona*, the frog. He knelt and kissed Hatuey's feet and placed the sculptures before him. "We give these to you in friendship." Huareo was proud to offer the sacred *cemí* to a brave warrior from the homeland of the Taíno.

"These stones of Yamaye will bring blessings to the people of Haití," Hatuey said.

"My uncle Guayacán and I engraved the stones."

"Then the gift is even more special, made by the hand of the man to be cacique." From the wrappings of a palm leaf, Hatuey uncovered a mask of white stone. He stood and placed the *guaísa* over the cacique's face. "This was made in the image of Behecchio. His spirit is with you when you wear it. With this gift, the great Cacique offers an exchange of friendship and invites you to visit him in Haití."

Majagua's wives and daughters, including Caona, brought out food for the guests. They served the cacique first and then offered the others a sumptuous feast of barbecued barracuda and *yaguasa* with casabe, freshly cooked on griddles.

Majagua bit into the dark flesh of the *yaguasa* and laughed. "The *arijuana* do not know food as delicious as this."

"And we will forbid them other pleasures as well." Hatuey joined in his laughter.

"You and your men are welcome here, Hatuey. As your gracious host, I remind you that we are one family and our relations can always be strengthened."

"Thank you, Cacique."

"How is my cousin?" Huareo blurted.

"Do you speak of Guababo?" Hatuey asked.

"I forbid my son's name to be called in my presence. Hatuey, we invite you and your men to be our guests at the *areíto*. Guayacán, prepare Huareo for the fast. He will lead the song, which will celebrate the coming of age of my daughter, Caona, and her marriage to our future cacique. I have consented to Huareo's request."

Chapter Ten

Huareo and eleven men followed Guayacán into the forest along a narrow path by the river Majó above Majagua's villages. Guayacán guided them through the *jiba* for the fast and for seven days and nights they ate nothing and drank only the juices of digo, the sacred herb.

On the last day, the men sat in a circle in a clearing by the river.

"Why do you think the strangers have been so wicked to the people of Haití, uncle?" Huareo asked Guayacán.

"We do not know who the *aijuana* are. I advised Majagua to call council." Guayacán was seated in the middle of the circle.

"We must have the cacique train warriors across the land," Hacona said.

"If there is an invasion, we will light signal fires by night and blow the conch by day," his uncle said. "Remember that greater power comes not from our weapons but from the *cemí* and the sacred truths of the *areíto*."

Next to Guayacán, the statue of a brown pelican held up a tray containing the sacred herb, its long beak wrapped around its bloated chest. The bird glared at Huareo with a fixed stare.

"The *aruna* will help us soar to the blinding light of *güey*." Guayacán stirred the mixture of herbs with his fingers.

Huareo received the *tobacú* from his uncle. He placed one end of the hollowed reed into the ashes and the other, which had two slender openings, he inserted into his nostrils. He gently snuffed the powder made from the pulverized seed of the *cojoba*. It did not burn him, and he did not cough or choke. He let the goodness seep within him and passed the snuff tube to the man beside him. When all had partaken of the substance, their spirits became as one, united with Yaya.

Guayacán called for the men to tighten the circle. He twisted his neck forward and around like a bird. "When you have children, you will teach them stories of our ancestors. These legends give power and tell truths about our people. In the beginning, our mothers and fathers were born from the cave of Cacibajagua in our homeland of Bohío. I will tell you about one of our ancestors, a man named Guahayona:

> Guahayona departed from the cave
> with all the women.
> "Leave your husbands,
> and let us go to other lands,
> and let us take much güeyo.
> Leave your children,
> and let us take only the plant,
> for afterwards we will return."
>
> Guahayona left the small children
> by a stream
> and went with the women
> in search of other lands,
> and he arrived in Mantininó
> where he left the women,
> and he went to another place
> called Guanín.
>
> Hunger troubled the children,
> and they wept and called to their mothers
> who had left them,
> and the fathers could not suckle the children
> who were crying for their mothers,
> "Mama, Mama."

They cried and cried for their mothers' milk,
"Toa, Toa,"
but their mothers did not hear them.
They cried so long,
"Toa, Toa,"
the children were changed into little animals,
they were changed into tona.
And this is what you hear
when the frogs of the land cry,
"Toa, toa."

"And were the women separated from their husbands?" Huareo asked.

"Yes, for the Spirit of Spirits willed it so."

"My father told me a story once," Huareo said, "of the day men went to bathe in the river, and when the rains came, they felt a strong desire for women. They found persons who fell from the trees, but the forms were neither men nor women. So they looked for the *inrirí*. The birds thought those creatures without the male or female sex were trees, and so they pecked holes in them. In that way, the Great Spirit granted the men their wish by creating Taíno women with whom to make love."

"He created another race of women who married the Taíno men and bore them children," Guayacán told the story as if it were a song.

The men's bodies and spirits were strengthened, not weakened by the fast. No enemy or *maboya* could ever steal their songs, the sacred history of the Taíno, as powerful as the *cemí*. Huareo would teach them to his children, who would teach them to theirs in turn. In that way, the customs of his people would never die.

"We must purify our bodies." The *bejique* summoned Huareo to sit before him. Guayacán pulled Huareo's head back as far as it would go so that his mouth opened wide and his eyes looked to the tops of the trees. His uncle then brandished the vomiting stick above his face. The bone handle was carved in the image of a crocodile with sunken eyes and bared teeth protruding from its jaw. Guayacán steadied the point of the curved blade above Huareo's mouth.

"You must cleanse your body before you perform the *areíto*," his uncle preached.

Huareo accepted the vomiting stick from his uncle's hands, and with his head still bent back, he forced the smooth, cold bone of the *manatí* down into his throat. He gagged. He swallowed, and gagged again, this time more violently, and his insides heaved. When he removed the spatula, he retched, and could not stop. He emptied all that was impure inside of him onto the ground beneath the sacred *ceiba*.

After all the men had performed the ritual, they descended to the river where they bathed with the soap of the *magüey*. They dried in the sun and used stamps to pattern themselves with images of the *cemí*. The men covered their naked bodies with paint, transforming themselves from beasts of the forest into men of the Taíno race, blessed by spirits of their ancestors.

Huareo's companions dressed him as a groom, with a headdress of green and red feathers, and golden rings in his nose and ears. On his arms and legs they wrapped bands of cloth, specially decorated with images of coloured feathers.

People travelled for the *areíto* from the distant *cacicazgo* of Yamaye and from the islands of Haití and Caobana. Musicians with wooden drums and dancers with maracas and scrapers lined the *batey* in joyful anticipation.

Huareo searched in the crowd for his mother and father. He wanted them to hear his storytelling, to watch him lead dancers in song, and to share the joy of his marriage to Caona. But they were nowhere to be seen.

Guayacán held the pink shell of the *guamó* and blew the signal to start the festivities. Thousands crowded behind the musicians to get a glimpse of Majagua's household assembled in front of the *caney*. The cacique was in full regalia. The *guanín* hung bright about his neck and his body was tall with the headdress of the feathers of the *guacamayo*. His wives and children stood on either side of him. An attendant carried the *dujo* whose golden eyes bulged and mouth opened wide with hunger. Majagua sat and called for a *naboría* to bring the sacred *cojoba*. He snuffed the holy substance, grasped his knees and leaned towards the head of the *dujo*. The cacique visited the world of the spirits and gave thanks to the Great One for the abundance of *yuca* and for his daughter, Caona, who celebrated the ritual of becoming a woman.

Caona stepped forward to face Majagua. She radiated a beauty as golden as the sun. She wore no paint or jewellery, she was as pure as the day she was born. She knelt before her father, who reached forward to place his hands on her forehead in blessing.

Her mother, Yabura, and sisters escorted Caona and Huareo to the centre of the *batey*. Caona crouched down and stared blankly in front of her. *Naboría* approached with woven baskets containing trappings and adornments for the bride. Huareo stood apart, silent and observant.

Her mother placed about her neck an amulet of Mother Attabeira on a string of white pearls that came to rest over her perfectly rounded *nati*. The bride stood and Yabura rolled bands of cloth high up onto her daughter's arms. Her sisters adorned her calves with cotton bands, her ankles with strings of pink shells, on her ears and nostrils, they fastened golden rings.

Caona's attendants prepared a red dye from the crushed seed of the *bija* and a black pigment from the fruit of the *jagua*. Two of Majagua's other wives decorated her skin, drawing red lines on her face and over her nipples. They dabbed their fingers in the black stain, marking her arms and legs with images of Attabeira, who brought her into the inner circle of Taíno women to prepare her for adulthood and shelter her from harm.

Her mother held the *nagua*. The cloth was elaborately woven, coloured a pale brown with red designs of the frog shape of Attabeira, the Giver of life and birth. She tied the loincloth below her daughter's waist to cover the innocence of her childhood and to clothe her with womanhood.

Huareo entered the inner circle of women and he and Caona looked at each other, sharing the expectancy of passion and love. Huareo knelt before her and bowed his head. He stood and placed in her hair a garland of red and yellow flowers and then lifted a vessel to her mouth. She closed her eyes and sipped the *cusubi*, the fermented juice of the *yuca*, wine transformed from the bitter poison of the tubers into the sweet drink of the sacred *cemí*.

He led her out of the circle to the end of the *batey*, where they knelt before the cacique to pay homage.

Majagua stood from the *dujo*. "You will lead us in song, Huareo, to celebrate the goodness of Yocajú Bagua Maórocoti, who brought us the *yuca*. Tell our people the story of the Taíno and welcome those who have come from far to celebrate with you and your bride, Caona. I give you both my blessing, and welcome you, Huareo, into my family."

The *mayohuacán* cried out. Huareo and Caona sounded the *maraca* and *guajey* to summon a group of young women to form a circle in the centre of the *batey*. The unwed virgins bore no *nagua*, but they wore red and white wreaths of flowers in their hair and bands of shells about their ankles, their arms and legs. The leaders chanted:

> *Bibi Atabey*
> *Coaiba Mamona*
> *Atte itaboera.*

> Mother Atabey
> Heavenly Mother of the Moon
> Mother of Waters.

The dancers and singers wrapped their arms about each other's waists. They beat the ground with their feet in time with the drums, and the bands of snail shells on their arms and thighs tinkled with the same tempo. They responded in chorus:

> *Acona Guakia Arawaka*

> Hear our sacred people.

Hundreds of dancers and musicians joined them, men alternating with women, forming larger circles until the *batey* was filled, their feet stomping the earth until it shook from the vibrations. The sun rose high above the chiefdom of Majagua, the heat of the *güey* giving strength to the dancers.

The cacique's attendants entered the circles with gourds filled with wine of the *yuca*. Men and women gave thanks, drank generously and passed the *jataca* from one to the next. The women jumped into the air, lifting one leg at a time, rattling the maraca in tempo with the drums. The *mayohuacán* beat harder and stronger. The men leapt up, pounded the earth with their feet, and linked together by each other's arms, they formed a tight circle around the women. The groups joined and danced in honour of Yaya.

Caona drank the *cusubi* until she was gratified. She flailed her arms when she danced, but her movements eventually slowed, and Huareo held her so she would not fall. Her mother wrapped the bride in a blanket and her attendants carried her through the crowd to the *bohío*, which had been built specially for her and Huareo.

After Majagua blessed the *casabe, the* women walked among the dancers and musicians to break the bread and share it with all.

Songs of the drums expelled the trickster spirit from that place, and the Taíno danced and sang into the night until they collapsed from exhaustion.

Yaya brought goodness to the *cacicazgo* of Majagua with the union of Huareo and Caona. The Spirit of Spirits granted the wishes of the cacique to restore happiness and prosperity to his people.

Chapter Eleven

Five moons after his marriage to Caona, a time when the one-legged man was nowhere to be seen in the sky, Huareo stood watch on the hills overlooking the villages of his uncle Majagua. Bagua was calm. No white caps showed on its surface, unperturbed except for the gulls diving for their evening feed.

The shapes first appeared as small clouds drifting on the horizon. He saw three groups of them, nine in all. They glided across the water as if they were formed into one, moving closer to the shores of Yamaye. They grew larger as they approached, appearing as peaks of mountains floating in the sea, darkening with the fading light of the setting sun.

Huareo blew the trumpet with his strongest breath. The sacred shell echoed its fateful message across the hills of Yamaye: *The arijuana are here.*

Men repeated the call of the *guamó* at each watch point on the hillocks stretching from Guayguata to Aguacadiba, to Maima and beyond.

Warriors descended the hills to board the *canoa* awaiting them on the beaches. The men were painted in black and wore *cemí* around their necks for protection; they carried spears with darts of flint and the *macana* made of the *guayacán*.

Forty men loaded each *canoa*. Half stood in the middle, brandishing their weapons, while the other twenty paddled in unison with a strength that sliced the water like a sharpened *buyón*. They beat the sides of the *canoa* and chanted fierce war cries as they surged forward towards the enemy.

Huareo's worst fears had come true. Three boats rose up out of the sea and were approaching the shores of Yamaye.

They were as long as the largest *canoa*, but much wider, and had wooden sides that reached out of the water, the height of two or three men. Three poles, five times the height of a man, carried broad white sheets that flapped in the gentle breeze.

The boats slowed and Huareo watched as the cloths were loosened to fall and wrap about the poles. Then the floating mountains changed shape, standing dead still in the water with their naked beams of wood.

With deafening cries, the Taíno encircled the dark creatures of the sea. Huareo's *canoa* approached the largest boat. He looked up to see the strangers, long hair bushed out from their white faces and, instead of feathers and paint, they wore clothes, and strange coverings on their heads. They waved white banners fastened to wooden handles, and smiled and fawned.

A boy who had the appearance of a Taíno leaned over the boat. "The *arijuana* come bearing gifts in friendship," he yelled in the Taíno language.

Huareo sounded the war cry of the conch. His warriors responded by shouting, and beating the sides of their *canoa*. The thumping noises quickened and strengthened like a storm. Huareo called upon the spirit of Guabancex, Lady of the Winds, to cast her spell on the strangers, to destroy them in her path with the forces of wind and water.

At that moment, from the bowels of the boat, a sound louder than thunder boomed through the air, fire burst a red shower of flames and smoke billowed everywhere. The Taíno panicked. Five smaller *canoa* capsized and the rest scattered to return to shore, but Huareo held his course to remain near the enemy. He would not let them land.

The strangers scrambled up the poles. The floating mountains took shape as the men pulled ropes to unfold the white cloths that started flapping in the breeze. The boats moved away, their long shadows chasing the fading sun.

Forty Taíno in each of five *canoa* paddled alongside to prevent them from coming ashore. As he followed the boats, Huareo noticed small blinking lights appear on board. He looked across to the land to see a string of torches burning on the hilltops lining the shore, a warning to the villagers of the impending danger.

After travelling the distance from Aguacadiba to Maima, the strangers' boats slowed and the white sheets dropped off the poles. Huareo sensed the threat and again sounded the conch to warn the *guaribono* on shore. Eighty *canoa*, already equipped and manned, quickly filled the bay in front of the village of Maima.

The strangers did not approach. They dropped heavy anchors in the open sea outside the bed of coral reef, and the *canoa* from Maima remained on guard in the water all night as a buffer between them and the land. Huareo and his men went ashore and lay on the beach to defend it from invasion.

As the first rays of orange light appeared, the strangers lifted their anchors, hoisted the white sheets and floated into the distance away from the rising sun. Huareo followed by sea with five *canoa*, while others of his men walked the paths along the shore in the direction of the boats.

The first bay the strangers tried to enter was shaped like a *bohío*. Low mountains and a smaller area of honeycomb rock formed the curved lines of the land, and a coral reef closed the circle at the entrance to the bay. The strangers lowered their own *canoa* from the boats. They were oddly shaped, fat and squat, and shorter than those the Taíno cut from the wood of the *ceiba*.

Fifty *canoa* rushed from land to block the narrow entrance of the bay. The Taíno howled angry war cries as they neared the enemy, forcing the strangers' *canoa* to scatter in every direction, taking flight to return to their boats waiting at sea. The Taíno stood waving their hands, celebrating with a thousand voices, screams of joy and victory.

"They are desperate to land because they must be hungry and thirsty." Huareo's muscles ached and his eyes burned for lack of sleep.

"Ha! They are afraid of the *guaribono* of Yamaye." Hacona stood with Huareo at the front of the *canoa*. "We will fight them, cousin. We will not let them invade Yamaye."

Ahead of the strangers' boats, Huareo and his men entered the next bay along the coast, which he knew had an abundance of fresh water. They drank from the streams, they washed in the mouth of the river and gave thanks to Attabeira for her bounty.

The three giants entered the bay, which was open to the sea without the protection of a coral reef. From their boats, the strangers lowered and boarded three *canoa* that they paddled towards shore.

Thousands of Taíno crowded the beach, curious to observe the unnatural figures of men and boats approaching the land. Fifty *canoa* of warriors pushed off from the beach to attack the invaders.

This time, the enemy *canoa* did not change course. Five stranger men, with thick grey coverings on their bodies, stood in the middle of each of the small boats. They held weapons different from the Taíno's, the bows more similar to those of the Caribe, but shorter and thicker, and attached to heavy wooden handles.

The Taíno assaulted the intruders with spears, but their weapons bounced off the hard coverings on the strangers' breasts and off the sides of their *canoa* into the sea.

The enemy's heavy arrows bolted through the air, stabbing six *guaribono* in two of the Taíno's *canoa*. The warriors fell instantly into the water. Their bodies floated in pools of blood, soon to be food for the *tiburón* that frequented the open bay.

The Taíno struck the sides of their *canoa*, retreating to shore in panic and despair. When they landed, Huareo and his warriors, armed with spears, stones and *macana*, withdrew behind the sea cotton trees lining the beach. They waited to engage the enemy in one-to-one combat.

The first stranger to come forward appeared to be their chief. He was taller than the others, walked in long strides and wore brightly coloured clothing that flowed behind him. Two other men followed, bearing poles with banners of yellow and red cloth.

Huareo and ten of his men stepped forward from the cover of the trees, the crowds behind them sounding the war cry.

An animal five times the size of a Taíno dog jumped out of one of the *canoa*. Its shark-like teeth were long and sharp. It growled, baring white fangs and drooling from opened jaws.

From the opposite side, the frightened Taíno hurled spears at the massive animal, but the weapons fell astray into the sand. The predator lunged at four men who had ventured out onto the beach. The dog pounced, throwing its first victim face down in the sand. It wrapped its jaws about the Taíno's neck and snapped his bones. The man lay dead on the sand. As the others scrambled to escape, a stranger aimed a long heavy weapon, which thundered and spat fire at one of them. The Taíno's body was blown apart. The giant dog bounded a second time, felling the other two *guaribono*. It ripped the legs of one man and tore out the entrails of the other.

Huareo shuddered from the howls of the wounded men, and vomited at the bloody savagery that unfolded before his eyes. He felt the comforting embrace of Hacona who placed his arm over his shoulder. Other men close by bent over in pain, retching from the sight of the disembowelled Taíno. Huareo then signalled for his men to retreat into the forest.

A man dressed in long, brown clothing called on the strangers to gather around. He clasped his hands and raised his head. "*In nomine patris et filii*," he spoke in a strange tongue.

His companions knelt, and with outstretched arms, repeated the words in solemn tones and sang praises to their spirit. Their chief stood and planted the red and yellow banner in the sands of Yamaye and repeated the words, "*Santiago, Santiago.*"

Huareo and his men watched in silence from the hillsides as the bearded ones returned to their boats. Huareo instructed two *guaribono* to remove the dead bodies, but to leave the *canoa* in place. The Taíno walked for an entire day along the paths of the seashore to return home to the *cacicazgo* of Majagua.

Chapter Twelve

The villagers of the bay where the strangers had landed appeased the enemy by offering them food and water on the day following the attack. The clothed men repaired their boats and left peacefully two days later without harming anyone or destroying the *canoa*.

After three moons had passed, two caciques from beyond the mountains reported that the visitors had returned to Yamaye. Their chief was friendly, and in return, the Taíno offered them supplies. The caciques received beads of many colours and a shiny stone the strangers called *vidrio* and in exchange, the Taíno gave them *yuca* and water, *jamaca*, and jewellery made of stones and shells. The visitors inquired about gold, but the Taíno had none to give them.

Huareo hoped that the bearded men would not return if they knew Yamaye did not have gold. He prayed to Atabey, Mother of all Waters and he nourished the *cemí* upon whose powers he would depend when he became cacique.

"You are now fully grown into manhood." Majagua raised himself in the *jamaca*. The cacique had become wasted with a sudden illness; his body showed shapes of bones beneath his skin.

"You must rest, uncle." He supported Majagua's shoulder to help him lie back in the bed.

"You are ready," Majagua said.

"Rest, uncle, do not speak."

"Ready to be cacique."

"I am grateful to you and Guayacán for preparing me."

"You will be a more powerful cacique than I am." Majagua coughed and gasped for air.

"You are a respected leader, uncle."

Guayacán entered the *caney* with two assistants.

"I called for the *bejique*," Huareo said.

"I do not want him here," the cacique spat his words.

"We will take the sickness from you, Guami," Guayacán comforted him.

"Take me into the forest." Majagua sat up in the *jamaca*. His bowl-like eyes bulged from his head. "Arrange for a *jamaca* to be tied between two trees in the forest." He looked about the room. "Where is the *yuke*?"

Guayacán reached for the ceremonial belt and, at the cacique's command, lifted the hulking stone to rest on Huareo's left shoulder.

"When you wear this, you have power to divine the wishes of the Great One," Majagua's voice strengthened.

Huareo lifted the heavy *cemí* to ease the pressure. He traced with his fingers the outlines of fish scales and of tona, the frog-like *cemí* carved in the image of Atabey.

"Others will want to take your power." Majagua fell back into the *jamaca*.

Huareo's hand reached for the shape of the headless snake engraved at the base of the *yuke*, which reached almost to his waist.

"Come closer." Majagua removed the *guanín* from his own neck. "Place this over your head, Huareo."

The golden disc rested snugly in the middle of Huareo's chest, warm and smooth like the touch of a woman. He fondled it, and inhaled, taking in the sweet smell of wild mushroom. It possessed its own light, a life like that of *guëy*, the sun.

"I was a fool, for I did not listen. I did not take advice from my *nitaíno*. Strangers have come and attacked our people. When you become leader, you must listen to those who give counsel and you must heed the word of the Great One.

When you sit on the *dujo* inherited from our ancestors, you will learn how to gain dominion over the sacred seat, and when you partake of the *cojoba*, you will commune with the spirits to divine truths and acquire wisdom."

"I will be honoured to serve our people, Cacique."

Majagua continued, "Make sure you guard the *cemí*. If you lose them or fall into disfavour with them, imposters will take away your sovereignty."

"I will acquire as many as I can, Cacique."

"Guayacán, take me now to the forest. The Cacique of the Spirit World calls me. Huareo, listen, for these are my last words: beware the *arijuana*, they are full of mischief and danger."

'Yaya would let no harm come to his people,' thought Huareo. 'Yocajú would rain fire from heaven to burn the strangers, and Guabancex would make the rivers and seas rise up to drown them.'

Two men cut the belly of the dead cacique with the sharp *buyón*. Hacona removed the liver, stomach and entrails, and severed his father's heart from the chest. The *naboría* laid the remains in a *jamaca* in the middle of the *batey* where the carcass smoldered for days until it was dried.

Guayacán removed the skull, wrapped it in a white cotton cloth and carried it to the prayer house. Huareo prayed to the sacred *cemí*, repository of the *opía* of his uncle, the spirit that lived after the body was dead.

Huareo arranged for a feast of *casabe*, the bread of the *yuca*, and *maisí*, the liquor made from corn. Caciques from the islands of Caobana and Haití and thousands of mourners from Yamaye gathered for the *areíto*. He presented his strongest warriors for the ball game and his most prized virgins for song and dance.

Dressed in the full regalia of a cacique, Huareo was carried on a litter from his house out to the *batey*. Feathers of the *guacamayo* and the medallion of *guanín* gleamed in the sunlight, patterns of red decorated his body and cotton bands accentuated the strength of his arms and legs. The attendants lowered him from the litter and placed the ceremonial stone belt over his shoulder. Standing with him was his wife, Caona, holding in her arms a newborn son whom they named Amayao.

Huareo raised one arm in praise of the Great One and in gratitude for the life of Majagua. He sat on the *dujo*, his royal seat of power, to partake of the *cojoba*. A melody of drums sounded in triumph and dancers performed in front of him to celebrate the new Cacique of Yamaye.

As leader of the dancers, Hacona told the story of Guahayona, the famous cacique of their ancestors, who returned to the land of the Taíno to bring home the *guanín*, and who thereafter was called *Guanín* by his people.

Dancers responded in chorus. Musicians joined them, playing the *mayohuacán*, the *maraca* and *güira*, flutes and whistles. Virgins decorated with garlands entered the *batey* bearing baskets full of *casabe*, which they presented to the cacique for his blessing. The maidens distributed the bread and danced and sang to give praise to Yaya.

The *areíto* lasted three days after which the remains of Majagua's body were placed in the ground. Huareo gave permission for Yabura to be buried alive with her dead husband. She was old and had suffered an illness that the *bejique* could not cure. She wanted to travel to be with Majagua in Coaybey, free of pain and sorrow in the resting place of their ancestors.

Her attendants dressed her with a *nagua* about her waist and on her ears placed the golden rings that Majagua had given her on their wedding day. They curled the willing wife of the cacique in the shape of a ball in the grave with the remains of her dead husband and gave her *casabe* and naiboa, the poisonous juice of the *yuca*. She bade her last farewell with a smile.

Her daughter, Caona, did not attend the funeral and for days refused to visit her husband, Huareo.

Part Two

The Chiefdom of Huareo
1498–1509

Guahayona stayed in the land of his father, who was called Hiauna. His father called him Híaguali Guanín, which means son of Hiauna, and henceforth he was called Guanín, and this is his name today.

Fray Ramón Pané

Chapter Thirteen

One evening, during the time of the second rains, Haureo lay with Caona on the grassland above the village. Normally the trees on the island in the bay were visible, but that day they were covered with a green haze, which hung low over the water. To his right on the mainland, the rounded peak of a mountain pushed itself through the mist in the form of the *cemí* of Yocajú Bagua Maórocoti.

"Your father chose a wonderful place for his *yucayeque*." Huareo broke the silence.

"Yes, but it is dark and gloomy today," Caona said.

"Every morning, the mountain peak of Yocajú casts its shadow of protection over the *cacicazgo*."

"Yes, He shelters us from harm."

"He has no beginning and no end. We cannot see Him, yet every day, the Blue Mountain peaks of Yamaye remind us of His presence." Huareo cut the fruit of the *jobo*, revealing its bright yellow pulp. "Do you want a bite?"

"You are tempting me, Huareo. You know what they say about those who eat the *jobo*?" She leaned towards him.

"Yes, of course. Those who wish to be lovers crave the *jobo*." He removed a slice from the blade of the *buyón* and placed it in her mouth.

"Huareo, I have never spoken to you about this." Her voice was low.

"What is it, Caona?"

"I was horrified by my mother's burial."

"I know you were angry. You did not speak to me for a long time, but it was her wish, Caona, to be with your father."

"I blamed you because she was overcome with grief and did not know her own mind."

"She lived a long life and wanted to be with him." Huareo pulled his wife close and felt the full length of her body against him.

They remained silent for a while in each other's embrace. *Toa, toa, toa, toa.*

"Do you hear that?" He cocked one ear to listen.

"Yes."

"This is the time that the *tona* are loudest, when the rains are heavy."

"The babies are crying for their mothers."

"We are hearing the mating call. The male feels close to the female, he wants to be with her." Huareo caressed her, tracing the curve of her shoulders with his fingers.

"Am I still your principal wife, Huareo?"

"I made you a promise."

"You have acquired many wives."

"Yes, but you know you are my first."

She gently pushed him from her. "You spend many nights with Yari."

"I have known her since childhood, Caona, from the *cacicazgo* of my father."

"I do not want her to bear your children."

He moved to close the distance between them.

Caona continued, "She steals you away in the night." She sat upright. Her breasts were riper, her body stronger after the birth of Amayao, her spirit brave, her voice as strong as the breath of the winds.

He had accompanied her to the river on the morning she gave birth to Amayao. He remembered how she squatted with legs spread wide in the water, supported by two *naboría*, one on either side. She exhaled deep breaths several times, quickening with each movement of her body as she heaved herself out of the water and twisted in pain. She held her tightened belly and pushed, bearing the full weight down on her assistants, and kept pushing, screaming, with her legs spread wide. The infant's head then emerged from her womb, his little body finding its way into the sacred river, into the safe arms of Attabeira.

"What are you thinking of?"

"Of the time you birthed Amayao."

"He swam so naturally into the river, we could have lost him after we cut the cord." She laughed. "I must know that you love me." She fondled his hair.

"You know I do." He held her breasts with both hands.

She stiffened and pulled his arms from her. "A messenger has told you my brother, Guababo, is coming to visit."

"His *canoa* will arrive soon from Haití."

"We must welcome him, Huareo."

"But your father banished him." He swallowed his anger.

"Majagua is dead, Huareo. You are cacique now."

"Our people will think me weak."

"Your people will never think you weak; they will judge you to be noble if you forgive my brother."

He gathered dry sticks from under the tree of the *majó*. He held one upright and placed another flat on the grass, and rubbed them together until the brittle wood sparked. He smothered the sparks with handfuls of dried leaves and kept blowing until smoke appeared. Flames twirled into the night as Huareo and Caona stoked the *guatú*.

"I suppose you are right. Macú is the one possessed with the *maboya*, not your brother." His face burned from the heat of the fire.

He grazed his hand over her navel and reached under the *nagua* that covered her waist. She did not pull his hand away. "You will give me many children."

"Yes, but I must be the only one to give them to you." She chuckled.

"I cannot promise you that, but I want to be the only man you love."

"I desire none other, Huareo." She let him remove the cloth from about her waist.

Their shadows, formed by the light of the fire, danced madly in the night.

Chapter Fourteen

"You are a brave Taíno, or a stupid one," Huareo said to Guababo.

They sat around the centre pole of the *caney*, Huareo on the *dujo* and Guababo on the floor next to their uncle, Guayacán. Two men stood guard outside the entrance to the home of the cacique.

"I have come home to ask your pardon, Huareo."

Guababo's face was as he remembered, round and youthful, but he had grown bulkier and more manly. His speech and actions were spirited and agitated.

Huareo rolled red and green beads between his fingers. He handed them to Guayacán. "Are these gifts from the *arijuana*?"

"Yes, they call them *vidrio*." Guababo's eyes darkened.

"We do not want these gifts." Huareo waved his hand for his uncle to return the beads to Guababo.

"I do not bring them as gifts, Huareo. The strangers gave us these, thinking we would have use for them," his cousin said.

"The bearded men already came to Yamaye, Guababo, we want nothing more to do with them."

"They have taken our women without permission, slaughtered our children and burned our *yucayeque*." Guababo shouted. "They are at war with us, cousin. They want to take the land. They value gold more than life itself and tell us their ruler will be pleased if they take it home. They force our people to abandon the fields to spend all day gathering flakes of gold from the rivers."

Guayacán straightened his back. "The prophecy is fulfilled, Huareo," his voice rattled.

"No one is going to take the land from us, uncle." Huareo lifted his hands from the head of the *dujo* to reveal the golden eyes of the *cemí*.

"Huareo, the strangers are destroying our homeland, Bohío. They capture our caciques and kill them. They imprison our people by the thousands and take them as slaves if the gold they trap is not sufficient. They tie men together with ropes and load them on their boats and we never see them again."

"Do you speak the truth, Guababo?"

"My word is true, cousin. The Taíno who are not being murdered and imprisoned are dying of hunger."

"How is Hatuey?

"He is well, he watched over me during my banishment and is now a cacique who assisted Behecchio in raising a force to fight the strangers."

"Guayacán, call a meeting of our *nitaíno* and caciques of Yamaye. They must know of these happenings." Huareo stood from the *dujo*. "Guababo, my council will decide whether you remain with us in Yamaye."

"He is innocent, Huareo," Guayacán said.

"This is not for you to decide, uncle."

"What do you know, Guayacán?" Guababo blurted his words.

"We know it was Macú who tricked Guababo into stealing the *cemí* of Yocajú," Guayacán shouted.

"Yes, but my cousin was the one who removed it from the *conuco*."

"Do you know why the crazy man wanted to trick me, uncle?" Guababo asked.

"He wanted to destroy your father."

"Why?" Guababo asked.

"Macú was the one chosen to be cacique. He was the eldest nephew but Majagua persuaded my father against it." Guayacán held his side in pain.

"Why have you not told me this before, uncle?" Huareo asked.

"I had no reason; Macú disappeared and so did his trickster spirit."

"I do not think he is dead," Huareo said. "Guababo, I want you to help me find and destroy Macú."

The three men shared a meal of *ajiaco*, the pepperpot soup, fish and *casabe*, served in *canarí*, clay bowls, moulded especially for the cacique in the shape of the sacred turtle. They feasted long into the night, and drank the liquor of the *maisí*.

Chapter Fifteen

"The *maboya* has possessed some women and children of the *yucayeque*," Guayacán informed the cacique.

"Do not bring me foolish tales," Huareo said.

Caona cried out from the *jamaca*.

"You must rest, Caona." Huareo kept vigil beside her bed.

Caona's hair fell loose and straggly about her shoulders, her body sweated and shivered as if the day were cold and she coughed and complained of a pain in her chest.

Huareo normally slept with one of his wives, but he was alone that evening with Caona and Guayacán. He admired the way Caona kept his home. She had enhanced the *caney* with latticework and paintings etched on tree bark, baskets containing food provisions hung from the ceiling on one side and, on the other, her personal *cemí*, body seals and jewellery, amulets and necklaces decorated the walls. Close to these, he secured his weapons, spears, axes and *macana*, and the prized *cemí* of the stone belt with the headless snake.

"I will not live long, Huareo," Caona whispered. She leaned forward and rubbed her belly in circles. "But I promise to keep our baby safe."

He bent over the bed to kiss her navel. "Why did you not tell me?"

"I have only known for a short while."

He rested his head on her to feel the baby.

"The baby is fine." She held his hand.

"Huareo, you must take your wife to rest in a *bohío* outside the village where no one lives, and I will treat her illness there," Guayacán said.

"I will stay with her."

"She must be alone until I cure her, Cacique."

Huareo felt his anger rise inside him. "Guayacán, if you take her from me and do not heal her, you will suffer the horrible fate of the *bejique* who does not cure the sick."

"My life depends on it, Huareo."

The naked man crept on all fours like Opiyelguobirán, the dog of darkness, into the centre of the *batey*. "Hua...re...ooo, Hua...re...ooo," he howled in the night.

Huareo approached.

The moon hid her face behind low hanging clouds so as not to show her smile, and raindrops pelted the open ground, making deep pools of mud.

Guababo emerged from the house of the cacique with three companions carrying wooden clubs raised above their heads.

The man stood, his skin pale and his hair, white and ragged. He wore no paint, no jewellery, feathers or bands of cloth, his body withered as if he were already dead.

The cacique faced the man and waved his hands before him. "I am Huareo. What do you want, Macú?" He realized the former *bejique* must be fully blind for his eyes darted madly in his head. His breath was foul, his teeth long and yellow.

"You have taken the seat of power that does not belong to you," the man screeched.

"You are a fool. You do not belong here." Huareo butted the end of the *macana* against the man's hollowed chest, which forced Macú to fall backwards into the mud.

"You are an imposter like Majagua," the man muttered. He lay flat on his back, unable to move.

Guababo approached, and looked to Huareo for permission. He flattened his foot on Macú's chest. "Old Macú, do you remember me? I am the one you sent into the fields."

Macú scrambled in the mud to raise himself, but Guababo pushed him back down with the fat, blunt end of the *macana*. The man lifted his arms to guard his face from blows of the club.

"You are a blind old fool." Guababo looked again at the cacique for his consent. Macú's legs were spread wide in the mud, his manhood exposed.

"I meant you no harm, Guababo. I did it for your good," Macú whined, writhing in the mud.

"Shut up, your words are foul. You have the *maboya* within you." Guababo stood astride Macú, facing his feet, he raised the *macana* and smashed it between the old man's legs. Macú shrieked with pain, a howl more horrific than Huareo had heard from man or beast.

"This is just punishment for your crime, Macú, you will never again walk as a man."Huareo spat at the man squirming in the mud.

The men dragged Macú off the ceremonial ground, and they cast him in the dark forest where yellow snakes came to lick his wounds.

The following day, the villagers found him in the woods, removed his genitals and beat him to death with the *coa*. They built a pyre in the middle of the *batey* and burned his body in homage to Yaya.

After his death, Huareo's people were satisfied that Macú was destroyed, but they would always be watchful of the *opía* with the straggly white hair.

Chapter Sixteen

Huareo's father, Ameyro, offered him the *cemí* of Yocajú as a gift. "I bring this from the place of your birth."

The smooth grey stone was similar to the one Guayacán buried in the *conuco* except that this *cemí* was wrapped in an image of the serpent.

"For some, it is the breast of the female, for others it is the young shoot of the *yuca*." His father rubbed the hump in the middle of the stone.

"Yes, Baba, and for others, the top of the *bohío* or the organ of the male." Huareo laughed heartily.

"He is half *cemí*, half human." His father laughed.

"But the face is carved in the image of the deity." Huareo turned the heavy stone. "On the other side, I see the carver has sculpted legs of the frog."

"I hope it will bring you continued prosperity."

"Thank you, Baba. I will place it in the prayer house with the others."

"I bring it in amends, Huareo. Your mother and I were sorry we did not come for your wedding."

"How is she, Baba?"

"She has passed, Huareo, to the land of Coaybey."

A sharp pain stabbed his chest. "Why did you not tell me?"

"She did not want you to feel sad, Huareo."

"I would have wanted to see her. Did she suffer long?"

"The *bejique* tried to cure her, but the sickness would not leave."

"Her love will always be strong even though she is dead. Her spirit is in a good place. I thank you for your gift, Baba. Let us join the assembly."

On that day, Huareo hosted the chiefs of the *cacicazgo* of Yamaye: Maima, Aguacadiba, Guayguata, Anamaquique, Caguaya, Guanaboa, Guatibacoa, Yama and Caobana. They were dressed in the formal array of the cacique. The venerable Cacique of Yama wore a magnificent cotton headdress of feathers, embroidered with golden thread, and a belt sewn with beads of black and white pearls.

"A stranger people from a land we do not know arrived many moons ago and we are blessed that they have not returned. But they have settled in our homeland, Bohío, where they have ravaged women, captured caciques and massacred thousands of our people," Huareo spoke in his position as paramount chief of Yamaye. "I welcome home my cousin, Guababo, who long ago was banished by his father, Majagua, for a crime that was not his fault. I also welcome my father, Cacique Ameyro, whom we thank for travelling from Anamaquique, and to all of you here for coming to meet in council, I extend my friendship."

"The strangers left us alone because they know we do not have gold," Huareo's cousin Mamyo, Cacique of Maima, responded. He was a short man with broad shoulders and muscular arms and legs.

Huareo, in an attempt to expand his chiefdom, had sworn friendship with Mamyo. They exchanged two virgins to become their respective wives. But his cousin was not ready to surrender his authority. Many more favours would be demanded before Maima became part of the *cacicazgo* of Huareo.

"We cannot be sure, Mamyo, that they will stay away. They are greedy, they will want to search our rivers and land for gold."

The Cacique of Yama leaned forward. "Some of you know the strangers returned to Yamaye and visited us," he offered. "Their cacique was kind, he gave us clothes, knives and beads, and in turn we paid him homage by bringing food and water so he would not harm us. A young Taíno, whom he named Diego, was his interpreter. He told us the strangers live in a land governed by mighty rulers."

"We must be cautious. These are the *arijuana* who have killed our people in Haití." Huareo chose his words carefully out of respect for the Cacique of Yama.

The visiting cacique continued, "But they were kind to us. I even asked their cacique if he would take me to their rich land, but he said it was too far, that he did not want to remove me from my people."

Huareo stood. "We must not trust the bearded ones. If they return, we give them food and water, only if they ask, but we do not make bonds of friendship and we do not offer them our women. We do not allow them to land or build their houses here. Their spirit is hostile, we do not understand its power over us."

"They will return, my son," Ameyro prophesied, "and when they do, we should not anger them for they will harm us."

"Their chief asked me to give you this message: his rulers, whom they call, *los reyes*, promise to be respectful of our people. They will work with us to make our land rich," the Cacique of Yama announced.

Guababo clenched his fists. "The *arijuana* are cruel and not to be trusted. The people of Haití tried to appease them, to bring them into their company, but the spirits of the Taíno would not accept the bearded ones. The strangers are wild and our powers cannot tame them or make them human."

"Did the *arijuana* kill the Taíno in defence?" Mamyo asked.

"No, Mamyo. At the start, the cacique welcomed the stranger people." Guababo raised his voice. "They accepted our offerings but they showed no goodness in return. Instead, they destroyed our villages. Only then did we fight them, but we had no defence. Our arrows were useless against the hardened shells of their clothing and our spears too weak to kill their ferocious dogs."

"My fellow caciques, we need a plan in case these strangers return." Huareo signalled to an attendant for food to be served. "Yaya did not send them. They are cruel and heartless. When they visited us, they set their wild dog on us, killing seven of our men."

"That is because we tried to prevent them from landing," Mamyo said.

Huareo felt his body tense with fury. "Cousin Mamyo, you do not listen. Even if we are good to them, they hurt us, they rape our women and steal the land." His voice was resolute. "We must stand united and pray for guidance. We have attained prosperity and will not allow a stranger people to take this from us. Do you understand, cousin?"

Mamyo did not reply.

The caciques agreed they would seek advice from the *cemí* and from their councils of elders, and they would train warriors to defend the land and people of Yamaye.

Chapter Seventeen

With the passing of the rainy seasons, Huareo's chiefdom grew to be the most prosperous of Yamaye. It supplied neighbouring *cacicazgo* with surpluses of fish and ground produce and received *sarobey*, the sea island cotton in exchange. Men and women from other parts of Yamaye settled there to work, and serve the cacique.

At Huareo's request, Hacona supervised the building of a *canoa* specially carved from the trunk of the *ceiba*, the longest boat of any in Yamaye, big enough to hold sixty men.

"We have decorated it as you asked, Cacique, with the face of Guabancex and with carvings of *tona* on its sides." Hacona beamed.

"It will give us power over the enemy," Huareo said, admiring the detail of his cousin's handiwork.

"The *cemí* will make you master of the sea."

"You are a fine *nitaíno*, Hacona."

"Thank you, *Guamikeni*. I promised my father I would serve you."

"I was not always sure."

"I gave you my word, cousin."

"When we were younger, you were angry."

"We must forget this. We are men now. I was not certain my father would approve of your marriage."

"He would be proud of you, Hacona." Huareo's face saddened. "Your sister is not well, and I am worried the *bejique* may not cure her."

"You are blessed that your child was born safely, Cacique."

"Yes. We have named her Aquiana. I shall raise her to be strong of spirit like you so she may be a ruler of her people."

According to plan, the *bejique* placed Caona in isolation in a *bohío* built in the forest far from the village.

"I am worse, Huareo." Tears welled in her dark eyes and her hacking cough persisted.

"You are strong, Caona." He grasped her hand to comfort her, biting his bottom lip to stem the flow of emotion he felt rising inside him.

"You should not hold me."

"The sickness will not enter me," he said. Her hands felt frail and clammy.

"The *bejique* has tried to remove it from me."

"Then he will try again and again until he cures you."

"Make me a promise, Huareo."

"What is it, Caona?"

"Promise me you will keep our children safe."

"Yes, from all danger. I shall also teach them all I know. They will grow to be Taíno wiser than their father." He squeezed her hands.

"Huareo, do you believe in the *opía*?"

"Yes, but your *goiesa* is alive, Caona."

"Do you believe my spirit will travel to another place?"

"At the time of death, it escapes to Coaybey where Maquetaurie Guayaba dwells. But you must not worry for the *bejique* will cure your illness."

"I am afraid. Guayacán is old and has lost his power to cure the sick."

"The *bejique* knows that if he fails, the villagers will punish him." He looked at her ailing face. "But if it is your time to leave, you will never be far. You will wait for the *güey* to go down and then you will come to me, and I will lie with you. You will feast on the succulent *guayaba* and your *opía* will be joyous. You will have sex and rejoice, you will sing and dance."

"Will you make me another promise?" She raised herself in the *jamaca*.

"Anything you wish."

"Do not cut or burn my body when I die. Instead, wrap me in cotton cloths and keep me whole." Her eyes regained their life. "Huareo, I must tell you a secret I have kept in my heart."

"What is it, Caona?"

"My mother is dead, so I can reveal it, but only to you."

"What is your secret?"

"We are not cousins, Huareo." She lowered her head and hid her face in her hands.

"Look at me, Caona." He pulled her hands away. "How do you know this?"

"My mother told me."

"Told you what?"

"Majagua was not my father."

"Did he know that?"

"No, she dared not tell him."

"I do not care, Caona. It is not our shame to bear."

"But you must speak this to no one."

"I always keep my word. Caona, tell me, would you have married me if you had thought we were cousins?"

She extended her hands to his. "Yes, Huareo, it would have changed nothing, for I love you more than life."

A shadowy figure parted the canes that blocked the entrance of the *bohío*. The person entered, his face blackened with charcoal and the rest of his body obscured by the dye of the *genipa*. He was gaunt, more ghastly than the patient, with white hair draped over his darkened shoulders.

The *bejique* approached Caona. He breathed heavily and stared at her in silence. His upper arms and legs were bound with cloth that framed his limp, bony joints. Bright feathers of the red-tailed hawk decorated his hair and dark plumes of the ground dove covered his groin.

Caona lay back down in the *jamaca*. She shivered and her eyes widened, frightened at the spectacle before her.

Huareo broke the silence. "What cure do you bring her this time, uncle?"

Guayacán did not answer. He unwrapped the herb of the *güeyo* from the leaves of the wild onion, and mixed it in a bowl with ash and the crushed leaves of another herb. With a stone pestle carved in the image of the night owl, he kneaded the concoction, sneezing and coughing from its pungent smell. He placed the emetic in a bowl and then into his nostrils and mouth. The *bejique* gagged and choked. He bent over in pain, withdrew to the entrance of the *bohío* and vomited violently, his impurities spilling onto the ground outside.

At Guayacán's beckoning, Huareo reached under his wife and scooped her up to place her on the *dujo*.

The *bejique* gathered a portion of the mixture from the *canarí*, the clay bowl which had handles carved in the shape of the wings of the night bat. He moistened the herbs with his saliva and fed Caona the substance. She grabbed her belly, convulsed and retched uncontrollably but she had neither food nor water to purge.

Guayacán watched in silence.

Huareo lit a torch and waved the flames up and down her body, from head to foot. He swung it wildly so the blaze would scorch the *maboya* that consumed her body. He cursed the spirit that made her sick and prayed for her to be cured.

Guayacán encircled the patient three times, beating the ground with his feet in rhythm to the sound of the *maraca*, humming incantations to Yaya for the wisdom to know the cause of the illness. The old man crouched before Caona and stretched out her legs. He dragged his healing hands over her body, rubbed her legs and feet, and pulled on her limbs to draw out the *maboya*. He commanded the spirit to depart that place, to go far away into the forest or the sea, and in a fit of rage, flailed his arms to expel and smash the *maboya*.

The *bejique* cupped his hands to his face, breathed out and then inhaled the smell and taste of Caona's illness. He puffed repeatedly and placing his trembling hands over his mouth, sucked them hard. After he sought Huareo's consent, he asked Caona to recline in the *dujo*. He spread his legs and leaned his frail body over her to rest his hands on her shoulders.

Huareo was disgusted to see his uncle bent over his wife, his mouth about to envelop hers, but he knew that for Guayacán to cure her, the *bejique* needed to suck the sickness from her into his own body.

Caona jerked her head away and violently pushed him off so he fell back onto the ground. She arched her back and screamed in pain, widened her legs and rubbed the sides of her belly for relief. "Be gone from me, Guayacán," she shouted. "You disgust me, you have lost the powers of the *bejique*. Let me alone to die."

Guayacán escaped punishment, for the villagers understood that Caona refused the *bejique's* treatment. If she had accepted and he failed, they would have beaten him, broken his arms and legs with the *macana*, cut out his eyes and penis and left him to die in the forest.

The cacique went into mourning for many moons. He secluded himself, incredulous that Yaya would have taken away his wife, so young. He had thought the Spirit of Spirits may have been displeased because their blood was too similar, that Caona's father and his mother were as the sun and the moon, born of the same parents. But this was not the case. He would never fully understand the world of the *cemí*. He had consoled her about the pleasures of Coaybey, but he hated Maquetaurie Guayaba, the Spirit of the Dead, who took his beloved from his arms on a journey into the underworld. The Watchdog of the Dead had waited for her and when the sun went down, he captured her in his cave on the Island of Soraya. He was the one without life. His eyes were empty sockets, his mouth a cavern wider than his face and his nostrils the cavities of a skeleton. He was the *cemí* who changed Huareo's loved one into the form of a bat to dwell within the cave, where she stayed deep inside the darkness with her ancestors, afraid to leave in the light of the day lest the sun turn her to stone.

Huareo's people warned him that he should not walk alone at night, but his desire for Caona was too strong to resist. He ventured out at dusk, a time when the *opía* hunted for the fruit of the *guayaba*. He roamed unafraid through the forest, until in the middle of the night, her form appeared as if she were alive. He recognized her even though she was not of the living. His passion was aroused with a burning desire to be with her. She welcomed him, and so he lay with her in the forest. When he thought he held his Caona in his arms, he felt nothing. Her shape, which had been so real, swirled up and away from him and disappeared into the night.

Chapter Eighteen

On the hill overlooking the village of Maima, Huareo and ten of his trusted *nitaíno*, including Hacona, Guababo and Yabey, gathered with Cacique Mamyo and a group of men of the region. Many moons had passed since the death of Caona, but even more horrible than that loss was the spectre Huareo beheld that morning. Two *navíos* sat squat, rammed fast into the sandy shore of the bay inside the coral reef. Waves reached up the sides of the boats, splashing the decks of the leaning giants.

"What are they building on top of their boats?" Huareo asked.

"Their *bohío*. They are using what wood and thatch they find by the shore," Mamyo replied. The *guanín* about his neck glistened in the early morning sun.

"They are afraid, cousin." Huareo chuckled. "It seems they are hiding from us; they are keeping to their boats. How many are there?"

"We do not know. Only a few came ashore last night to gather sand and materials. We saw a couple men take turns on watch while the others slept."

"So these are the mighty strangers who rape our women and burn our *yucayeque* in Haití. And now their boats have come to ruin on our shores." Huareo turned to the hills so all of Yamaye would hear him. "Yeaaaaaaaaaaooooooooooow!" The *nitaíno* joined him, repeating his cry of defiance and victory.

Below them, tiny figures scrambled out onto the decks, scattering across the length of their boats.

"Ha! Look at them, Guababo. They are cowards running about. There must be at least a hundred of them." Huareo blew the conch to tell the neighbouring villagers they were safe, but that they should remain on guard. At the sound of the shell, the strangers disappeared, insects scurrying into their holes for safety.

"Their hearts are not brave like the Taíno." Huareo was confident he had power over the *arijuana*, strangers to the land.

"They may want food and water," Mamyo remarked.

"Yes, Mamyo, but we will starve them so they die." Guababo burst with raucous laughter.

"Guababo, you laugh like a fool. Don't you know that if we give them what they want, they will leave us alone?" Mamyo replied.

"How will they leave us? Their boats are wrecked. They cannot move." Guababo stood warlike, weapons in hand.

"We need to feed them and repair their boats so they can leave Yamaye," Mamyo said.

"I do not trust them." Huareo picked up his spear and *macana* to prepare for his descent. "What do you say, Yabey?"

"They are a stranger spirit, Cacique. My father tells me I should fear them."

"Fear will destroy you, *guaribo*. You are to be brave of heart."

"We will make them starve and die," Guababo interjected, glaring at his older brother, Mamyo.

Huareo sounded the *guamó* for warriors of neighbouring villages to assemble by the beach. He and his men pushed their way through the brush at the top of the hill and slid, iguanas on all fours, down the cliffs of white marl to land on the flat below. They trekked through the swamps to join other Taíno who were gathering in the red mangroves behind the sea cotton trees.

Four bearded men, fully clothed and wearing pointed hats, climbed down the side of their boat onto the beach. They carried pointed weapons, the ones used to spit fire at Huareo and his men when they first landed in Yamaye. The strangers walked in a straight line to the centre of the beach, the man in front carrying a pole with a white cloth that ruffled in the wind.

The strangers fell prostrate on the sand and covered their heads with their hands. Huareo commanded his men not to attack.

"Look at them, they act like children hiding in the sand," Huareo said as he and Mamyo moved out from behind the trees onto the beach. With his hand on his mouth, the cacique bellowed the sounds of victory, raising his voice louder and louder to see if he could scare and disorient the strangers. But they lay motionless in the sand.

Huareo waited. Eventually, the man holding the white flag stood to face the caciques. "We come in friendship," he shouted in the Taíno language.

Huareo and Mamyo stepped forward.

"My name is Diego Méndez." The man's beard was long and pointed, dark against the white skin of his cheeks and forehead. Every other part of his body was covered with a grey shell, stiff and hard as stone.

Huareo and Mamyo remained silent.

"We are hungry. Our food is spoiled and rotten from the heat."

Huareo was nauseated by the man's stale, fish-like smell.

"Our *navíos* are damaged and full of seawater."

"You are not our friends. We do not want you here," Huareo spoke.

"We do not intend to stay, Cacique, but we need your help. Our men are without food or drink."

"In the morning, my village will provide your men with *casabe* and water," Mamyo blurted. "How many men do you have?"

"Over a hundred." The man called for his three companions to stand.

At Huareo's beckoning, hundreds of Taíno emerged from behind the trees.

"And what will you give Cacique Mamyo in return?" Huareo asked the stranger.

"We will give you whatever you want. We have gifts from our land, clothes, beads and hats."

"The finest gift would be for you to leave Yamaye," Huareo said.

"This is our intention, Cacique, to find rescue so we can leave your land, but first we must save our men. We are grateful for the offers you make."

"You must promise to keep your men on the boats and away from our *yucayeque*. We will kill you if you steal or hurt our women and children."

"These are also my Admiral's wishes. I will hold to these promises, Cacique."

Huareo knew the man's words to be false, spoken with the tongue of a stranger whose friends had betrayed and killed the Taíno of Haití.

As the bearded men turned to leave, the warriors formed a blockade in front of the sea cotton trees to ensure that the four men returned directly to their boats.

Chapter Nineteen

"**W**hy do our homes form a circle, Baba?"

"Yes, the *yucayeque* are built in a circle and each *bohío* is round." Huareo lifted Amayao onto his lap.

"Why, Baba?"

"Well, Amayao, we do not know all the answers, but look at the *güey*, it is round. Look at his sister, the moon, she is also round. Look at the curve of the blue above us." Huareo lifted the boy's chin for him to see the cloudless sky. Amayao reminded him of Caona, his smooth skin and tender eyes.

"It feels as if the *turey* is a big cover, Baba."

"Yes, Amayao, and the roof of the *bohío* covers us like the blue covers the earth. When you learn to climb the middle pole of the house, you will feel as if you are ascending into the *turey*."

The boy jumped. "Look, Baba." He pointed to the branch of a dogwood tree where a yellow snake curled its scaly body. The boa was as thick as Amayao's fist, and longer than he was tall.

"He will strangle and eat the *jutía* but you do not need to worry for his bite has no poison." Huareo stretched out his hand to touch the snake. The boa turned its head, flicked its tongue and slithered up the branch a short distance, showing its yellow underbelly and black tail. "Do you see? He will not hurt me."

"I do not like his look, Baba."

"Only cowards show fear, Amayao. You are to be brave like Baba."

"He is big and scary. He is looking at me. I hate his eye."

"He is not our enemy. He is the son of Boina, the dark

serpent who brings black clouds full of rain." Huareo reached out again but the serpent wound its way down a vine and vanished into the thicket.

Huareo felt Yari staring, but as he turned towards her, she looked away. The morning light brightened her face, tinting it with a touch of pink. She wore bands that showed the firmness in her legs and arms, and a belt that supported the *nagua* decorated with images of the *tona*. She was so perfectly formed he thought *the cemí* must have sculpted her.

"The strangers have returned," Yari said.

His wife stood between two poles to which she had tied a set of strings with evenly spaced knots. She moved a wooden needle in and out, releasing strands of blue spun cotton.

Huareo fingered the weave of the *jamaca*. "It is beautiful. Are you making this for the cacique and his wives?"

"Whom do you want it for, Huareo?" Before he could answer, she said, "Hold this, Amayao. I will teach you." Yari passed the needle to his son and guided the boy's hand to make a triple weave, moving the needle under two of the strings, over one and back around.

"He is a boy, Yari."

"Yes, and he will make a good weaver."

Amayao's nimble hands moved swiftly. "Yari, the pattern looks like peaks and valleys," the boy said.

"I think we will make this *jamaca* for you, Amayao." She picked up a second needle and threaded it with red yarn. "How long will the strangers be here, Huareo?"

"We do not know."

"I hope they starve on their rotted ships," Yari said.

"They need our help to find a way home."

He stood close.

"You have been absent since the death of Caona." She teased him with her smile.

"I want to thank you for caring for my children."

"I love them as my own, Huareo."

"Amayao," Huareo pulled him up onto his shoulders, "I will take you to see the boats in the bay of Maima."

"He is too young, Huareo."

"He must grow to know the enemy," Huareo said.

"He alone cannot defend Yamaye."

Huareo smiled. "Then you will have to give me children."

The night fell quickly and they retired to the *caney*, where they fed on pepperpot soup, turtle and *casabe* with *aguacate*, the succulent avocado pear of Yamaye.

Hacona led two strangers up the path from the beach.

"Have you found two stray dogs, cousin?" Huareo shouted from the entrance of the *caney*.

"They plead for mercy, Cacique." Hacona brought them closer.

"I am Diego Méndez and my companion is Bartolomeo," said the man with the pointed beard.

Both strangers were completely clothed. They wore tight fitting fabric on their legs and puffy, bright red coverings on their shoulders and arms. A *nagua* was fastened about the waist, covering the upper parts of their legs. They wore long hair tied in the back and red hats with feathers to match.

"I know who you are," Huareo said.

"We come as your friends, Cacique."

When the stranger spoke the Taíno language, the words sounded peculiar and unnatural as if they should not belong to him. "Where did you learn to speak like this?" Huareo asked.

"I learned many languages in my travels," Méndez said. "We have come a long way from home, Cacique, and we are hungry. We begged for food from the generous Cacique of Aguacadiba but what he gave us is not sufficient."

"You promised us to remain on your boat."

"The food Cacique Mamyo offered us did not last a day."

Huareo nodded to Hacona to escort the visitors into his house where Guababo, Hacona and Guayacán joined them. The stranger's stench of rotted fish was as strong as the first time Huareo met him. "What did the cacique of Aguacadiba give you?" Huareo pulled his weight forward on the *dujo*.

"*Yuca* and fish."

"What would we receive in return if we helped you?" The cacique did not trust him. His words were slippery like the boa in the grass.

"We will give you whatever you want."

"I have told you what I want. My wish is for you to leave Yamaye."

"We did not come to your land by choice, Huareo. Worms ate our *navíos* and seawater came through the holes. We were forced to beach our ships to save our men from drowning." The stranger grabbed the handle of his shiny weapon that lay on the floor beside him. "We call this the *espada*." He kissed the blade. It was long and pointed, extending almost the full length of his legs.

"How many Taíno have you killed with this?" Huareo asked.

"It is our defence in battle, Cacique. The *espada* is strong and sharp enough to cut off a head or slice a body in half in one fell swoop. This is what we call *el lazo*." The stranger pointed to the decorative handle. "Here, hold it. You must never grasp the *espada* by the blade."

"This weapon reeks of the blood of the Taíno. I will not touch it." Huareo glared at the stranger with hatred in his heart. "Why would I befriend a stranger with a weapon that has murdered our people?"

"We are not here to hurt you, Cacique."

Huareo looked at the other stranger. "Your friend does not speak."

"He does not know your language well."

"*Díle que yo comprendo mucho y le agradezco su bondad,*" the man named Bartolomeo spoke in a strange tongue.

"He says he understands what you say and is grateful for your kindness."

Méndez rested the *espada* back down on the floor and reached for a bag next to him. "Our leader, Almirante Cristóbal Colón, gives you his word that we will not enter your homes uninvited, we will not trouble your women and children or roam through the land." He pulled out a shiny, flat object. "This is an *espejillo*. I give it to you as a sign of our friendship."

"How did you reach here if you were not roaming through the land?"

"Huareo, please accept this *espejillo*."

"*Espejillo*," Huareo repeated, finding it easy to say the stranger's word. The object was broken with uneven edges, a fragment of something larger. He held it to his face and saw his reflection as if he were looking into a pool of still water. He breathed on it and the surface became foggy. "Does this come from the earth?"

"No. Our people make them from materials we call metal and glass."

Huareo passed the *espejillo* to Guayacán.

"Our Admiral has more of these to offer you."

Huareo was still not sure he could trust him, daring not for a moment to entertain his friendship.

Guababo shifted his legs beneath him. "Why have you killed our caciques in Haití?" His cousin raised his voice.

"We have been away a long time on our travels and do not know what has happened there. Besides, the new governor and our *almirante* are not friends. I have told you, Huareo, we do not intend to stay here or give you trouble."

"How can I trust you?" Huareo asked.

"You have my word. You have a custom in these parts you call *guatiao*."

"We will not exchange names. You are the *arijuana* to me. You know that we are stronger than you in one-to-one combat. My men could overpower you, take your *espada* and disembowel you."

The stranger grasped the handle of the sword. "Yes, Cacique, but if I do not return to the *navíos*, you know what would happen."

"I think we understand each other's wishes."

"Yes."

"We will provide you with the food you need so your men can leave Yamaye."

"You are kind, Cacique. On my travel here through your land, *it pleased God that I have found some people who were very gentle and did us no harm, but received us cheerfully, and gave us food with hearty goodwill*, as you have done. I am most grateful. I will appoint one of my men in charge of receiving your provisions."

Huareo called an attendant to arrange for *casabe* and fruit to be brought for the strangers.

The stranger continued, "We have more *espejillos*, and red *bonetes* like the one I wear on my head. We can offer you coloured beads of *vidrio* as lovely as your jewellery and clothes to make you warm at night. Best of all, we have the gift of the *cascabel*, which makes a wondrous sound, more pleasing than your musical instruments."

"What foods do you want from us?"

"My *almirante* would ask you in person but he is old and sick. I come as a brave lieutenant on his behalf to ask for *yuca, jutía*, and fish."

"We will provide what we can, but will judge if the trade is fair. If your men are unruly and harm our people, we will stop the supply. What is your plan for rescue?"

"I will need *canoas* and the assistance of your men to travel the ocean to La Española where I will equip a ship for rescue."

"The waters are deep and turbulent. Our men are capable of such a journey, but yours would likely perish."

Huareo's attendants arrived with food which they lay before the cacique: white cakes of *casabe* and an assortment of fruit, slices of *papaya* and the succulent *yayama*.

The strangers remained in Huareo's chiefdom for three days. The cacique kept his promise to gather provisions and also arranged for two *naboría* to escort Diego Méndez and Bartolomeo Fieschi with *jamaca* and food to the *cacicazgo* of Anamaquique, the home of his father, Ameyro. The strangers wanted to visit the extreme end of the island to find a suitable spot from which they could launch *canoa* for their sojourn to Haití.

Huareo and the caciques of Maima, Aguacadiba and Guayguata continued to supply food. The Taíno dug fields for the tubers, hunted through the night to capture *jutía*, and laboured to catch enough fish to satisfy the ravenous appetites of the *arijuana*. Women grilled food on fires for the useless men, one hundred strangers who consumed more food than a thousand Taíno.

In exchange, Diego Méndez and the son of their chief, a boy named Hernando Colón, handed out mirrors, bells, cups and coloured beads, but these were soon exhausted. Once the supplies stopped, the Taíno cut back on food. The

bearded ones were angry and made more demands; they
wanted discs of *guanín*, golden earrings, finely woven cloths,
jamaca and cotton belts. Their lustful appetites led them to
wander from their boats into the villages in pursuit of Taíno
women. In time, the *arijuana* broke all their promises as
Huareo had expected. They ravaged the land like savages.

Chapter Twenty

Huareo climbed the side of the strangers' boat with Hacona, Guababo and the caciques of Maima and Aguacadiba.

Their chief, Cristóbal Colón, sat on a chair inside the makeshift *bohío* with its wooden poles and thatched roof. He was dressed in long white clothing that fell loosely about his body. His eyes were sunken in his thin face, which was mostly covered by straggly white hair. Standing next to him was a man he introduced as his brother, Bartolomé Colón, and a younger man, his son named Hernando Colón.

"I know you," Huareo blurted the words at Cristóbal Colón.

"I do not believe we have met," he answered in the Taíno language.

"You killed our men with arrows and ripped out the entrails of others with your dog."

"Ah, this was many years ago when I first set eyes on this fair island. You must have been a boy then. Now you are a cacique and I have asked you to visit me because I am displeased with your conduct. You stopped providing us with food."

"You did not keep your promise. Many moons have passed and you are still here. Your men have stolen our *canoa* and raped our women." Huareo spat his words in defiance.

The stranger chief held his legs in pain. "The men responsible for this are evil, Cacique Huareo. I lost forty-eight men who disobeyed me and have left the ships in search of their own rescue."

"They took with them Taíno who did not return. They cut off their hands and threw their bodies into the sea," Huareo shouted.

"I do not want you to raise your voice before me. We must forget these men who have done us both wrong. Our God is wise; He punishes evil and rewards good. They will receive their just punishment in due course. But all my men do not behave this way. I have good officers such as Diego Méndez and Bartolomeo Fieschi, whom you kindly helped. I am confident they arrived safely in La Española and that they will send a ship for us."

"Why are your men so helpless? They do not fish or hunt, they do not repair your boats," Huareo said.

"My fortunes are no more, Cacique Huareo. My misery weighs heavily on me," the old man whined. "I have been confined for months in this place, *lodged on the open decks of our ships*. The friends who remain with me are sick and dying. My brother and son, whom you see here, are in danger of perishing from hunger. I am old and infirm with pains I can no longer tolerate and I lack the medicines necessary to cure myself. I am the *unfortunate and miserable Cristóbal Colón*, once the Great Admiral of the Ocean Seas, now old and sick. I depend now on your mercy and kindness for my survival. You see me here, fallen from riches to this pitiful state. *I have suffered much for the glory and service* of my Queen."

Huareo did not feel sorry for him. "You and your men are not starving. You have eaten so much that our *yucayeque* can no longer supply you. We are not fooled by broken pieces of *vidrio* or remnants of old clothing. We gave you precious food and water and you gave us objects of no value in return. You are desperate because you have nothing left to trade."

The old man's face reddened, his arms and legs trembled. "Huareo, our God is good, He wants us to be fed and to be rescued." He reached for his son's arm to help him stand. Leaning on a crooked stick, he held his head up and shouted, "Our God will bring wrath upon your people if you do not help us. He will bring a sign of His displeasure tonight. He will cover the light of the moon so its fullness will not shine. He will cast darkness over your land to show his anger for the Taíno who will not feed His chosen people."

The angry caciques left in disbelief that the old admiral would have powers to make his Spirit cast darkness over the land. But later that evening, as the full moon rose in glory, its light gradually changed, losing its golden lustre and turning blood red. The people of Yamaye were alarmed and terrified at the supernatural powers of the white-haired old man.

Huareo had heard of unnatural occurrences in the sky. His father told him he once saw the light of the moon fade, but the cacique remained astonished at Cristóbal Colón's knowledge and power. Could this man have commanded the *cemí* to change the colour of the moon? And if he did, what else could he do to control the lives of the Taíno?"

The stranger chief remained locked inside his houseboat. Frightened Taíno gathered on the beach all night to plead for mercy, until finally, the old man heeded their cries and said he would forgive them if they renewed their supplies of food and water.

Before the sun rose the following morning, the moon regained its light. The Taíno were jubilant but remained fearful of the mad stranger whom they believed was possessed by the *maboya*. Huareo and the other caciques agreed to his terms but they rationed the supplies.

Not long after, a *navío* came to the Bay of Maima to rescue the miserable strangers, many of whom had died from sickness and from killing each other in battles they had waged among themselves.

Chapter Twenty-one

Huareo held a heavy, yellowish-white rock close to his body, seated with his uncle in a *bohío* specially built for training sculptors.

"Why did you choose this one?" his uncle queried, looking at the assortment of rocks and sculptures.

"You know that the white stone is rare, difficult to find." The cacique rubbed its rough edges, moving his fingers into every crevice to feel the spirit of the stone. "We have acquired *cemí* from other places, Guayacán, but we need to create more of our own."

"Are you worried?" His uncle inquired.

"Yes."

"The *cemí* favour you, Huareo, so you do not need to worry," Guayacán patted him on the forehead, where the cacique wore a *cemí* of Guabancex tied to his brow.

Huareo rested the stone on the ground and picked up the *manaya*, an axe made of greenstone, set snugly within a wooden handle. The celt had sharpened edges, pointed at one end, and flat, chisel-shaped at the other. "The cacique of Boriquén knows the art of creating sculptures with three points."

"You are able to make them too," his uncle said.

Huareo shaped the rock by splitting off unwanted pieces with the *manaya*. A form quickly emerged, rounded at each end with the rise of a mountain in the middle. "The tail will rest at the top." He felt the pointed rough edges of the stone and moved his fingers across and down to where it rounded in front. "I will carve the head of the *majá* below."

"Its yellow scales will match the colour of the stone," Guayacán spoke as if he knew Huareo's thoughts. "Who is this for?"

"My father, Ameyro, gave me a *cemí* of Yocajú with the serpent wrapped around it, so I make one for my children." Huareo picked up another tool to mark the stone. The black celt was the length of his forearm, rounded in the middle to enable him to grasp it firmly. It was flattened on each end with a chiselled edge for cutting, which he used to make shallow grooves in the new sculpture to show the outline of the snake. Huareo inhaled the smell of the stone to absorb the power of the *cemí*.

"Yaya shows you how, Huareo." He covered his mouth to control a hacking cough.

"You are not well, uncle."

"You will soon need the assistance of a *bejique*, Huareo." The cacique rested his tools and sculpture on the earthen floor of the *bohío*.

"Huareo." His words were gloomy like the clouds of Boinayel.

"You must be happy of spirit, Guayacán." Huareo reached up to smell the ground seed of the *cojóbana* contained in the bowl resting on Boinayel's head.

"Your people are in danger, Huareo."

"But you told me I should not worry."

"The *arijuana* will come again."

"So what advice do you give me?"

"I have no advice, Huareo."

"Then why do you tell me empty words?"

"The words are spoken by Yocajú to Cacique Cacibaquel, father of Guarionex. You must guard the cemí, so they are not stolen."

"I will feed them and they will keep us safe." Huareo lifted the stone and with the flat edge of the black celt chipped the form of the legs of a frog into one of the rounded ends. "The Taíno will procreate to give us strength."

"And you will cast the stranger spirit from the sacred land of Yamaye." Guayacán finished the cacique's words as if they were reciting words of a song together.

"*Buibá maboya, Buibá maboya*," Huareo shouted the words, stabbing the air with the sculptor's tool to banish the trickster spirit.

"My son, Yabey, will help you."

"What will he do?"

"Serve as your *bejique*. I have trained him."

"I no longer need the help of a *bejique*."

"Then who will be your priest?"

"I will be my own priest, Guayacán, and commune with the Great One." Huareo placed the *tobacú* in the sacred herbs and inhaled the snuff. "If your son has special powers, I will use him to cure the sick and dying." He passed the inhalator to his uncle. "You have been my father and teacher, Guayacán, and I will always be thankful."

"Ameyro is your father."

"My father is absent like the *opía*. He did not want me here but he sent me when I was a boy. I expected him to celebrate the *areíto* when Caona and I were married but he was not there. He came bearing gifts to make amends, to say my mother had passed."

"You give away your power when you blame others," his uncle counselled him.

"I am grateful for everything, my wives, children, cousins, especially Hacona and Guababo.

"They would die for you."

"I have made a gift for Hacona." Huareo unwrapped a wooden staff from the folds of a palm leaf.

"The *matuko* is beautifully carved, Huareo. It resembles Baibrama, the *cemí* who makes the *yuca* grow."

"It is a *guaribo* made in the image of his father, Majagua. It was carved from the wood of a specially chosen tree."

His uncle looked closely. "I see his big round eyes filled with the light of the *guanín,* a headdress of cotton, and the *macana* in both hands ready for battle. The *cemí* will give Hacona protection." Guayacán's voice faded.

"Nothing will defeat him, with his nobility, and strength of manhood.

"I must rest, Huareo." His uncle's hands trembled.

"I will help you return to your *bohío.*" Huareo reached up to place one end of the *tobacú* on the head of Boinayel and pushed the forked end of the hollowed stick into his own nostrils. He snuffed the holy substance and passed the reed to this uncle. "I ask for Bibi Atabey to be with you." Huareo squatted before his uncle.

Tears formed in Guayacán's eyes. "I loved you since you were a boy. You saved my brother and his *cacicazgo* from ruin."

"In what way, uncle?"

"Majagua did not have the power to combat the *maboya.*" Guayacán placed both hands on Huareo's head.

> *Bibi Atabey,*
> Mother Atabey,
> *Bibi Mamona Turey,*
> Formless Mother of the heavens.
> *Okama guakia Taíno,*
> Hear our good people.
> *Matun'aru,*
> Generous woman.
> *Busica guakia kakona,*
> Grant your blessing
> on us, your humble men
> and on this great cacique,
> Huareo.

Huareo stood and prayed in turn:
  Bibi Atabey,
  we are your servants.
  I ask you to accept
  the spirit of this good man,
  Guayacán,
  into the hands of
  Maquetaurie Guayaba
  so that he may dwell
  with the absent ones
  in the house of Coaybey,
  to be with our ancestors,
  to love and to feast with them
  in the sacred place.

By placing his hand under his arm, Huareo supported his uncle who shuffled his way back home, an old man, bent and crippled.

That evening, Guayacán passed peacefully to the land of Coaybey.

Guababo stood squat in the middle of a clearing in the forest. He beat the air with a *macana* and fanned his mouth to sound the war cry, "*Guasábara! Guasábara!*"

Huareo stood facing him ten paces away. His only form of defence was a spear tipped with the barbed spine of the stingray.

Two groups of warriors, one led by Hacona and the other by Yabey, stood watching on the side.

"You are the master *guaribo* of the Taíno," Huareo shouted to his opponent.

"Hatuey of Haití trained me. I do it in your honour, *Guajeri* Huareo." Guababo's blackened skin glistened in the sun.

"Then pretend I am the bearded one. Show me how you fight."

"I do not wish to hurt you." His cousin laughed.

"Show me you are the fearless *guaribo* of the Taíno."

Guababo charged, narrowing the space between them. He raised the club behind his shoulders, howling like a wild dog and swinging the weapon in front of Huareo's face. Its force and weight cracked the cacique's spear in two. Guababo then stood back, waiting for Huareo to attack. Blood dripped from his right shoulder where the tip of the cacique's spear had grazed him. He spread his legs wide with knees bent and raised his head, eyes fixed on the enemy.

The defenceless Huareo rushed his opponent trying to reach around his legs to grab the upper calves but Guababo butted him with his head. Huareo fell back. He recovered and then moved in higher to place both hands on his attacker's shoulders.

But Guababo was fast. He threw the *macana* to the ground, yanked on Huareo's left arm, forcing his victim's body to twist, and shoved his right hand under the cacique's other arm and over his shoulder.

Huareo felt his position weaken, the strength of his opponent pulling his body out of control.

Guababo turned his back with Huareo in an arm lock. He spread his legs shoulder-width and bent low.

The cacique did not struggle. In a smooth, easy movement, he felt himself being lifted up over the hips of his opponent. He landed on his side, breaking the full impact of the fall with his hands.

The warriors moved closer to defend their cacique as they sensed he might be in danger.

In triumph, Guababo pushed his foot down on the
shoulder of the cacique to force him to lay prostrate in the
dirt. He leaned to pick up the *macana* and, brandishing it
over his victim's head, he released Huareo, smiled and
stepped back, still bleeding from the point of the barbed
spear.

Huareo stood. "You have brought your cacique to the
ground in defeat. I am confident the *guaribono* fight as well
as you."

"*Nabori daca*, cacique, I am at the service of the cacique,"
Guababo spoke in reverence. "*Guasábara! Guasábara!*" he
yelled the war cry across the green to command the two sets
of warriors to engage in battle.

The men moved in straight lines until they met face to
face. They swung the lethal *macana* attacking one another
with brutal force. Hacona's team was fierce. It felled the first
two *guaribono* of Yabey's men with blows of the wooden
club which left the men unconscious on the ground.

"You may stop the fight, Guababo. We must spare their
lives, preserve them for battle with the strangers. I am
proud of you all and to Guababo for training you to fight
like the *Caribe*, the fierce and brave ones. The Taíno are not
a warlike people but we would be foolish not to prepare
ourselves." Huareo called to Hacona, "I have a special prize
for the victor." He handed his cousin the wooden staff
carved in the image of Majagua. "I give you this in praise
of your skill as a Taíno *guaribo*, in memory of your father
whose spirit lives with us."

Hacona bowed before the cacique to accept the gift.

Chapter Twenty-two

He held her as she floated on the waves. Her nipples showed on the surface and her thick, black hair spread wide in the water.

"You are absent again, Huareo." Yari splashed him.

Huareo was remembering Caona swimming in the river, how she was faster than the river mullet.

"I am here with you now." He stood waist deep in the water. He rubbed her navel and then turned her so her legs wrapped around him. Her softness aroused a passion of fire in him.

She caressed his face and chest. "You do not need to search for my navel, Huareo. I will not vanish like a shadow." She laughed. "I will bear children so they will inherit the land. You are my cacique, *d'aniki*, my heart and my love."

"Let me show you a special place." He carried her to where the *cayuco*, a small canoe, was beached on the sands of Aguacadiba, a neighbouring chiefdom.

They paddled through inlets that opened into a deep bay and as they broke the stillness of the water, cranes took flight from the honeycombed rocks lining the shore. For a moment, Huareo wished he could drift with her out to sea to explore the lands of Caobana and Haití but he knew he must remain in Yamaye.

Yari sat in front. She straightened her body as she pulled the oar, the muscles in her back flexing with the motion. She was thicker and more voluptuous than Caona.

"You are my principal wife, Yari."

She turned to face him. Her eyes were sparkling. "I will make our home prosperous, Huareo."

"I know you will." He rested both hands on the sides of the *cayuco* and rocked it so hard she lost her balance and fell backwards off the seat into the bottom of the boat. Their laughter travelled far across the bay.

They secured the *cayuco* in a cove enclosed on two sides by cliffs of jagged, black rock. They swam from shore across the bay beyond the coral reefs and dived together into the deep water where they scavenged for large pink snails. Huareo was watchful for predators of the sea. The conchs were food for the manta ray, the bird of the sea, which chopped and smashed their shells with its powerful jaws.

He guided her to a feeding spot, a sandy area at the bottom of the reef. The sea was calm, so the *cobo* were not hiding, easy for Huareo to spot their trails of double lines in the sand. As he and Yari came to the mouth of a huge cave, they saw hundreds of them almost indistinguishable from the pink coral, crawling on the open seabed to feed on pieces of broken coral and grass. The swimmers each pulled four out of the sand, the most they could carry to the surface at once.

When they came ashore, Huareo used a stone to break a hole in the spiral of a conch, releasing the suction that held the snail anchored within its *bohío*. He pulled the animal out of its shell with the tip of his knife and peeled the dark skin to show the white meat beneath. When he reached inside, he felt a hard stone hidden in the flesh. He cut open the thick membrane and pulled out a gem, which was shaped like a seed. It was the pearl of the conch, deep pink with streaks of white on either end.

"This is a charm, Yari." He handed her the pearl. "It is yours; guard it with your life. Bibi Atabey blesses and protects you with this gift from the sea."

"I have never seen the pearl of the *cobo*." She rubbed the stone.

"It is rare, encountered once in a lifetime."

They fed on the raw conch and roasted the *cigua*, whelks which they gathered from the shallow pools within the rocks.

"If the strangers come back, Yari..."

She interrupted him, "Yes, I know, your children..." She lay back on the sand. Her beauty was stunning, her skin dark like the evening, her full breasts ripe like the fruit of the *jobo*.

He caressed her arms. "You must look after all the children, not only mine. My uncle's words troubled me."

"What did he say?"

"He told me the prophecy would come true."

"The *bejique* had lost his powers, Huareo." She stroked his face. "Come this way." She led him from the shore to a grassed area shaded by branches of the *mamey* tree. She lifted herself into his arms wrapping her legs about his waist.

He carried her nearer to the tree.

She released herself from him and lay face down, resting her breasts on the fallen leaves.

Huareo lowered himself over her, and with the full strength of his manhood, he loved Yari in the mad heat of the night, on the damp ground under the branches of the spreading *mamey* tree.

Chapter Twenty-three

Streaks of light brightened the interior of the cave, illuminating the smooth damp stone that formed its roof. Huareo extended his arms to finish small incisions in the rock with the sharpened end of a petal-shaped flint. He hoisted his son, Amayao, up onto his shoulders so he could reach the drawings.

The boy dipped the shredded end of a small stick in the *jataca* filled with the black dye of the *genipa* seed. His hands were small and smooth, not yet a man's, but his movements as skilful as those of an adult artisan.

"Who are these people you have drawn, Baba? They are happy."

"Yes, they are Taíno, celebrating the goodness of our land." Huareo craned his neck to view the etchings he had made.

His son moved forward and painted the heads of the dancers, making broad strokes to create images of masks.

"We take on a new form when we cover our faces with the *guaísa*. The mask creates whatever spirit we want, birds of the sky or fish of the sea." Huareo held still so that he would not disturb his son's brush strokes.

"They are moving, Baba, and looking at each other as they dance." Amayao marked them with black outlines to create their necks and arms.

"Maybe they are lovers. They are happy for they are one in spirit."

"What do they hold in their hands, Baba?" The boy followed the markings of the long thin drawing.

"What do you want them to be, Amayao?"

"They are spears, Baba, to kill the strangers."

"But they are lovers. Aren't they, son?"

"They can be *guaribono* too." The boy's voice was playful and confident.

"Make them whatever you want them to be. You have a gift, Amayao. Let your hand move freely and the spirits will guide you."

His son put the finishing touches on the dancers.

"They are beautiful, Amayao. Their heads are like Inrirí Cahubabayel, the bird who formed the sex of the woman. You will learn about this one day."

"*Toa, toa.*" The boy turned his brush to paint another of the etchings.

"The babies want their *bibi* for they have no milk."

"I miss my *bibi*, too," Amayao said.

Huareo chuckled. "Yes, but you are too old to suckle your mother's *nati*."

"What was she like, Baba?"

"She was loving and gentle. You remind me of her."

"I feel her spirit is with me."

"Bibi Atabey, the Spirit of all Mothers, also looks after you."

Amayao made black strokes to follow the lines of the squatting frog. "See, Baba. She is bending down, she is Bibi, giving birth to me in the river."

"Yes, she gave birth to you under Attabeira's watch."

"Baba?"

"What is it, son?"

"Do you think the bearded strangers are bad?"

"You must never trust them."

"Are they from the *turey*, as people say?"

"They are not good spirits, Amayao. They are from a strange place we do not know. They will kill us if we allow them to make Yamaye their home."

"I am afraid, Baba."

"Remember what I told you. Do you recall the *boa* we saw on the dogwood tree? The serpent will only hurt you if you fear him."

"I want to be like you, Baba."

"You will grow to be strong if you will it that way."

He and his son carved another image into the rock. Together they created the form of the iguana, Macocael, who sunned himself by day and was guardian of the cave by night.

"Here, I want you to wear this." Huareo removed from his neck the amulet of Attabeira that Caona had worn on her marriage day. "This belonged to your mother; it is a *cemí* of the Mother of all Waters who will teach you the mysteries of life and keep you from harm."

"It is lovely. Who will guard you, Baba?"

"Do not worry, for I possess many other *cemí*."

As father and son emerged from the underworld, twin rainbows painted the sky from one end of the land to the other. They spanned the horizon, arched above the still waters of Bagua, forming a perfect reflection in the sea, a complete circle in stripes of coloured light.

Huareo received a visitor named Bobuyo from Haití with a message from Hatuey.

"It must be urgent for you to have come so far," Huareo said.

"*Guami* Huareo, they are loading their boats. You must warn your people. The strangers are coming to Yamaye," Bobuyo said.

"How many men?

"Eighty."

The visitor told Huareo and his men stories of the horrors that beset the Taíno of Haití. "The *cacicazgo* of Xaragua is no more, the land where caciques and *nitaíno* once lived in great numbers. They killed Anacaona, cacique of that region. The governor, a man named Ovando, arrived with horses and men and invited three hundred of her *nitaíno* to a meeting. Her people agreed to assemble in the *caney* for they thought the governor had come in good faith, bearing gifts of friendship. But the man locked them in, Huareo, and he blocked the opening of the cacique's house so no one could leave. Three hundred of our nobles were closed in. We knew they were in danger for none of the strangers remained inside with them. Our worst fears came true. The governor gave the order for no reason that I can understand. Our caciques had done nothing to offend them. His men lit torches, they encircled the house and threw balls of fire onto the *caney* from all sides. The wind swept the flames, ravenously eating the canes until the whole house was ablaze. I heard our people scream for mercy above the sound of the crackling fire but the strangers only laughed and rejoiced. A few Taíno managed to escape when the burning canes fell to the ground but they were quickly run through with swords and chopped to pieces. The fire consumed everyone else, three hundred of them, Huareo. Not one survived. All were burned to ashes."

"What became of Anacaona?" Huareo asked.

"They spared her life for they wanted her to watch the slaughter and hear the cries of her nobles as they burned to death. But afterwards, they took no pity on her. They hanged her and laughed to see her strung naked on ropes and to hear her neck snap in two."

"They are *tuyra*, worse than excrement," Huareo said.

"I was lucky to escape with some women and children;

others of them were caught, stabbed through with spears or sliced with *espadas*."

"These happenings are too horrible to be true." Huareo was nauseated from the tale of carnage and suffering.

"I have no reason to lie, Huareo. The man, who comes as ruler to Yamaye, is called Esquivel. He has murdered thousands and captured Cacique Cotubanamá of the Cacicazgo of Higüey.

"Then we must prepare for the worst," Huareo said.

The dujo, the special seat of power, reserved for the cacique and his guests of honour (p.4).

Boinayel, the spirit of the rain (p.8).

*A wooden stand made for the cacique in the image of
Boinayel, the Spirit of the rain (p.6).*

Cemí of Yocajú Bagua Maórocoti (p.8).

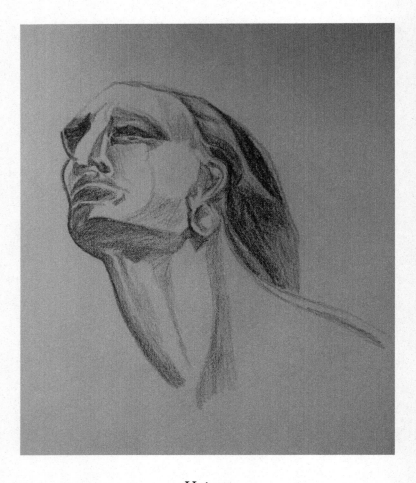

Hatuey

His hair was pulled back, which showed the strength of his chiselled jaw and thick neck (p.34).

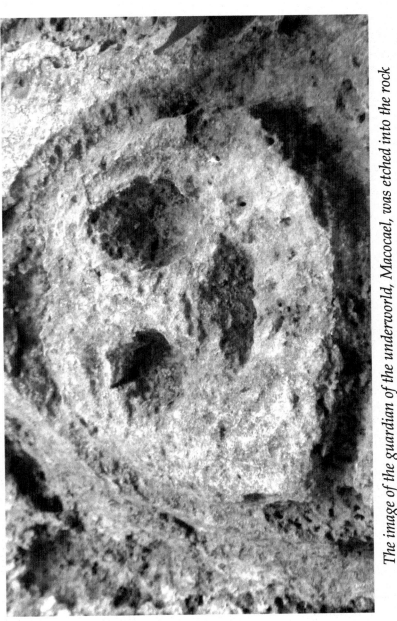

The image of the guardian of the underworld, Maocael, was etched into the rock at the cave entrance (p.39).

Baibrama would no longer punish the Taíno, no longer bring them sickness and hunger (p.40).

European portrayal of Christopher Columbus' encounter with the Taíno.

...the statue of a brown pelican held up a tray containing the sacred herb (p.65).

As the others scrambled to escape, a stranger aimed a long heavy weapon, which thundered and spat fire at one of them (p.77).

"It is a guaribo made in the image of his father, Majagua"
(p. 124).

"They are moving, Baba, and looking at each other as they dance" (p. 132).

Opiyelguobirán guards the dead, not the living (p. 177).

They died nobly like the hero Hatuey (p. 210).

"But these are not angels, Diego, they are little monsters"
(p. 249).

Part Three

Sevilla
1509–14

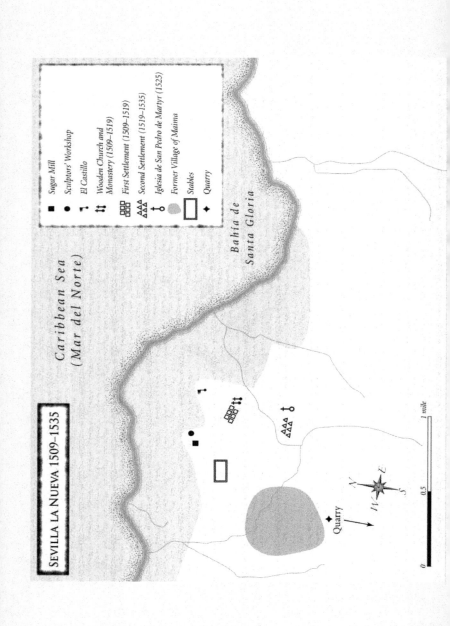

SEVILLA LA NUEVA 1509-1535

Caribbean Sea
(Mar del Norte)

Bahía de
Santa Gloria

■ Sugar Mill
● Sculptors' Workshop
⚓ El Castillo
⛪ Wooden Church and
   Monastery (1509–1519)
▦ First Settlement (1509–1519)
▲ Second Settlement (1519–1535)
⛪ Iglesia de San Pedro de Martyr (1525)
● Former Village of Máima
▭ Stables
◆ Quarry

Quarry

N
W E
S

0   0.5   1 mile

Most Sacred, Catholic Majesty of the Holy Roman Empire, from your humble servant, Diego del Castillo:

I place in the hands of your Royal Majesty this, the narrative of my people, with the hope that you have been entertained thus far, that you have found both informative and interesting the descriptions of the ways of life of the Taínos in the Island of Jamaica.

As a young boy of eleven years of age, I remember clearly that fateful day when the first Spanish governor arrived.

I beseech your Majesty to now give attention to the continuance of the narrative.

Despite all odds, my people remained strong and valiant, true to their hearts, more that I could say for myself.

Santo Domingo
Anno Domini, 1535.

Chapter Twenty-four

The friar stood on the hot white sands of Santa Gloria, the bay that Cristóbal Colón had named as the most glorious place he had ever seen.

"*In nomine Patris et Filii et Spiritus Sancti.*" Antonio Díaz del Castillo made the sign of the cross in the sweltering sun. He felt sweat trickle beneath his thick brown tunic woven from the fabric of the Indians of La Española.

"*Benedictus Deus. Benedictum Nomen Sanctum eius,*" the young Franciscan spoke the prayers, his voice nervous and uncertain.

Don Juan de Esquivel, Captain and first Governor of the Island of Jamaica, knelt before a wooden cross in reverence and dignity, his lieutenant, Pánfilo de Narváez, beside him, carrying the banner of King Ferdinand. Their eighty crewmen also bowed their heads and genuflected before the cross, driven deep into the sandy shore of their new colony, Jamaica.

"*Benedictum nomen Jesu,*" the friar stumbled on his words. He raised his head to gain solace from the blue expanse of sky, but he could see nothing. The scorching sun blinded him and sweat from his brow stung his eyes. He had an eerie feeling of Taíno concealed in the nearby forest bordering the beach. His hands had the fresh smell of the blood of Indians slaughtered by Esquivel in the Province of Higüey on the battlefields of La Española. He was unable to find his voice to continue praying.

The new governor stood from his kneeling position and turned his back to the friar to address his men. "Today we take possession of this fair isle in the name of the Holy Sovereign, don Fernando el Católico. Don Diego Colón,

Almirante and *Gobernador de las Indias*, has given me orders to colonize this land, to subjugate the natives and to convert them to our Holy Faith. We shall build a town in this place that will be named Sevilla."

His men stood up, applauded and shouted in jubilation, unsheathing and brandishing their *espadas*.

Fray Juan de la Deule, the friar's religious companion, whispered, "Do you wish me to conclude the benediction, Fray Antonio?"

"No, thank you, Friar, I will be fine. The Good Lord gives me strength." The Franciscan approached the wooden cross that towered above his head. He blessed the relic with holy water and incense in the name of the Trinity:

> *Oremus*
> Blessed are you, Lord God, King of the universe,
> you have made all things for your glory.
> Bless this wooden cross,
> a sign of our Saviour
> who died for our salvation.
>
> Father,
> We praise you through Christ our Lord.
> *Gloria Patri, et Filio, et Spiritui Sancto,*
> *sicut erat in principio, et nunc, et semper,*
> *et in saecula saeculorum.* Amen.

He turned to peer through the sea cotton trees to see moving shadows of naked savages painted in red and black.

Fray Antonio Díaz del Castillo, twenty-six years of age, was born to an aristocratic family in Sevilla, Spain. Even though he was of noble stock, his complexion and features were more African than Castilian. He often wondered whether his mother was of Moorish origins but he had never dared ask the question.

He had been in search of new adventure when don Juan de Esquivel asked him to join the expedition to colonize the island of Jamaica. The Almirante, don Diego Colón, Governor of La Española, favoured Esquivel to head the mission because of his proven military prowess in waging war against Cacique Cotubanamá. They both knew the friar to be suitable for leading the Franciscan ministry. He demonstrated the Christian zeal necessary to help the new governor subdue the natives of Jamaica.

The men slept aboard ship with instructions from the governor not to venture ashore without permission from an officer. Even though Cristóbal Colón had not reported raids by Indians while he was marooned in Jamaica, it was common knowledge that the natives were not friendly. Juan de Esquivel thought it prudent to confine his men on board until they had an opportunity to meet the prominent chiefs of the island.

That first evening, the governor summoned Pánfilo de Narváez, first lieutenant, Rodrigo de Villareal, second lieutenant and Friar Antonio Díaz del Castillo to report to his quarters situated on the upper deck of the ship's stern.

"Diego Méndez, of whom we have acquaintance, spoke of a cacique named Huareo," the governor said, stroking his beard and leaning back in his chair. Juan de Esquivel was heavy set with jowls hanging from his face and a belly that bulged from his doublet. He was a well-seasoned *conquistador*, having first sailed to the New World with Cristóbal Colón in 1493.

"Yes," Narváez responded. "The Almirante referred to him as one of the main chiefs, aggressive but not particularly violent." The lieutenant was a ruthless colonizer, a man born to be a leader, but careless in his duties and morals. Tall, handsome and intelligent, he charmed women and men alike.

"We must begin construction of the town as soon as possible. We will need the full cooperation of the caciques." The glass in the governor's right eye jumped as he spoke.

"Señor Esquivel, we start whether they cooperate or not," said Narváez.

Antonio took a deep breath. "Don Juan, it is prudent to meet first with the caciques, as you suggested. If they are not as rebellious as those in La Española, they will help us to build the town." He looked to Rodrigo for support.

"The good friar, my Lord, speaks from experience. Our exploits in La Española, although successful, were fraught with perils." Rodrigo de Villareal had faithfully served the Crown and as a young man distinguished himself in the fight to defend Spain in *La Reconquista*, the reconquest of territories captured by Muslim states. He was fondly called *la roja furia*, the red fury, a name fully deserved. He always wore a red waistcoat with a feather in his cap to match, in honour of his exploits.

"I am surprised, don Diego, a *conquistador* of such notable fame, that you would come to the defence of our Franciscan," the governor responded.

Before Rodrigo had a chance to reply, Pánfilo de Narváez interjected, "Fray Antonio, our governor is a seasoned officer. You and Fray Deule are here to tend to the spiritual welfare of the Indians, to ensure that they are instructed in the tenets of the Holy Catholic faith. Remember, Antonio, you are subordinate to civil administration. You must leave the matters of conquest to the governor and me."

Antonio swallowed his unease and nodded. "I must take my leave, gentlemen. Your lordship, don Esquivel, I urge you to allow no harm to come to the Indians." On returning to his cabin, the friar heard the mocking laughter of the first lieutenant echo through the narrow passageways of the caravel.

Before falling asleep that first night in Jamaica, Fray Antonio gave thanks to the Virgin Mary and saints for his safe arrival. He examined his conscience and asked God's forgiveness for breaking the vow of chastity. He loved a woman of Sevilla named Ana María. Daily, he relished sweet memories of their intimacies. He wondered how it was possible that natural thoughts of his beloved could be void of the love of God, as the teachings of his Church would want him to believe.

He knelt in reverence before the crucifix next to his bed. The silver image of Christ glowed in the dark against the duller bronze of the cross. The crown of thorns pressed deep into the Saviour's head, yet His eyes showed no pain; they were compassionate and forgiving. The friar prayed to Our Lady of Sorrows that through her intercession his sins might be pardoned. He recited verses of bedtime vespers from his breviary to expunge feelings of guilt and shame. Fray Antonio finally slept, but fitfully, that hot November night in the year of Our Lord, 1509, with nightmares of raids on the colonists by the inhospitable Indians of Yamaye.

Chapter Twenty-five

Huareo, Guababo and Amayao were guests in the home of Mamyo, the cacique's brother-in-law, whose villages overlooked the bay where the strangers' ships were anchored, dark and motionless in the early morning mist.

"The filthy ones are here among us," Huareo cursed. He narrowed his eyes and twisted his face. He was exhausted for he had remained awake the whole night, keeping watch in the forest that lined the Bay of Maima.

"They have only enough men to fill one *canoa* and we have thousands of *guaribono* to fight them." Guababo held petal-shaped pieces of flint sharpened on all sides.

"They will want to take our women for pleasure, cousin." Huareo was defiant.

"I shall kill anyone who takes a Taíno woman." Guababo picked up the *buyón* and carved a deep slit in one end of along wooden spear.

Visions of dirty, bearded men forcing themselves on his wives and children flashed before Huareo's eyes. "I want to kill them too, cousin. The strangers are like *canica*, the waste that comes from the animal."

"Help me, Amayao. Push the flat edge of the flint into the cleft as hard as you can." He and Amayao wedged the sharpened stone so it could not move. "We must prepare the sap of the *tibey* and of the manchineel apple for the tips of the arrows and spears."

The haze lifted to reveal clear images of the decks and poles of the strangers' ships. Flocks of *aruna* and other birds that normally dived for fish in the Bay of Maima were nowhere to be seen.

"Bobuyo told us their leader's name is Esquivel," Huareo said.

"Yes, the one who captured Cacique Cotubanamá. He asked his governor if he could pull the skin of the cacique to tear it from his body." Guababo scraped the knife hard on the edges of the flint. "But the governor was merciful, Huareo; he gave permission for him to be hanged instead."

Mamyo passed a *túbano* to Huareo who puffed on the rolled tobacco and blew thick rings of smoke.

Guababo continued, "Esquivel swore a solemn oath with the cacique and in an act of *guatiao*, they became brothers, each taking the other's name. You would have thought this to be an honourable bond between two men. But do you know how cruel the strangers are, Huareo? When they captured Cacique Cotubanamá, they asked him for his name, and when he told them that it was Juan de Esquivel, what do you think the enemy did?"

"I tell you, Guababo, they are worse than excrement."

"They mocked the cacique saying their governor would never have given his name in friendship. They spat on him and took him prisoner."

"Let the curse of *the cemí* be on Esquivel." Huareo passed the *túbano* to his son. Amayao inhaled the cigar smoke and coughed uncontrollably

Guababo laughed. "Your son is still young, Huareo." He ruffled Amayao's hair.

"You will be a man soon, son, ready to take a wife," Huareo said.

"Here, stand up, let me see if you are a man." Guababo teased the boy.

The bashful boy stood with his shoulders hunched forward.

"Let him be, Guababo. My cousin is only joking with you, Amayao." Huareo worried his son was vulnerable, an easy target for the enemy. He heard that in Haití the strangers took away sons of the caciques to special places where they taught them how to speak their language and pray to their spirit they call God.'

"I will teach you to be a *guaribo*," Guababo said. "You are a noble one, heir to the *cacicazgo* of Maima as eldest nephew of Cacique Mamyo. You, son of Huareo, will help us defeat the enemy, to use the poisoned spear and *macana*, mightier than their sword."

Huareo nodded. "When the time is right, we will use our weapons, but first we must keep the peace in the hope of finding a way to send them home. We make no offers or promises for they are murderers and thieves and cannot be trusted."

A stranger guarded the shoreline of the bay where the *navíos* were anchored. He sat high on a white animal, which twitched its tail and bulged its eyes at Huareo. The cacique could never have imagined a creature so enormous, with its back as tall as he was, and legs so strong, capable of running ten times faster than a man. Huareo looked into the eyes of the *caballo*, and there to his surprise, saw a spirit, intelligent and kind.

Huareo and his companions climbed up the side of the *navío*, which rose from the water the height of two or more men. The cacique looked back across the land where the smoke of cooking fires spiralled from the hills of Maima, the tops of *bohío* barely visible, hidden in the thick green forests of Yamaye. He squinted in the sunlight to watch a man climb one of the poles to adjust ropes that made a creaking sound in the breeze.

The stranger men and boys stood gaping at Huareo, Amayao and the caciques of Maima and Guayguata. The spectators' faces were fearful and their spirits disquieted as if they feared the presence of Taíno among them. Huareo scowled at them as he and his companions climbed into the cave of the boat, leaving the brightness of the day behind them.

The stranger spoke in the Taíno language, "I welcome you, caciques of the island of Jamaica. It is good for us to meet. Please be seated." He introduced himself as Juan de Esquivel, Lieutenant Governor. When he spoke his left eye widened with a murderous look, his right eye blank and unseeing like that of Macú. His greying beard fluffed out from his face but had two points growing from the chin in the shape of the *magüey* leaf. His skin was fat and floppy, as white as fish flesh.

"Our ancestors call the land Yamaye," said Huareo. "It is sacred ground, the place of many springs. We ask you to tell us why you are here and why you have called us to speak with you." Huareo fixed his stare on Esquivel.

Two other strangers were in the room, Pánfilo de Narváez, whom Esquivel introduced as his friend, and Antonio Díaz del Castillo, their priest. Narváez was taller than his leader. His beard bushed out from his face, his hair yellow, the colour of dried grasses and his nose swollen with bumps like the prickly pear. He wore a pointed hat with a skin hard as stone. Their *bejique* wore long brown clothing. He was slim with black hair and darkish skin, his eyes kind and sparkling.

Huareo glanced around the small space. The roof of Esquivel's house was lined with broad pieces of dark wood, not reaching upwards as they did in the *bohío*, but sitting flat and low above their heads. The strangers' familiar smell of rotted fish was stronger in the closed-up room.

"You are the one they call Huareo, the preeminent Cacique of Jamaica." Esquivel stroked the hairs on his face.

"My name is Huareo. This is Amayao, my son and this is Mamyo, Cacique of Maima, and Iguaca, Cacique of Guayguata."

"The great Admiral, Cristóbal Colón, spoke of you and of the kindness your people showed him."

"We met your Admiral. We supplied him with food, water and *canoa*, but his men were cruel to our people." Huareo lifted his legs to ease his discomfort on the oddly shaped seat.

"We expect that you will help us, Cacique." The stranger squinted his left eye and puffed his cheeks like the *guanábano*, the soursop fish, when it is bloated and threatened.

"What help do you want from us?" Huareo asked.

"Pánfilo de Narváez and I come here under the command of Don Diego Colón, son of the Great Admiral."

"With what purpose?"

Esquivel raised his shoulders. "I invited you here to tell you that we come in the name of King Ferdinand, who serves our Pope, Lord of the entire world. This Father and Governor of men, Pope Julius II, has commanded the King to bring the lands and nations of the New World under one ruler so its people may be taught that there is only one God and one faith."

Huareo interrupted Esquivel, "Have you come to tell us that you are the new Cacique of Yamaye?" He stood, and signalled to Amayao, Mamyo and Iguaca to do the same.

Pánfilo de Narváez banged his fists twice on the table and two men with *espadas* in hand, burst through the entrance.

"You will sit until I finish speaking," Esquivel shouted.

Two hands pushed on Huareo's shoulders from behind, trying to force him back down on the seat.

"Do not touch me." Huareo sat down after the stranger removed his hands.

"You must not be angry, Cacique. We are your friends. We do not want to war against you in this land."

Huareo turned to Mamyo. "It is time for us to leave."

"We have not finished our business here," Esquivel spoke slowly and in a deep voice.

Huareo caught the priest looking at him with pleading eyes as if to say he should stay and listen.

"Now that we understand each other, I wish to tell you the purpose of our meeting." The governor snorted. "Our King does not want us to use force against you. He wishes for your souls to be saved, and it is necessary for this purpose that you be taught the tenets of our faith. Our priest, Fray Antonio Díaz del Castillo, will build a church and a house where he will teach the sons of caciques." Esquivel grabbed Amayao's arm. "Your son will learn the Catholic Faith so he may teach others the way to salvation."

"Take your hands off my son," Huareo shouted. "We must leave, Mamyo." He fondled the *guanín* on his chest to gather the strength of the *cemí*.

"Is this alloy that you call *guanín* made from gold found on the island?" Esquivel inquired.

The governor's question irritated Huareo. "Our rivers do not contain much gold. This *guanín* belonged to my uncle and came from another place."

"Our Admiral has ordered us to secure gold. It will be necessary to use the services of your people for this and other tasks. We have inspected the land around the bay and find it suitable to build a town."

Huareo held his breath to contain his anger before speaking. "We have our own *yucayeque*. One is already in this place called Maima. We do not need you to build another village."

"Yes, of course, you may remain in your villages, but we will build our own and we will need your help to do this." The man waved his hands about and spoke excitedly. "You must tell your people who live close by that we will require them to clear land and cut trees to make our houses. Our men will not be scattered through the countryside, but live in this place that we have called Sevilla. Just as you helped the Admiral, you will supply us with food until we can grow our own."

"What do we say to our people?" Mamyo spoke for the first time. "Do we tell them they must build a *yucayeque* for strangers? They will not want this."

"You must tell them they are now subjects of a king and their new ruler will not ask them to work for free like you do, but will pay them for their services. The finest reward will be the salvation of their souls."

"What will you give them?" Mamyo inquired.

"The payment will be the teachings our holy friars offer them. We will determine what else to pay them depending on the nature of the work and their willingness to help."

Huareo stood to leave, and said, "We do not work for rewards like these." The cacique felt trapped in a place with stranger spirits.

"We do not want war, my friends. We come under the command of the supreme ruler of the world. If you do not help us willingly, we will force you."

"We will hold council in the morning and send a messenger to you with an answer," Huareo said.

"We part in the spirit of friendship, Caciques," Esquivel motioned to the priest who held out red coloured beads and broken pieces of glass. "We want to present these to you as a sign of our promise."

Huareo shook his head. "You are strangers to us, not *guatiao* with whom we exchange our names and gifts. We leave now."

Esquivel bade his farewell. "Our *navíos* are anchored in the bay and are not leaving. We trust you have the wisdom to instruct your people to work willingly for us."

Chapter Twenty-six

Huareo did not return in person after meeting with the governor, but Cacique Mamyo agreed to have fifty men from his village assist with building houses for the new settlement. He bargained for nothing in exchange, but the Spaniards promised him favours if the Indians worked diligently.

Fray Antonio Díaz del Castillo stood with Amayao on a patch of cleared ground, the site his fellow Spaniards had chosen for their town. Pánfilo de Narváez, overseer of the project, walked among the Indian labourers with a *perro de presa canario* at his side. The dog strutted in time to its master's gait, ready to attack on command. Naked in the hot morning sun, the Taíno felled trees with axes and saws, which the Spaniards showed them how to use. Under Narváez's strict surveillance, the Indians hauled the logs hundreds of feet away and made piles to be used for construction and cooking fires.

"I am gradually getting accustomed to this heat," the friar said.

"You speak our language," Amayao remarked.

"Yes, my companion Fray Deule and I learned to speak Taíno when we were in La Española. He knows it better than I do. Your language is somewhat different from what I am used to, but I understand what you say." Fray Antonio pulled the woollen cowl of his tunic to free it from rubbing the back of his neck. "Generally, we find Taíno easy to understand, you speak as clearly as the learned men in our country speak Spanish and another language we call Latin."

"Why do you wear such long clothing?"

"It is called *un hábito*, a religious robe. The man who founded my group dressed this way, and we follow his example."

"You would be cooler if you did not wear it."

"Thank you for your concern." The friar was curious about why the young man was alone. "Did your father not come with you today?"

"He lives far from here, in another *cacicazgo*," he spoke quietly.

Antonio studied the Indian. He was eleven or twelve years of age, still boyish in appearance, his hands slender, his chest and shoulders not fully developed. His face was broad and forehead flattened, his skin lighter than most, similar in colour to the wheat of late autumn. He strode naked as was the custom, his body adorned with a pendant about his neck, green feathers tied about his forehead and cloth bands on his arms and legs.

"Did he give you permission to be here?"

"Yes. He asked me to report to him what the strangers are doing."

"Here, help me with this." Fray Antonio handed him the end of a cord. "Hold this and walk in a straight line towards that tree. Do not stop until I tell you and do not let go of the string."

The friar measured out a rectangle, using pegs to mark each of the four corners.

"What are you doing?" Amayao's eyes were wide with curiosity.

"This is the place where we will build the house of God, our church of worship." He walked to one end. "This is where the altar will be, facing east, the direction of the rising sun." He took ten long paces. "Here will be the entrance." The priest pointed west. "The doors will face the setting sun. I want these to be magnificently carved."

The boy let go of the cord and turned sideways to face the bushes. "My father has a holy place where he makes offerings to the *cemí*."

"When you learn the teachings of our Holy Faith, Amayao, your life will change."

The boy urinated on the fallen leaves. "What kinds of changes, Friar?"

"Among other things, you will learn to urinate in private, and to clothe yourself."

Amayao looked perplexed.

"Our church will be bigger than your father's, Amayao. People from all over will come to give praise to God." He studied the Indian's bright eyes. "I can tell you are an intelligent boy."

"My father has taught me many things."

"Would you like to learn more? About faraway places where there are mighty kingdoms?

"I do not know of these places, Friar."

"I want to teach you and other sons of the caciques. You will reap great rewards."

"How will you do this?" The boy's voice was excited.

"Do you think you can bring them to me?"

"They will need the permission of their fathers."

"Bring as many as you can. We will have a meeting as soon as my house is ready. Fray Deule and I will build a *monasterio* where we will teach you all you want to know."

An elderly Taíno shouted from a distance, "Amayao, Amayao, we are thirsty. Go to the river and fetch us water."

Fray Antonio held the boy by the arm to prevent him from leaving. "The man in charge will give them water when he thinks it is necessary, Amayao. You should go directly home. Do not fetch water for the workers without permission."

"But the man will be sick, Friar. We are not accustomed to working like this; when we are hungry we eat and when we are thirsty we drink. The man with the dog is cruel, Guami Antonio." Amayao was defiant.

Antonio admired his bravery in speaking out, but he dared not show sympathy. "Remember what I told you, the governor wants it this way, our village must be built, and if your people cooperate, they will be rewarded for their labour."

The Indian moved his arms and legs nervously.

"I know it is hard for you to understand. Look here." The friar removed a small medal from his pocket. "I want you to have this."

"What is it?" The boy leaned over to inspect the object.

"It is a *relicario* of the most Blessed Virgin. Her name is Mary, the Mother of God. She will protect you if you pray to her."

The small brass medal was engraved with the image of the Virgin Mary holding the infant Jesus with cherubs on either side. Before he left Spain, his friend Ana María had paid an artisan to make relics for Antonio to carry as reminders of their friendship and as protection in the barbarous regions of the Ocean Sea.

"The mother of our Great Spirit is Attabeira who is the giver of life." The boy showed the friar the pendant his father had given him.

"We bring a new religion to your people, Amayao. The times will be dangerous, so you will need to be safe. If your heart is pure, the Blessed Virgin will grant what you ask and you will no longer need the help of Mother Attabeira."

Amayao rubbed the brass medal. "Even if I ask her to send the strangers away from Yamaye?"

"Ask her to lead you to know the one true God."

"I will take her and feed her the way I do the *cemí* in my father's house."

"Take her, Amayao, but do not feed her. If you pray to her, she will give you the food of life, the knowledge of the Son of God. Go, and remember your promise to bring me sons of the caciques."

As Antonio moved closer to the construction site, he saw Narváez loosen his grip on the leash. The dog growled and surged forward, frothing at the mouth and snapping its fierce teeth.

"*Levántate, hijo de puta.*" Narváez motioned for the man to rise.

The elderly Indian who had called out to Amayao had fallen from exhaustion.

The priest approached. "He needs food and water, don Pánfilo. He has worked too long in the sun."

Ignoring Fray Antonio, Narváez shouted above the animal's attack growl, "There is no resting here." He gave the command and the beast sank its teeth, tearing the man's ankle and dragging him face down through the mud, the Indian's cries muffled and deadened by the thickness of the swamp. Those who looked on cowered and whimpered at the sight of their fellow Taíno being ripped apart.

Pánfilo de Narváez was entertained by his sport. He fondled his yellow tresses shining wet in the midday sun and laughed aloud to himself. When he called off the dog, the victim's body lay mangled and lifeless in the mud. The Indians returned to work in silence, Narváez had taught them a lesson: no food or water unless offered by the master.

The friar stepped back into the cool shade under one of the few remaining trees and the taskmaster continued his patrol. Neither man spoke.

Like many Spaniards, Narváez had developed the dual nature of a conquistador. When he related to the governor and his friends, the lieutenant was friendly and jocular, conversing freely and with the quickest wit; when he dealt with the Indians, he was a bloodthirsty monster, indulging in sadistic pleasures.

This first incident of violence occurred too soon after their arrival in Jamaica, Antonio thought, it was going to make it more difficult to subjugate the natives and settle the new colony.

The settlers continued to live aboard the caravels. Their temporary shelter carried provisions for the new colony, food and supplies that they would not have found in Jamaica. The governor ensured that these were rationed, and he appointed his trustworthy lieutenant, Rodrigo de Villareal, to monitor their distribution and consumption. Antonio had the opportunity on more than one occasion to scan the ships' bills of lading, which his friend Rodrigo kept. The cargo included items such as two thousand kegs of wine, three hundred quintals of biscuits, bacon, thirty casks of olive oil, dried beef, cheeses, nine hundred bushels of garbanzos, garlic, onions, medicines, artillery, fishing nets, hooks, tallow, nails and iron fasteners for construction.

The Spaniards brought wheat and barley, and stalks of sugar cane from the Canary Islands in the hope that these crops would supplement the local produce of the Indians. But until these were planted and reaped, they had to be satisfied with monthly rations. In addition to food crops, the Spaniards loved their meat, they brought pigs, chickens and cattle, with the plan to clear patches of land and build pens and ranches. In La Española, these animals reproduced at a phenomenal rate, providing adequate sources of food for the settlers. The friar was hopeful that the same would happen in Jamaica.

Eighty men, who comprised the human cargo, were a sufficient number, in the opinion of Diego Colón, Almirante de La Española, to subdue seventy thousand natives. Besides the regular ship's crew, the governor had chosen tradesmen, carpenters and masons, the best *escuderos* for defence, and persons of the elite class, the *caballeros andantes*, who would serve as *alcaldes*, accountants and assistants.

For building the town, the governor depended on Antonio's architectural genius. At his request, Fray Antonio had sketched a plan for Sevilla. Second only to the higher calling of converting souls to Christendom, the friar loved draftsmanship. He had studied architecture at the University of Valladolid in addition to the compulsory disciplines of theology, Latin and Greek. He was also a skilled sculptor and hoped to train the Indians to improve their pottery and learn rudimentary masonry. He wanted to build a church adorned with friezes to rival those of Spain and Italy, but for this he would require the assistance of a European artisan schooled in modern architecture.

He had objected to the governor's choice of the town's site. Fray Antonio was aware of the problems associated with the swamp and had advised Juan de Esquivel about its unsuitability. "Will you not reconsider, Señor don Juan?" he had asked, pointing out where the terrain gradually changed to sandy soil. "Close to the bay, the land is below sea level and overgrown with thick red mangrove forest, but farther up, only a few hundred feet from shore, it rises to fifteen feet above sea level. We could use the swamp as a buffer between the sea and the proposed fortress."

The governor dismissed him with a curt reply. "Build closer to their village? No, Antonio. We take too big a risk as it is with these savages."

The governor distributed land plots, using a design with the church and plaza as the central focus and the houses

located on either side of a single street. He appointed
Narváez to supervise the building of the settlers' homes,
twenty-five wooden *cabañas* with thatched roofs and *tapia*
walls, made of rammed mud and limestone, like those used
by hunters in Spain. Esquivel was confident these would
be adequate, for the Indians knew how to make roofs
impervious to rain and houses sturdy enough to withstand
the force of *huracanes*.

Fray Antonio often asked his friend, Rodrigo de Villareal,
to assist with surveying and inspection of work.

"Is this the proposed site of the governor's house?"
Rodrigo asked, pointing to a large piece of cleared land
with a stone foundation already built.

"Yes, on sandy ground, too close to the sea. We are more
than a thousand feet north of the town." Fray Antonio pulled
out sketches from the pocket of his tunic. "It measures fifty-
two by fifty eight feet, the external walls being four feet
thick. You may help me measure it to ensure accuracy, if
you like."

"The governor will not be living in mud and thatch, I take
it." Rodrigo laughed.

"You are right. The *Casa Fuerte* is of limestone, sturdy
enough to hold armaments. Here," he showed Rodrigo
his plans, "the castle tower will face the sea in view of the
caravels, its entrance on the opposite end, pointing south
towards the town."

"It reminds me of Cristóbal Colón's house in La Isabela."

"I also want a hospital and a solid structure for the
church and *monasterio*, but I do not think I can persuade the
governor."

"The governor has given me permission to return to
Sevilla for a while," Rodrigo said.

"On what business?"

"I told him it is a legal matter to do with my father's estate."

"I was not aware your father died."

"In truth, Antonio, I wonder if I am losing my zeal for adventure and, besides, I miss my Beatriz. I am not sure how you deny yourself the pleasures, my friend."

"God works in mysterious ways, Rodrigo."

"I suppose." His friend chuckled. "I believe the Governor is in some sort of trouble."

"How so?"

"I am not exactly sure. The *tesorero* of La Española has asked for a report of his activities."

"I can see nothing amiss in his administration. We should go, everything here seems in order. The Indians have effectively cleared the area and the dimensions and structure of the foundation are fine."

Fray Antonio and Rodrigo walked along the muddy path towards the town site. They turned to hear the muffled sounds of a Taíno woman who was pushed up against a tree. Narváez stood in front of her with his pants down and his hands covering her mouth.

"Let us turn around and return to the ships," Rodrigo said.

The friar did not try to stop Narváez and hated himself for it. He wondered if the lieutenant would spare the Indian woman's life. Men changed in ways he did not understand. They lusted for Indian concubines, coveted gold and murdered for sport. He realized *el fuego de la sangre*, the passion of the conquistador, knew no bounds.

"Forgive us, Father, for we know not what we have done," he said aloud so Rodrigo could hear. He made the sign of the cross, his head throbbing with the pain of guilt. He was reminded of the words of Yahweh, Isaiah 1:15:

When you spread out your hands.
I will hide my eyes from you;
even though you make many prayers,
I will not listen;
your hands are full of blood.

They stepped into one of the *canoas* stolen from the Indians. He said a novena that evening to pray for peace in the new colony and for the salvation of souls of both the natives and his countrymen.

Chapter Twenty-seven

"Wear this on your belt tonight." Huareo attached the wooden *cemí* of Opiyelguobirán to the cord tied around his son's waist. "He will be your guide in the night."

The boy held up the face of the *cemí* resting above his groin. The dog spirit stared at Amayao with its bulging eye. "He scares me, Baba. Opiyelguobirán guards the dead, not the living."

"The son of the cacique is not fearful. Hold Opiyelguobirán close and tight so he does not escape."

In the cool of the night just before dawn, blue soldier crabs marched in hordes from the hills above the villages to deposit sacs of eggs into the seawater.

Men carried torches for the hunt to make a path through the darkness. Huareo and his cousins, Guababo and Hacona led the group, followed by Amayao and ten friends of the cacique. Painted with the *genipa*, they crept through the thick brush like moving shadows of the *opía*. As they entered a clearing, the clattering of crabs filled the air. The female *juey* scurried and climbed madly on one another's backs in a race to the sea.

The cacique told the hunters to spread out in a wide circle. They flashed torches low to the ground and the creatures immediately screeched to a halt, blinded and confused by the light. They arched their backs and opened their front claws in defence, their beady eyes popping out in fright.

Amayao screamed in pain when a blue crab viciously snapped his finger. In the excitement, he had bent down to hold it without waiting for instructions from his father.

Huareo grabbed the shell of the *juey* and pulled down on its two hind legs and with his other hand, he twisted and broke the claw that was fastened to Amayao's finger, ripping the flesh as he removed the crab. "Always hold the warrior from behind, surprise him by jumping on his back," Huareo advised his son.

The hunters gathered hundreds of blue crabs to fill nets and baskets, and when the light of morning showed, they built a fire and filled clay pots with seawater to place them on the embers.

The crabs shrieked as they were thrown into the boiling water, their shells turning bright red like the seed of the *bija*. They clamoured to crawl out, but kept pulling each other back down the slippery sides of the pots.

The men sat in a circle, their legs crossed on the cool sands. Guababo removed dried leaves of tobacco from a basket and rolled them into cigars that he shared with the group.

"They have come to take the land from us." Huareo leaned towards the fire to light one end of a *túbano*. "What do we know of cousin Mamyo and his people?"

"F-fifty of his men have worked h-hard to build h-houses for the s-strangers," Amayao stuttered.

"Is this all we know?" Huareo asked and then he whispered to Amayao, "What is the matter with you? I want you to talk like a man." The cacique pulled a steaming crab from the pot, blew on it to cool the shell, then cracked open the claws with his teeth to suck out the soft white meat. The frothy juices of the *juey* dripped freely down his chest.

Guababo said, "The strangers needed more than fifty men to build their houses, so they used dogs and *caballos* to capture men from other *yucayeque*."

"What happened when our people refused to go with them?" Huareo inquired.

"The *tuyra* set dogs on them to tear flesh from their bones." Guababo stood and spread his legs in protest. "We need to give them the *naiboa* to drink as a sign of friendship.

'Here, Guamikeni Esquivel, Chief of the Earth, Sea and Sky, welcome to Yamaye, accept this juice of the *yuca*. It is the sacred drink of the Taíno, made especially for you.'" Guababo's sinister laugh filled the morning air.

The men repeated the joke and laughed heartily.

Hacona rose to stand with Guababo, holding a *macana* above his head. "Guajeri Huareo, we are the brave ones, the *guaribono* of your *cacicazgo*." He beat his chest, his spirit cried out, a long wailing sound in mourning for the people of Yamaye. "The strangers are our enemy, Huareo. If we do not fight them, they will become our rulers and we will become the absent ones."

"You have the spirit of your father to look over you, Hacona." Huareo thought of the *cemí* he had given his cousin.

"Hacona speaks the truth." Yabey stood to face the cacique. "They cut down the trees, burn the land, and force our people to work as slaves. Soon, they will rape our women and give us their sickness."

Guababo addressed the men, "When our people in Haití first saw the bearded white men, they thought they were creatures from the *turey*. They called their leader, Guamikeni, Cacique of the Earth and Sky. But we know that these strangers are not born of the Spirit of Spirits, they did not come to us from the sky, but from another land, a place of darkness we do not know."

"I must seek counsel from the Great One. Our people are in danger," Huareo said.

"The *maboya* lives within them, Huareo." Guababo swung the *macana* in a circle above his head. "Cacique Huareo, I await your command to surprise their village."

"They will never be satisfied," Hacona joined in. "We will never provide them with enough food. The stranger eats more than the *manatí*."

Huareo laughed and his men shared the moment of levity. He inhaled the tobacco smoke that tasted sweeter after he had feasted. He savoured it, then jutting his jaw forward and curling his lips, blew thick smoke rings that floated above the fire. He looked into the half empty pot. "We need to hunt more. We have left none to take home," the cacique joked. He looked around at his men and felt a closeness of spirit with them. "My *nitaíno*, we must protect our women and children. Esquivel wants to divide us and put his own men in charge of our *cacicazgo*."

"We shall die before we allow this," Guababo shouted in defiance.

"They want to seize the land to grow more cotton so that we weave the *jamaca* for their use, and they want to raise animals so they will have enough meat to eat. They work our men day and night to find gold in the rivers of Otoao, the Place of the High Mountains, but there is none to be found," Huareo said.

Hacona clenched his fists. "They will destroy us, *Guajeri* Huareo. They will force our *naboría* to labour until they are sick and dying, they do not allow us to perform the *areíto*, our songs and prayers we must do in private."

Guababo whispered to the cacique, "There is trouble, Huareo." He pointed to a boy who had arrived from the village moments before.

"What message do you have for us?" Huareo asked.

"They have captured Iguaca, Cacique of Guayguata, they burned his houses and made his people slaves." The messenger's lips quivered as he spoke.

Huareo stood, and for a moment, his vision was blurred, his feet unsteady as if someone had beaten his head with a *macana*. He looked at Guababo whose eyes were full of fire.

Guababo pounded his feet on the sand with the tempo of the war dance and gave voice to the howling of the battle cry.

"If they do not return Iguaca, we will murder them and burn their village," Huareo heard the voice of Yaya speaking through him.

Then all fell silent.

The men stood, bowed in deference to their chief, and raising their heads, they danced in a circle.

"Guababo, gather two hundred *guaribono* and make preparations in secret for a surprise attack. The Taíno are not accustomed to fighting, we have had no reason to defend our *yucayeque*, no need to use arrows before the bearded man came to our land. But now the Great One has said we must act, he will give us the wisdom to know when to strike. We return to our women to share the remainder of the hunt, but we bathe first in the river to give thanks to Bibi Atabey. We will no longer do as the strangers ask. It is against the will of Yaya for the *arijuana* to hold our cacique prisoner."

"I believe he is a holy man, Baba." Amayao sat with his father in the shrine Guayacán had prepared within the cave.

"How do you know this?" Huareo placed pieces of *yuca* before the *cemí* of Baibrama, careful not to spill the *naiboa*, the poisonous juice of the tuber contained in a calabash bowl by his side.

"Their priest is like our *bejique*, Baba. He cures the sick."

"That is the *maboya* within him, Amayao. He tricks you to believe that he has the power." The cacique rubbed his hands with the poisonous *naiboa*.

"What are you doing, Baba?" The boy held his hand to cover his mouth and opened his eyes wide, startled at his father's actions.

"We are making an offering to Baibrama." Huareo

continued to rub his hands. "Amayao, you must have faith, you must know that Yocajú Bagua Maórocoti, the Great Spirit who has no beginning and no end and who is invisible, lives in His own house. He sees everything you do and hears everything you say."

"I have this faith, Baba."

"Then you will be strong. If you walk in the night and are fearful, the *opía* will consume your spirit, you will not be able to return to the world of the living because the enemy will defeat you." Huareo dipped his hand again into the bowl of poisonous juice.

He looked around the cave. Boinayel stood in the middle of the other *cemí*, with tears streaking down his cheeks and hands resting on his hips above his groin. In the corner was a grey stone, carved by Guayacán, of Attabeira, the Mother of Waters, Lady of the Moon and Tides, Mother of All.

Huareo scooped up the juice into his cupped hands. "Place your hands here next to mine," he instructed Amayao.

"What is this for, Baba?"

"Hold still so you do not spill the juice. Pour it over his head and rub it on his body."

"Why, Baba?"

"Do as I say, but do not touch your hands to your mouth."

Amayao rubbed one side of Baibrama with the *naiboa*, his hands trembling as he smeared the smooth wood of the *cemí*.

"He will guard us against sickness that the bearded ones bring. If you do not feed him the *yuca* or care for his house, our people will suffer.

"Baba, the bearded priest also teaches me how to protect myself." He showed his father the rounded object that resembled a *guanín*.

Huareo grabbed it from his hand. "You are not to take what belongs to the stranger."

"It was a gift, Baba."

Huareo cursed his son, raising his voice in anger. "Amayao, you are not to accept gifts, they possess the stranger spirit."

Amayao reached to recover the object, but he was no match for his father's strength. He pushed the boy backwards and hurled the stranger's *cemí* through the opening of the cave.

"You are a fool." Huareo raised his fist to Amayao who lay flat on his back. He knelt down next to his son, grabbed his neck with both hands and tightened his grip. The skin was soft and tender.

The boy's face turned red, and he choked and gasped for air. "P-please, Ba-b-ba."

Huareo took a deep breath. No, he would not do it. He lifted himself off, and he saw wet marks pulsing red on Amayao's neck. He looked at his own hands stained with the juice of the yuca. He reached for the bowl. No, he would not make him drink it; Amayao was his son and future cacique of Maima.

His son sat up, his hands raised to guard his throat.

"Listen to me, you are the son of Cacique Huareo. You are not to attend to the stranger, not to visit him, not to listen to him, not to take instruction in their language. Do you hear what I say to you?"

"Yes, Baba."

"My *nitaíno* tell me you speak in the strangers' tongue. If you speak like them, then your thoughts and spirit will become theirs, like the *maboya*. I forbid you to be with them. You must see them no more, and if you disobey my command, if you do not keep watch, you will be carried off by the sun like Macocael and be turned to stone."

Huareo looked about for Opiyelguobirán. He saw the wooden *cemí* of Boinayel but the Guardian of the Dead was absent. He knew now the *cemí* were in danger, he needed to hide them, to bury them deep within the ancestral caves. He fondled the *guanín* for comfort, smooth and warm to his touch. His uncle Majagua was right; it possessed its own light, a life like that of güey, the sun.

"Where is the amulet of Opiyelguobirán I gave you the night of the hunt?" Huareo's tone was accusatory.

"I left it in our home, Baba."

"You must always carry it with you. The *cemí* of Opiyelguobirán is not here. We tied him to a rock, but he has escaped." He extended his hand to his son to help him stand. "We will be brave, Amayao, the Great One will not forsake us. Let us go to the river and cleanse our hands of poison."

Huareo's heart was heavy as if someone had tied it to a stone and dropped it to the bottom of the sea. The words of the prophecy haunted him: *When the strangers come to our land, Opiyelguobirán will walk off into the night, and we shall not find him.*

Chapter Twenty-eight

Milady,

I have arrived safely on the island of Jamaica, praise and thanks be to God and the Virgin Mary, with the Governor, don Juan de Esquivel and eighty other men to settle a new town, which we have named Sevilla. He asked me to join him because of the bravery I showed in battles against the Indians of La Española. We thought the natives here in Jamaica to be fierce, but this is not altogether true. There are some, especially a cacique named Huareo, who is resisting our settlement of the land. He is the principal chief of the island and has a negative influence over the others.

The ways of the natives are as strange to us as they were in La Española. They walk naked in public, men, young girls and boys alike, just as their mothers bore them. They decorate themselves with paint, black, white and red, which makes for a ghastly sight. They worship statues they call cemíes, which I believe, are little devils. They claim the objects protect them from danger.

On the matter of their sexual behaviours, I cannot elaborate at great length, for their habits are lewd. They show no shame for the naked body, they share their wives and daughters freely and copulate as the beasts do. Generally, however, they are docile and good-natured, suited to conversion to our Holy Faith, and innocent to the ways of the world, paying little attention to possessions. They are very clean. They bathe in the cold waters of rivers, and even though this is a daily practice, it does not seem to harm them.

I am sure you do not care to hear of these Indians, but rather to know that I am, thanks be to God, in good health. I have not received a letter from you for three years even though I have sent correspondence with good and trusted friends on two different occasions, including 200 maravedís of coin each time. I hope that letters from you have not been sent to La Española since I have been here in Jamaica, but if they have, I will soon receive them, for travel between the islands is frequent. I wish it were the case that you could join me here in the colony, but you understand my position. I think of you daily. The love I hold for you in my heart gives me solace on lonely nights in these uncivilized regions of the world.

I entrust this letter to a gentleman, don Rodrigo de Villareal, a trusted friend with whom I made acquaintance in La Española. I am sorry that I cannot afford to send money at this time, for we are still a new colony. The Indians are not obeying our orders to mine gold from the rivers, so we have not yet acquired the riches of La Española. Rodrigo will be returning to Jamaica, so before he leaves, I implore you to write and tell me of your situation. Please send my love to our son, Francisco, and tell me in your letters how he is and how he has grown, and what he is doing *in school. Education is important for his future success in life. Make sure that you help him with his studies and that he remains in school so that he may study Latin and Mathematics and learn to read and write the Spanish language.*

My brother's son, Martín, is now fourteen years old, of an age when he would benefit from a voyage to the Indies. I ask for you to encourage my nephew to accompany Rodrigo on his return to Jamaica. There will be fortunes to be made here once we are able to subjugate the Indians and instruct them properly in the Holy Faith.

May you and all your relatives prosper, and I send you love from the father of your child and loving admirer, Antonio, who wishes for your well-being always.

Jamaica, 1511

Fray Antonio knelt on the dirt floor of his new home. He mouthed the words of the Hail Mary as he fingered the rosary beads, *Ave María, gratia plena, Dominus tecum.* He had recited the prayer by rote so many times its true meaning was lost to him. His knees hurt from the rough ground, but this was a pain he would tolerate, a small penance for sinful thoughts. He meditated on the Ten Commandments to examine his conscience, and then reached for the scourge that lay by his side. He positioned the thick handle above his head, admiring the thongs dangling before his face.

A thump of boots sounded on the front steps. The

governor abruptly entered without knocking. "Pardon me, Fray Antonio, I did not mean to interrupt."

"Please come in, come in, Don Juan," the friar said.

The governor's odour was unpleasant. Even after years of living in La Española, he dressed like a Castilian. He wore a shirt with long, puffed sleeves, hose that covered the entire length of his legs and a tight-fitting doublet that wrapped about his torso.

"I believe it to be warmer here than in La Española." He wiped his beard and neck with a silk handkerchief.

"Please, be my guest, have a seat, Governor." The friar pointed to a wooden stool made by the Indians.

"Thank you, Fray Antonio." The governor examined the furniture. "The natives are learning from our carpenters." He glanced at a dark brown water jug sitting on a table. "Is this also their handiwork?"

"Yes, don Juan."

The governor felt the contours of the jug. "Was this made using hand-made coils?"

"Yes, the Indians are skilled at pottery, don Juan. They have been quick to copy the styles of our Spanish ceramics."

"I suppose you must find your lodging somewhat more humble than the monasteries of Spain." When the governor chuckled, his drooping moustache lifted from the sides of his mouth, deep wrinkles beneath his eyes making him look more advanced than his years.

"I must congratulate you, Antonio."

"Why is that, sir?" He moved up a chair.

"We have met with success in the new colony in a relatively short period, we have already pacified many Indians, ensuring their allegiance to the Crown of Spain. Don Rodrigo tells me you and Fray Deule have converted many to the Holy Faith."

"It will take more work, don Juan."

"They will quickly learn their lesson. We have captured one of their caciques and punished him for refusing to serve us. The Indians will soon come over to our side if we take their chiefs, they are lost without their leaders."

"God willing, don Juan, we do not resort to the bloodshed we saw in the capture of Cotubanamá."

"Friar Antonio, that was my crowning glory, the subjugation of the Province of Higüey." He snorted like a pig.

The friar chose his words carefully. "We will build a more prosperous colony, I believe, sir, without the massacres. I know I can appeal to the natives' affectionate dispositions."

"That is your duty, after all, Friar." The governor stifled his laugh. "You know Pánfilo de Narváez would not agree with you, he would say the natives are malicious beings, incapable of natural judgment."

"They are not beasts, don Juan. Our monarchs charged us with the duty of benign subjugation for the conversion of souls."

"Indeed, our mission is a holy one, Friar." The governor forced a smile. "Our deepest disappointment is that we have not found gold in quantities that would please the Crown."

"There are reports of finds, don Juan."

"Not enough to satisfy the courts of Spain. We must concentrate on growing food. Jamaica is more fertile than either Cuba or La Española, *yuca, maíz* and cotton grow in abundance and pigs multiply at a rate never before seen. We produce the sweetest pork and finest beef Spaniards will ever taste."

"We are short of labourers, Governor. Indians are escaping to the mountains to hide in caves."

"We will remedy this." He stood and stretched his arms. "It is time we take ownership of the land, Friar. We will create

our own *vencindades*, communities in which the Indians
become our vassals, we will assign them to our men in lots
of one hundred and fifty and two hundred. The colonists
will be the proprietors of the land, their allotments granted
in the name of the Crown. With the help of the Franciscans
soon to arrive from Sevilla, you will serve the King, my
dear friar, to ensure the Indians are treated with care and
respect."

"This is my duty, Governor."

"The popes of Rome granted us the right of propagation
of the Holy Faith to the barbarous nations. You have work
to do, Friar. The Indians are prone to idleness, wiling away
hours sitting on riverbanks. Our form of governance is new
to them, as is employment to mine gold, build houses and
work the fields."

"We know this, sir." The friar hated himself for overtures
of deference to the governor but knew that any objections
he made would be futile.

"Thank you, Antonio, I rely on your allegiance. I need your
support in a matter of government. As you know, the King
did not appoint me, it was don Diego who commissioned me
as lieutenant. My fate now lies in the hands of the Tesorero
of La Española, the estimable Miguel de Pasamonte,
who has authority with the King. He disapproved of my
appointment from the start."

"I am sure the King holds you in high esteem, sir."

"He can be persuaded otherwise. Opposition will be
made to my governorship, Friar, so I will need to depend
on your loyalty. You are fired by Christian zeal and a sense
of duty to both King and country."

"Thank you, sir. It is not always as fervent as it should
be." He smiled.

"I am sure you are a more devout Christian than I." The

governor chuckled. "You see, Antonio, my father, Pedro de Esquivel, was forced to convert from Judaism. He was captured by the Moors but was fortunate enough to escape. Our family received royal favours for which I am grateful, but I carry with me always the stigma of the *converso*. I tell you this in utter confidence."

"You have my word, don Juan."

"We will do what we can to succeed for the Crown but we are in desperate need of women. No settlement can prosper without families. We also need labour, the Indians have been unsatisfactory. So we may have to resort to the importation of African slaves, they are hardier and more productive."

"This would be of tremendous benefit to the natives, don Juan."

"I thank you for your time, Antonio. I hear your companion, Fray Deule, is not well."

"He is tired, Governor. Deule is a holy man who has worked relentlessly for the conversion of souls."

"Be sure to give him my best wishes for a speedy recovery."

"I believe the Good Lord will soon be calling him to enjoy the next Kingdom."

Fray Antonio saw his guest to the door.

The governor's pompous talk and obsession with failure tired the friar. He yearned for the comforts of home and the company of Ana María. Perhaps he should lie to the Governor like Rodrigo to earn a passage to Sevilla, but his vocation to the priesthood was strong and he would resist temptations, both of lust and deceit. He was reminded of the Founder of his Order, St Francis of Assisi who threw his body onto thickets to be pricked by thorns in order to rid his mind of sinful thoughts.

Antonio Díaz del Castillo and Juan de la Deule sat at either end of a long table within the main hall of the monastery. Antonio looked at the sleeves of his frayed and moth-eaten Franciscan habit and thought how proud St Francis would be of him, a true mendicant devoting himself to a life of poverty and humility. Ten Indians sat with them, nine were sons of caciques, and one, a man named Mamyo, former Cacique of Maima.

Deule pushed his chair back and stood. "Let us begin with the Nicene Creed. Each of you may take turns reciting a verse after me. When we say this prayer, we remember one important truth: Jesus Christ, God made man, is our only Saviour. You are aware that through the sacrament of baptism we embrace the risen Lord, we die with Christ on the cross to give up our sinful ways and we rise triumphantly with Him to enjoy eternal life."

Credo in unum Deum, Patrem omnipotentem,
factorem caeli et terrae, visibilium omnium et invisibilium.

Each recited a verse in Latin until the prayer was finished.

The Indians had memorized most prayers of *la Santa Fe* and believed in the Catholic doctrine that *Nuestro Señor* was Son of the one true God. They had developed a devotion to the saints, in particular *la Santa María*, the Mother of God. Antonio was satisfied that they were ready to adopt Christian names through baptism. Amayao was to be called Diego because of his love of the patron saint of Spain.

Fray Deule took a deep breath before beginning instruction. "You must tell your fathers the idols they worship are of the devil and the dances and songs they perform are sacrilegious. You know how beguiling the ways are of *el demonio*, he will trick you into believing falsehoods. *La Santa Cruz* will be erected in each of your villages and your houses of worship and idols destroyed."

Amayao interrupted, "Fray Deule, may I speak?"

"Yes, my son, what do you wish to say?"

"Many of us are in danger of being banished or killed by our fathers," the young Indian spoke in Spanish.

"No harm will come to you while you are with us, " Fray Antonio replied. "I am proud of how you have learned Spanish, Amayao." The friar was drowsy in the afternoon heat. The mud walls retained humidity, making the air heavy and musty. He straightened his back and looked around the room, these men seated at the table of the Franciscan Monastery were his *discípulos*, new soldiers of Christ.

Fray Deule nodded. Rays of sunlight that streaked through the window caught tufts of his crimson hair. "This is part of Christian sacrifice, my son. You are called to leave your father and mother to follow in His footsteps." He coughed a wheezing sound.

"Some of us cannot return to our villages," Amayao said in a sad tone, "for our relatives believe we have betrayed them."

"Your faith will save you from evil," Fray Deule interrupted him. "Do you remember what we taught you? We are different from other living creatures of the earth for we alone have souls that the Lord nourishes through baptism. Fray Antonio and I dispense God's grace through baptism so that once you are cleansed with Holy Water you will be ready to enter the Kingdom of God, you will have no fear in your heart for you will be saved from the sin of Adam."

The young men's faces brightened. Fray Antonio noticed they had acquired the graces of civilized society. They said prayers in Latin as devoutly as any Castilian, they knew the rules of *La Gramática Castellana* and were able to read and write Spanish, they did not paint their bodies with hideous markings nor walk about nude in public. Many, including Mamyo and his family, had learned the arts of masonry and sculpture.

Fray Antonio addressed them, "We want you to bring your mothers with their babies. Tell them the priests will baptize them to save their children from the devil. We want you to bring the sick and dying whom we will anoint with holy oils to prepare them for eternal life. Tell them Fray Deule and I have healing hands."

Fray Antonio had noticed that when Fray Deule laid hands on the sick, they were miraculously cured of disease. When the Indians saw this, they gave thanks to God, they wept and knelt before the friar. The Grace of God worked wonders through His minister.

Fray Antonio continued, "After you are baptized, you will be ready to receive the sacrament of penance and confession. You confess your sins because they offend God, who deserves all your love and, by the help of His grace, you will resolve to sin no more. If you are penitent, you will receive absolution and be purged of all sin. Poor as you are, you must bring your prize possessions, gold and other valuables, as restitution." Fray Antonio stood from his seat to stretch his stiffened legs and arms. "You are all welcome to reside here until it is safe for you to visit your villages."

"Fray Antonio," Amayao spoke with panic in his voice.

"What is it, my son?"

"Respectfully, sir, the Town of Sevilla may be in danger."

"How so?"

"Taíno warriors are planning an attack."

"Who has told you this, Amayao?" Fray Antonio asked.

"It is the talk of the villages."

"I do not think there is need to panic. If you find there is truth to these rumours, you should inform me and I will alert the governor. I retire now for afternoon prayer. Fray Deule will lead you in Vespers at sunset. May God continue to bless you all." Fray Antonio raised his hands and made the sign of the cross.

Chapter Twenty-nine

Huareo's face, arms and legs bore the black stains of the *genipa*, his back was patterned in red with the image of the serpent and his chest painted with the gaping mouth of Yocajú Bagua Maórocoti.

"The great spirits will guide you just as they helped Guahayona," Yari said.

"Yaya has decreed we must face the enemy." He kissed her forehead.

The dark night was good for an attack. The clouds covered the lights of the *turey* and the moon was hiding her face.

As Yari reached her arms above his shoulders, he felt the warmth of her *nagua* touch him between his legs, but he resisted the strong passion he felt for her.

"My eldest daughter comes with me tonight."

"Huareo, Aquiana is too young."

"You speak as if she were your own."

"I love her as if she were mine."

Her lips were red, the colour of the *curujey*, and her skin smelled of sweet grass. The chatter of expectant warriors outside jolted him, shifting his thoughts to the impending battle. "Aquiana is ready. Guababo has trained her with our finest *guaribono*."

"If you lose her, Huareo..."

"Do not worry, she is safe. I know the Great One has chosen her to be *cacique* of our people. Our natural order is no more, our *cacicazgo* are no more. My cousin Mamyo has betrayed me and like a fool become a servant of the strangers. I no longer have my son. Amayao is forever banished as a traitor, he is *arijuana* to me like the bearded one."

A moment of silence passed between them.

"You are distant, again, Guami Huareo." She caressed his cheek.

"Yari, the enemy has invaded us with a force more powerful than we could have imagined."

"No one will defeat you, Huareo. The *cemí* give you strength." She paused, and her eyes sparkled in the darkness.

"What is it, Yari?"

"You have wives and children who depend on you."

"No harm will come to me or to them."

"You will return to me victorious." She leaned her breasts to press against his, and he felt her spirit breathe life and strength into him.

He separated from her embrace and looked into her eyes. "My daughter and I will be safe."

The ground on the hilltop was cool and damp beneath his belly. Hugging a *macana*, Huareo lay still, waiting for the right moment to signal the descent.

His daughter stretched out by his side, her eyes wide and alert. She whispered, "I will be brave like you, Baba. Do not worry about me."

"*Shhh*, you must be quiet." He laid one arm across her shoulder.

They both looked out in silence with the sharp vision of the night owl. Yabey and his friend Cuayaoya guarded the cacique's immediate surroundings and a band of boys crouched in the nearby woods to keep watch.

Hundreds called to service from across the island formed a line on the hills above the strangers' village. Hacona and Guababo each led a group of men who made their approach from the opposite side closer to the former chiefdom of Maima. The *guaribono* carried spears pointed with sharpened flint and arrows poisoned with the juice of the *tibey* and manchineel.

Huareo had ordered a surprise attack because if he delayed any longer, he would leave the villages defenceless. He planned to capture a white man, not to torture him, but to hold him ransom. He intended also to destroy their village, to force them back into their boats.

He sought revenge for the capture of Iguaca, Cacique of Guayguata, for the destruction of Taíno villages and for taking his people by force. He would kill any stranger who assaulted him, his daughter or his men. He wanted justice, he wanted Yamaye to be freed from the hands of the *arijuana*.

A sole light flickered on the rooftop of Esquivel's house where a man stood watch, looking out at the hills where the cacique and his warriors lay hidden. Cuayaoya had orders to kill the guard, who would likely be the first to alert the villagers and to fire the *cañones*. Huareo counted twenty houses built not in a circle like those of a *yucayeque*, but in two straight lines with a road in the middle.

The cacique passed word for the approach to begin. Hacona and his men, who flanked the far side of the village below Maima, descended the hill to position themselves near the pens and stables. They had instructions to let the pigs, horses and cattle run free. Guababo and his group approached from the middle of the mountain to wait for the opportune time to release arrows of fire onto the rooftops. From the hilltops closer to the bay, Huareo, his daughter and their band of twenty men crept down the limestone rock to invade the strangers' village.

Huareo and Aquiana entered the first house while Yabey stood watch at the door. A fully clothed man was snoring, outstretched on a *jamaca*. Aquiana's order was to strike him unconscious with the *macana* so he could be taken prisoner.

In another *jamaca*, a second man lay asleep in the embrace of a Taíno woman.

She suddenly awoke, her eyes wide and frightened. Huareo motioned for the woman to be silent, but she leapt out of bed and started shrieking, breaking the silence of the night and waking the two men. Huareo reached to grab her but she slipped from him. Her companion fumbled for the *espada* on the ground next to the bed. Huareo snatched it first and in an instant, the cacique thrust the sword into the naked man's body, splitting his belly open and spilling his innards on the floor.

As the other man turned his back to pick up a weapon, Aquiana struck him from behind with the *macana*. He fell forward on his face with a thump.

Huareo sounded the war cry of the *guamó* but he knew it was too late. The frantic screams of the Taíno woman had already awakened the village. The cacique listened for Hacona and for the sound of animals scurrying from the corrals but he heard nothing. He wondered if Cuayaoya had done his murderous deed. He looked up to the roof of the governor's house and saw the guard still standing.

Yabey dragged the unconscious body of the man out of the house and with the help of others lifted him through the bush to a hideout in the hills.

Streaks of fire suddenly descended on the rooftops of the strangers' houses. Huareo knew then that Guababo was safe. The enemy turned its attention to saving the thatch-roofed houses from destruction, which gave Huareo the chance to retreat. He made his escape with Aquiana into the mountains. Fifteen of the twenty men returned safely.

As they reached the hilltop, the earth suddenly shook beneath their feet. Enormous boulders tumbled off the hillsides and crashed on the plain below. The *ceiba* and *caoba* of the forests split in two, blasted by the fire that burst from the mouths of the *cañones*. The earth cracked open louder than the storms of Guabancex, terrifying his men who fell, stupefied by the noise of the big fire.

Huareo and Aquiana met Guababo and a group of men by the river overlooking Maima. They formed a circle around the Spanish prisoner who lay flat on the grey sands of the embankment. Huareo watched anxiously for any signs of life.

With no paint, clothes or ornaments, the man's skin was bare, white as the flower of the *tibey*. His mouth gaped open, his arms and legs were stretched wide, stiff and cold. Huareo nudged the body with his spear but it would not move. The stranger was dead.

Guababo, with his spear held triumphant in his hands, stood astride the corpse. "We stripped him of his clothes to see if he had a navel and then carried him to the middle of the river, where it is deep. He awoke when we placed him in the water, Huareo."

"Why did you take him to the river, Guababo?" The cacique asked angrily. "Did he say anything?"

"We asked him his name but he did not answer. Then he begged us for mercy. We wanted to see what would happen if we held his head under water."

"You are a fool, Guababo."

"Your people wanted to know, *Guami* Huareo."

"What did my people want to know?"

"They wanted to know whether he was a spirit or a man like us."

"Guababo, you take orders from me, your cacique, not from our people. We wanted him alive for ransom." Huareo nodded to two of his men, who seized Guababo's weapon and led him away.

Huareo raised the corpse off the ground with his spear, and when he released it, the lifeless body flopped back down. "His spirit will not come back. We will not take him home for burial. Fetch leaves of the *yarey* and wrap the body in the palm, but make sure you do not touch it with your bare hands for it is unclean. Haul it into the bush where the strangers cannot not find it and leave it naked above the ground for the *aura*, the crows of carrion."

Chapter Thirty

Fray Antonio stepped close to the gibbet to which two Indians were tied awaiting execution. Despite the tropical midday sun, the friar felt cool, dressed in his newly sewn tunic made of *sarobey*, sea island cotton of Jamaica.

"What is your name?" the friar asked the man on the left.

"My name is Hacona."

Fray Antonio knew the other man to be Iguaca, Cacique of Guayguata, who was captured and imprisoned for refusing to surrender.

The men's wrists were bound with thick ropes above their heads, their bodies suspended from the crossbar of a long wooden beam that rested on posts eight feet tall on either end. Their legs dangled with their feet touching piles of dried wood arranged in pyramids.

Fray Antonio adjusted the religious stole about his shoulders. The gold-etched crosses that decorated the garment reflected the brilliance of the sun, shooting darts of light at the prisoners. "I am here to anoint you in preparation for eternal life."

The prisoners did not move or make a sound. They were naked as the day their mothers bore them, their skin glistening with sweat in the sunlight.

"How do you prepare me for eternal life?" Hacona asked.

"You must first accept Jesus Christ as your Lord and God." The friar fingered the pages of a black missal cupped in his hand. "If you accept Him as the Son of God and beg forgiveness of your sins, He will allow you to enter the Kingdom of Heaven."

"Do Christians like you go to this heaven?" Hacona inquired.

"Yes, good Christians go to heaven."

The Indian swung violently from the beam, the ropes creaking and the wood of the gibbet bending with the force of his sudden movement. The friar stumbled backwards to avoid being hit by the prisoner's legs.

"*Buibá maboya*. Be gone, trickster spirit. The Taíno are the good and noble ones. I do not want to go to your heaven, I do not want to go any place where Christians go."

The friar clasped the Holy Book to his breast and raised his eyes to heaven in supplication. As he retreated, the executioner and his assistants wrapped the bodies of the Indians with dried grasses. The afternoon breeze strengthened, whirling stray pieces of straw about the courtyard.

Don Juan de Esquivel stepped forward from the group of men present to witness the execution. "Your people will know that you are being put to death in the name of our God and King, and that anyone whosoever dares to capture or kill one of ours or whosoever dares to destroy our houses, will suffer the same ignoble death you face today." He raised his two-edged sword and placed it between Hacona's legs, then pulled it away with a sneer. He brandished his sword and with force and passion, twisted it into the sides of each prisoner, first Hacona and then Iguaca. Chilling, agonized cries of the victims echoed through the village. Blood gushed from their bodies to stain the piles of wood beneath them.

"Proceed," Esquivel commanded the executioner, who held flaming torches in both hands.

The friar turned away to enter the monastery just as the tinder ignited beneath the Indians' feet. "Father, these heathens know not what they have done. I ask you to be with them. Send your angel from heaven to look after them, and may the power of the devil over them be destroyed. This I ask in your Son's name, in the name of the Father, and of the Son and of the Holy Spirit." He made the sign of the cross, a benediction for the souls of Hacona and Iguaca.

A messenger summoned Fray Antonio to the governor's stone fortress for discussing a matter of grave importance.

"They did not listen, Fray Antonio, they fully deserved their punishment." The governor's glass eye rolled in its socket. "This cacique they call Huareo is deranged."

"Your men call him *El Loquillo* for he is crazy enough to dare the impossible," the friar said.

"He needs to be dealt with; he is a menace to our new colony. Antonio, I have received word from don Diego Colón." The governor coughed and spat phlegm on the floor. "Ay, *diós mío*! I fear I am not well."

"It may be pestilence from the swamps, Governor. I hope you will soon recover."

"Jamaica will be my grave, Antonio." He stroked his beard. "I think you are too innocent a soul to hear my confession, Friar." He laughed.

"Our Lord is merciful, don Juan."

"The *almirante* received letters from the King stating he is displeased that we have not found gold in Jamaica. He wants us to shift our attention to growing crops. He seeks support for the Spanish expeditions on *Terra Firme*, where explorers are discovering kingdoms rich in gold and minerals."

"We are already prosperous. You have been generous in assigning Indians to Rodrigo and other nobles. Our colony has filled ships to provide Cuba with an abundance of *yuca*. What more does the Crown require?"

"The King is not happy, Antonio. He believes we are negligent in the conversion and pacification of the Indians." The governor cursed beneath his breath.

"We have converted hundreds to the Holy Faith."

"The King's statements may be a pretext, dear Antonio. His Majesty has paid heed to malicious rumours that I am dishonest in my dealings with his *haciendas*, the properties of the Crown."

"I will attest to your good character if need be, don Juan."

"It may be too late for that, but thank you. He has given orders to have *la residencia* imposed on me. I shall be forced into confinement, and judges, of lesser rank than I, will investigate my governance and fabricate lies to remove me from office."

"How did this come about, Governor?"

"I am not sure if we have spies, but the Crown has little faith in our colony. I have lost Narváez along with thirty of our best crossbowmen who received permission to join Diego Velázquez de Cuéllar in the conquest of Cuba. This leaves the caciques without supervision, it leaves us stranded at the mercy of the Indians."

'Damn this wretched place,' Fray Antonio thought.

"My condolences, Antonio, for the loss of your friend."

"Thank you, Governor, the Good Shepherd has called Fray Deule to a better place. He was a faithful servant of God."

"He served his King and Church for a long time."

"Yes, Governor, he sailed with Cristóbal Colón in 1493."

"Your work is never done, Friar, thousands of barbarians to tame." Esquivel chuckled.

"The rewards are great, Governor."

"I know you will continue your good works. You must pray for me." He approached Antonio and hugged him, caressing both his cheeks. "May God bless and keep you, Fray Antonio."

"Thank you, Governor."

"Perhaps this is the reason for the King's suspicion."

"I do not know what you mean, sir."

"He may know." The governor pointed to the menorah with its seven gold and silver lamps. "My zeal to convert Indians to Christianity was not as fiery as he would have wanted."

"Yet you have managed the affairs of governing well, sir."

"I admire your spirit and innocence, my priest. Go with God, but remember not to take your devotion as seriously as our Dominican friends."

"The Dominicans are new to La Española, don Juan. We Franciscans are more accustomed to the ways of evangelizing the natives."

"So be it, Antonio. Promise that when this mortal body fails me or if the *almirante* devises a murderous plot against me, you will give me an honourable burial, but first and foremost, make sure my wife and children are cared for."

Fray Antonio walked away from the governor's *castillo* in the pouring rain. Each step darkened his spirit until he reached the monastery.

Part Four
Guayguata 1514–26

*And he returned to the mountain
called Cauta, which has two caves.*

Fray Ramón Pané

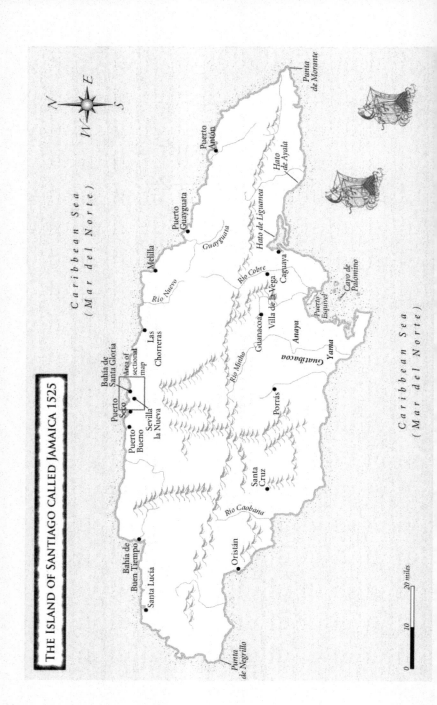

THE ISLAND OF SANTIAGO CALLED JAMAICA 1525

Caribbean Sea
(M a r   d e l   N o r t e)

Caribbean Sea
(M a r   d e l   N o r t e)

N
W · E
S

Punta de Morante

Puerto Antón

Hato de Ayala

Puerto Guayguata

Hato de Liguanea

Melilla

Guayguata

Río Nuevo

Río Cobre

Río Nuevo

Caguaya

Villa de la Vega

Puerto Esquivel

Cayo de Palomino

Las Chorreras

Bahía de Santa Gloria

Area of sectional map

Puerto Seco

Guanaboa

Anaya

Guatibacoa

Yuma

Puerto Bueno

Sevilla la Nueva

Río Minho

Porras

Santa Cruz

Bahía de Buen Tiempo

Santa Lucía

Río Caobana

Oristán

Punta de Negrillo

0   10   20 miles

Chapter Thirty-one

My son is banished.
I taught him the ways of our people,
I showed him the sacred art,
carved images of the *cemí*,
I taught him songs and stories,
the *areíto*.
He betrayed me,
betrayed our people,
the good and noble ones.
He gave his spirit to dwell
among the strangers,
tuyra,
from a strange land.
He is banished
forever,
from the tribes of Yamaye,
never to be forgiven,
never to be called my son.

His uncle, Mamyo,
was to grant my son
the Cacicazgo of Maima.
He is a fool also,
traitor to our people,
never to be forgiven,
never to be called my cousin.
We paid the *tuyra* homage,
we gave them masks of gold,
jamaca and cotton belts,
we gave them yuca,
bread of life,

goodness of the land.
We gave them *naboría*
guided them through the forest,
helped them build houses,
gave them *canoa*
carved with images,
the sacred *cemí*.
All these we gave them
for their respect,
they did not say
thank you.

They are strangers in the land,
invaders who take
our men as slaves,
our women as wives,
our children they slaughter.
They worship gold
we do not have,
they cut down trees,
raise cattle and pigs,
soil rivers with blood,
burn our villages,
our houses of prayer,
our *cemí*
they destroy.

I mourn for Hacona,
I mourn for Iguaca,
arijuana burned their bodies.
No harm will come
to their spirit,
they died nobly
like the hero Hatuey.

He travelled from Haití,
warned the people of Caobana
the strangers were coming.
The wicked ones burned him,
he refused to accept their god,
refused to go to their heaven
where Christians go.
Our dead *guaribono* are sons of Yocajú,
they enjoy now and forever
sweetness of the land
of Coaybey.

The strangers
wish to become our rulers,
I will not be conquered,
I am not afraid,
the Great One ordained
I should lead my people.
Yocajú rains fire
to burn them,
Guabancex, Spirit of storms,
makes the seas and rivers rise
to drown them.

The prophecy said,
bearded men would come
to destroy us,
but Yocajú Bagua Maórocoti
spoke to us,
'You will not perish,
you are my humble servants,
you have done me no wrong.
So weep not my people,
the Mighty One will save you,
the stranger spirit will die.

Yamaye,
Land of springs,
saved from
the stranger cacique.'

I make preparations,
remove the *cemí*,
take them to the cave,
Otoao,
place of the high mountain.
Women and children hide,
we send the stranger
away from Yamaye.

My men and I will stay,
work their crops,
tend their animals.
I know what we do is right,
we will plan our attack.

We are peaceful,
not trained to fight,
we had no enemies,
we used the spear to hunt,
now we must use it
to kill.

Buibá maboya,
Be gone, trickster spirit
Yukiyú jan,
Maboya uá,
good spirit, yes,
trickster spirit, no.
Jan, jan katú
So be it.

Chapter Thirty-two

One early November morning in the year of our Lord 1514, the newly appointed Treasurer, Pedro de Mazuelo, sailed into the Bay of Sevilla, arriving from Spain with a fleet of three caravels. To welcome the official at the wharf, the friar had joined an entourage of *alcaldes* including *Capitanes* Perea and Camargo, who had governed the island after the eviction and death of don Juan de Esquivel.

Soon after his arrival, Pedro de Mazuelo summoned Fray Antonio to the Governor's house. "This town is in shambles, young friar." Mazuelo looked over the thatched roofs of the wooden houses.

Fray Antonio did not correct the treasurer; he was almost thirty years of age and no longer felt young.

"I want you to take the sons of the caciques out of school so we can train them as masons. We need skilled labour to build stronger fortifications and a bigger castle-fort." Mazuelo's bushy eyebrows touched the brim of his helmet when he spoke. Sweat dripped from his beard and his eyes narrowed in the sunlight.

"We have schooled a convert named Diego del Castillo, versed in *la Gramática* and skilled in the art of sculpture," Fray Antonio said.

"We will need more than one, a cacique and his family perhaps."

"I know of such a family, don Pedro. His Christian name is Juan de Medina, former Cacique of the village of Maima."

"Very well, Antonio, you will bring this family of Indians to me. If I may impose upon your time, Friar, would you be so kind as to take a stroll with me through the town?"

An African walked with the *tesorero* and Fray Antonio along the main street of Sevilla. Baptized Pedro de León, the Negro was a former slave of don Juan de Esquivel, who had imported him from Spain. Thick and robust in stature, he was almost twice the size of an Indian. Thick lips filled the lower part of his face and his smile showed a pair of brilliantly white teeth.

As Mazuelo walked past the houses, he greeted the colonists by waving enthusiastically. With his other hand, he grasped the hilt of the *espada* hanging loosely from his left side.

"We have a river quarry where we could cut stone to build a new church. We are in drastic need of a new building, sir," the friar said.

"The King has instructed me to assign Indians to our men, who will become *encomenderos* as grantees of land and natives. We will desperately need labour and resources for new buildings, but I believe, Antonio, improving our defences and expanding the *Castillo* should take precedence over a church. Do you not think so?"

"The former governor already started allotments, sir, and we have Indians assigned to the King's *haciendas*. The church's mission is in critical need of funding; it has proven most difficult for the Franciscans to raise money because the *vecinos* do not pay their tithes."

"That will change in time, Fray Antonio, but our priority is to put idle Indians to work. We will take full charge of their villages, capture the caciques and put the *encomenderos* in charge of their chiefdoms. Your governor was too lenient. Under this new governance, we shall subjugate the entire population."

The party of three moved off the main street to a path that led to corrals that kept pigs, horses and cattle.

"We are the new Israelites. Did you not know, Antonio? Did not Moses instruct Joshua to abandon Jericho because it belonged to the people of Israel? God has given us this country." Mazuelo leaned over the fence. "Bring this horse closer to me," he instructed the slave. He grabbed the bridle strap of the stallion. "This is the *marismeño*, the most rugged horse of the Peninsula. But, look at him. He is being neglected. His head is hung low and he is tucked up in the flanks. The animal is listless, no life. What an utter disgrace! Who is responsible for tending the animals, Antonio?"

"You need to meet with your officials, sir. We have a most competent group of *alcaldes*. I do not deal with these matters."

Mazuelo approached the pigpens. "And these stalls are not clean."

"The pigs are not sick, sir. They breed so fast we cannot contain them. Many have escaped into the mountains where they roam wild. They are populating the woodlands of the island at a remarkable rate."

"Then we must contain them. We need to establish *hatos* throughout the island and place an *encomendero* in charge of each ranch with governorship over an assigned lot of Indians who will tend the animals and crops. The caciques, not the pigs, are our main problem."

"With all due respect, don Pedro—."

"As I said, the caciques will be removed from their positions and taken off their lands. If they resist, we kill them. Your good friend, Esquivel, did nothing to enforce the Laws of Burgos."

Fray Antonio led Mazuelo and his slave back along the riverbank, where a newly constructed road wound its way through the swamp from the quarry to the shoreline. A storage house on the wharf kept the King's produce for shipment: yuca, hammocks and dried meats. A distance of four hundred feet from the pier, stood the governor's house, which Mazuelo occupied immediately after arriving in Jamaica.

Mazuelo looked across the mangrove forest. "This swamp will be our death knell. We shall have to move the town one day." The newcomer stroked his beard as if he were deep in thought. "I must take no more of your time, Friar."

"It has been my pleasure, sir."

"As we trudge back through this godforsaken swamp, tell me, goodly Friar, what you know of the disposition of Indian girls on the island. I understand that the most desirable is the daughter of a troublesome cacique named Huareo. Do you know her?"

"Even if I did, sir, I would not divulge the information."

"Fray Antonio Díaz del Castillo, you are sounding like a self-righteous Dominican. I did hear from sources that you take your mission seriously." Mazuelo shifted his metal breastplate. "My God, this heat is unbearable. Very well, Friar, I shall make my own arrangements to become acquainted if that would please you more." He shrugged his shoulders, and turned to his slave for assistance. "Here, take this off."

Fray Antonio walked in the direction of the church.

"The hypocrisy of it all, my dear Antonio," Mazuelo shouted.

"I do not understand, sir."

"You pick your women well, Antonio. She is a good wench, indeed."

"I am not sure..." Blood rushed to his face.

"I come bearing messages from your lady. You may have noticed your friend Rodrigo de Villareal was unable to make the return voyage."

"And my nephew, sir?"

"Unfortunately, he was not able to join you. Your lady, Ana María, a delightful damsel, I might add, asked me to inform you that she received the coin you sent from Santo Domingo and that with this money, bought gifts for the poor and alms for the Franciscans. She was very appreciative and asked me to thank you profusely."

Fray Antonio struggled to keep his expression calm. "Did you come bearing a note from her, sir?"

"Ay, she did pen a letter, Fray Antonio, but alas, in the turbulent voyage across the ocean, I seem to have misplaced it."

The friar coughed nervously. "You must excuse me, don Pedro, but I must go."

"Thank you for your time, Antonio. I expect that as head of the Franciscan residence, you will make sure that the *encomenderos* do their duty to instruct the Indians in the Catholic faith."

"That has been my mission, sir."

"The Indians will gladly offer their services in return for the salvation of their souls."

"We will speak further, don Pedro."

"I will enact my orders with haste. Indians will be gathered into new towns and villages and their old huts burned. We will show them how to build sturdier houses for themselves. Remember what I told you, Antonio, when the people of Jericho did not give up their land, Joshua surrounded and killed them all."

He heard the imperious *tesorero* shout to him, "Send word to the troublesome Huareo that his villages at Melilla will be my first order of business." Mazuelo's sinister laughter travelled across the swampy ground to the monastery.

Chapter Thirty-three

The Spirit of the Dead was nowhere to be found. Opiyelguobirán had escaped into the darkness of the jungle. Huareo's people traced his tracks to the edge of a lagoon by the Guayguata River. They waited many days and nights for him to reappear but the dark water hid him from their view.

The people of Huareo's villages assembled at the mouth of the Guayguata River. Cuayaoya and other *guaribono* loaded *cayucos* with ground provisions, dried fish and turtle, and fresh fruit. In another *canoa*, Yabey guarded the cacique's prized possessions. Among these were the *cemí* of his chiefdom: the *dujo*, the *yuke*, the cloth belt weaved by his first wife, the wooden *cemí* of Boinayel and the white stone of Yocajú.

"We will enjoy a feast of fish and *casabe*." Huareo was confident the women and children would be safe in the mountains because the forest was too dense and steep for the white man to find his way. The Guayguata held no traces of footsteps and told no secrets of retreat. Attabeira, the Mother of all Waters, cared for her people.

Huareo held his head back and through the holes of the hollowed bone of the *manatí*, inhaled the powder of the *cojoba*. His nostrils burned from the potent mixture of pulverized seed and dried tobacco leaves. Images of ancestors shifted in differing patterns of light, and spirits of the land, of animals and plants, of rivers and wind, united with his.

Twenty virgins entered the circle formed by those who sat on the riverbank. They wore garlands of flowers around their necks and shells were tied to their arms and legs. Each played a pair of *maraca*, the stones and seeds rattling inside the dried gourds. They bowed to their cacique and danced before him. They formed a small circle and, wrapping their arms over each other's shoulders, they leapt in the air as one, singing and giving praise to Yaya. They saluted their cacique as *Guamikeni*, Great Spirit of the Earth and Water.

Huareo addressed the crowd, "The strangers are not good creatures; they did not come from the sky but from a place where their ruler is possessed with the *maboya*. Yaya, the Great One, tells us we must fight the bad spirit and send it away from Yamaye. We know that Yocajú Bagua Maórocoti will not forsake us." He raised his voice to make sure all could hear. "You are going to a new place where you will be safe and you will wait there until we defeat the enemy." He clasped the sacred *guanín* with both hands.

Aquiana stood beside him. She was dressed with the red feathers of the *guacamayo* on her forehead and she held the macana and spear at her sides. She radiated the strength of a warrior and she breathed the spirit of fire.

The cacique's voice was firm. "My son Amayao is not a Taíno, he is a traitor to his people, a stranger to my heart. My daughter will be with me to fight the enemy. Yaya has spoken his wish that when I pass to the land of Coaybey, Aquiana will be your cacique. When the time is right, I will give her the stone belt and the *guanín* of my uncle, Majagua. She will learn the *areíto* to possess the spirit of our ancestors who inhabit Yamaye."

Huareo extended his hand to bless his daughter.

> Let us give praise to Attabeira,
> Mother of all Waters,
> Lady of the Moon and the Tides,
> Mother of All.

Protect our women and children,
give us your blessing.
We are Taíno,
Your *naboría*,
Good and Noble Ones.

Women entered the circle with baskets of *casabe* for Huareo to bless, and the feasting began, lasting until the shadows lengthened.

Men carried the cacique on a litter along the riverbank up to the place where the *cayuco* were tied. Huareo bade farewell to his wives and children, satisfied that they would be safe, away from the wanton appetites of the white man, the hungry jaws of their vicious dogs and the terror of the lethal *espada*.

They did not choose to attack at night like the Taíno, but by day when the sun was bright. Huareo heard them approach from the direction of Maima. They came covered in steel, their shining armour flashing beacons of light across the bay. They marched with heavy boots and rode on white horses, attended by bands of barking dogs hungry for Taíno blood. They came before Huareo had time to meet with the caciques and before his spies had a chance to discover their movements. While only fifty in number, they were a powerful enemy, but they were cowards, Huareo thought. When they fought, they did not use the skill of their bodies like the Taíno; instead, they hid behind their weapons that shot fire and smoke, and they let loose animals to tear the flesh of their opponents.

Huareo sounded the war cry of the *guamó*. His attendants prepared him for battle: they drew images of *cemí* on his arms and legs and they painted his face black with rings of red around his eyes. They placed red feathers of the macaw on his head and gave him his weapon, the *macana* carved with the image of the headless fish.

The cacique descended the hill with Aquiana, Guababo and two of his warriors, stopping at the end of the path in front of the leader of the strangers. Hundreds of Taíno lined the ridges of the foothills; they gave voice to war cries in long, continuous tones.

"We come to speak to Cacique Huareo," the man on the horse shouted.

Huareo took one step forward. "I am Cacique Huareo."

"In the name of his Royal Majesty, King of Spain, don Fernando and of doña Juana, his daughter, Queen of Castilla and León, we, their humble servants, are here before you to read the declaration of sovereignty and war."

Huareo barely understood the meaning of the garbled words.

Two bearded men forced a young Taíno to the front of the line. One man was dressed in shiny steel, the other he recognized to be the priest, covered in long, loose fitted clothing. The Taíno bowed his head so his face was hidden.

The man on the horse unrolled a parchment and holding it in front of him, spoke words Huareo did not understand: *Como mejor puedo, vos ruego y requiero....*

The Taíno who stood next to the horse raised his head. In an instant, Huareo lifted the *macana* and yelled for the Great One to hear him, "*Buibá maboya*. You be gone, trickster spirit." He lunged forward to attack his son who stood before him, but Guababo grabbed the cacique and wrapped his strong arms about his cousin's chest to restrain him.

Amayao spoke in the Taíno language, "I beg and require of you as best as I can..."

Huareo reeled, blinded by angry thoughts that ran wild in his head. Cursed be the enemy who invaded Yamaye and cursed be his son who betrayed him. What punishment worse than this could the Great One have inflicted on him? Was he not right in wanting to murder Amayao? He should have made him drink the poison. Had not Yaya taken the life of his own son, Yayael?

Amayao's hands trembled and tears formed on his cheeks. His words cracked and fell to the ground as he spoke:

That you acknowledge the Church
as the ruler and superior of the whole world,
and the high priest called Pope,
and in his name the King and Queen doña Juana our lords…
But if you do not do this
or if you maliciously delay in doing it,
I certify to you that with the help of God…
we shall make war against you
in all ways and manners that we can
and shall subject you to the yoke and obedience
of the Church and of their highnesses;
we shall take you and your wives and your children
and shall make slaves of them.

The stranger on the horse gave the command, "*Tómalo!*" A dog bolted for Huareo, growled a vicious bark and frothed at the mouth. Its teeth were larger than the *tiburón*, its yellow eyes bulged from its head, fixed on Huareo.

The cacique dropped to the ground and curled tight and motionless in the shape of a ball. The animal's jaws wrapped around the *macana* that Huareo held at his side and yanked at the weapon, but the wood of the *guayacán* was too tough for its teeth. In defence, Huareo continued to play dead.

Thump! A sudden blow descended on the back of the animal's neck, knocking it lifeless to the ground. Guababo repeatedly beat the dog, clubbing it with his *macana* even after it had fallen dead. Huareo smiled at his cousin, and they lifted the hind legs of the dead animal in victory to show the strangers their spoils.

"Quickly, come stand behind me, away from them," Huareo called to his daughter. "The stranger chief wants you. I see the lust in his eyes."

"*Santiago, Santiago!*" The battle cry went out.

"Guababo, take her. Go, now!" Huareo commanded his cousin.

The onslaught began. The strangers knocked Huareo to the ground and tied a thick rope about his neck. The man on the horse secured the other end of the rope and jerking the horse to start moving, mercilessly pulled his prisoner alongside him up the hill to the village.

The *yucayeque* was deserted. Hungry for the flesh of the Taíno, the Spanish dogs scrambled to enter the *bohío*, barking savagely, crazed that they could not find their prey.

"You are a clever man," the stranger shouted to Huareo. "Where are your villagers?" Huareo's captor tightened the rope around his neck. "If we find your men, women and children, we will slaughter them before your eyes." The horseman jerked the rope again. "Burn the village," he commanded his men.

They torched Huareo's house first. In the strong wind, the fire spread rapidly to the rest of the village, tearing the cane walls and thatched roofs off the houses. *Jamaca* and fishing nets, vegetable gardens, cages with *jutía* and iguana were burned to ashes, and utensils of clay and stone charred and blackened beyond recognition. The strangers' dogs ran scared from the fire and the horses made hideous noises, trampling everything in their paths. The bearded ones danced and rejoiced to see everything destroyed. Waving their *espadas*, they ran about in a frenzy pretending to slice the Taíno in half.

"Where do you keep your idols? Tell me where your little demons are," the stranger shouted at Huareo.

The cacique did not answer.

The man leaned from the horse and spat in Huareo's face. "Damn you, infidel! You are as base as a dog that crawls on all fours. You are no longer cacique of your people for your chiefdom is destroyed. I am king now, and you are my prisoner, my slave who will do as I command."

Chapter Thirty-four

The new governor, don Francisco de Garay, spoke in an agitated voice, "Pedro de Mazuelo, there are complaints that you have appropriated five hundred Indians into your personal service and that others have fled the island due to your harsh treatment. Nothing is wrong with discipline, don Pedro, but we need labour for our farms and the King is anxious for us to convert more Indians to the Holy Faith." Garay was a guest in the home of the wealthy nobleman, Álvarez de Pineda, upon whose generosity he depended for his accommodation.

After Mass one Sunday, Fray Antonio accompanied the gentlemen to Pineda's home in the hope that he would receive permission to rebuild his church, which had recently burned to the ground. From rumours whispered by his pupils, Fray Antonio suspected arson, but he had no evidence. He understood the Indians' frustrations and felt increasingly uneasy about the cruel behaviour of the colonists towards them. Ever since the visit from Cuba of Dominican friar, Pablo de la Rentería, Fray Antonio had begun to question the morality of the *Encomienda* system, by which the Crown commended Indians to the Spanish colonists.

"You accuse me, sir, of wrongdoings that I have not committed," Mazuelo said.

"The worst affront, don Pedro, is that you continue to occupy my residence at Castle Fort. You refuse to afford me accommodation rightfully owing as newly appointed Governor of Jamaica."

The well-dressed governor had retained a trim, youthful figure. His greying beard was shaved close to the sides of his face but was long in the middle so that it rubbed on the embroidery of his high-necked doublet. Gold rings with insets of diamonds and ivory adorned his fingers.

Mazuelo snorted. "If it pleases you, sir, I saved the Island of Jamaica from ruin. After don Juan de Esquivel's dismissal from office, neither *Capitán* Perea nor Camargo could control the local population. One riot succeeded another until both men were relieved of their duties."

"Nonetheless, I have been more than tolerant, don Pedro." Francisco de Garay sipped red wine and swished it in his mouth. "Ah, at least the dreadful heat has not yet spoiled the taste of Madeira."

"Castle Fort was my official residence during your absence, sir."

"Yes, don Pedro, but I carry royal papers appointing me Governor of Jamaica, manager of the King's estates and *Repartidor* of the natives, the one responsible for distributing Indians among the colonists." He turned to Fray Antonio. "Would you care for wine, Friar?"

"Thank you, but no, don Francisco. Spirits induce certain reactions." Fray Antonio chuckled.

"Ah, might I ask what kinds?"

"Let us say, I act somewhat like Bacchus or Dionysus."

"Ah, my dear Friar, no one ever said that you should completely deny yourself the pleasures of life." Garay emptied his glass with two gulps.

"Indeed not, don Francisco, but in all seriousness, I must travel far this afternoon to visit the *encomiendas*."

"Very well, Friar." The governor turned his attention to the treasurer. "So, don Pedro, I trust you understand my position."

"Pardon me saying this, sir, but since the date of your appointment, you delayed almost twelve months before assuming your post," Mazuelo said.

"Don Pedro, with the authority vested in me as Governor," don Francisco flared his nostrils, "I command you to vacate the premises of Castle Fort with utmost haste. I have indulged your excuses too long."

"I shall conform to your wishes, Señor don Francisco. I know you are in favour with don Diego Colón, *Almirante, Virrey y Gobernador de las Indias,* and I am aware the King, whom we both serve, appointed you directly," Mazuelo sneered.

"Fray Antonio, you have been quiet." The governor ignored the treasurer's remarks. "There is a matter of importance that needs discussion." Don Francisco adjusted the belt of his doublet. "Could Juan de Esquivel have chosen a hotter place?" He unbuttoned the tight-fitting garment to show beneath, a shirt of fine silk.

"I am at your service, don Francisco," the friar said.

"I have complaints from the colonists, Antonio."

"Of what nature, sir?" Fray Antonio knew of the gossip about his outspokenness.

"They are displeased with your Sunday sermons."

"We would be more comfortable if we had a building in which to worship, Governor."

"I am not speaking of that. I am referring to your interpretation of the scriptures. I do not want a repeat of what happened in Santo Domingo. The Dominican friars disgraced the good name of their religious order, of the colonists and the King. You would be best to follow the example of the humble friar de la Deule whom we both knew well."

"What untruths have I preached, Señor Garay?"

"You know, dear Antonio, that the pontiff grants us full dominion over the lands of the New World."

"Señor, with all due respect, I believe we have disobeyed the church and our sovereigns. They never wished us to harm innocent souls. We hold Indians as prisoners and slaves and have killed thousands without mercy."

"I am not asking for a debate. We have challenges to bring this colony back to order. Henceforth, Friar, you shall not publicly say anything that discredits the names of our *encomenderos* and you shall not deprive any Christian the right to the Sacraments. If you do not obey me, I shall have you removed from your mission." He stood, his face flushed with anger. "Don Pedro, we will work together to increase the King's revenue."

"I am at your command, sir," Mazuelo said.

"Records show the royal revenue is short."

"There must be a mistake, don Francisco. I will explain the accounts to you when you have a chance to meet with me," Mazuelo said.

"We want proper governance of Jamaica, the island that our King now wishes to be called, Santiago. I have requested of his Majesty that all business of the island be entrusted to me."

"Señor Garay, I ask that we review —"

The governor interrupted Mazuelo. "You are to determine the exact value of the royal assets and make provisions for me to occupy Castle Fort as soon as possible."

"I give you my word, sir."

"We shall carry out and complete the job of *repartimiento* that you have begun, to distribute thousands of Indians in the name of the King and don Diego Colón."

"We are in need of more settlers, don Francisco, and more servants to work the *haciendas*," Mazuelo said.

"I am fully aware. If we find gold and increase production, the King will send more families. I also intend to build a sugar mill, but we need a new labour force because the Indians are physically weak, not suited to hard labour."

Antonio rose from his seat. "I bid you farewell, gentlemen." The friar was anxious to rest before his daily trip to the *encomiendas*. He also planned to visit the prison cell in town.

As the friar left the house, he glanced at the bare hill where the *bohíos* of Maima had once stood and across at Castle Fort with its stone tower and forbidding cannons. He thought how much had changed for the natives in six or seven years. He looked over to the Bay of Sevilla, where five vessels were anchored near to shore. He marvelled at how Spanish ships had advanced in a relatively short period. They now carried ten times the tonnage of the early caravels of Columbus' voyages.

The friar returned to the monastery. He had moved the crucifix to hang it on the wall above a mahogany prayer kneeler, which Amayao had made for him. He knelt in adoration, humbled by his own transgressions and those of his fellow Spaniards. He opened the Bible to read from Isaiah 1:18:

> *Come now, let us reason together, says the Lord:*
> *though your sins are like scarlet,*
> *they shall be as white as snow;*
> *though they are red like crimson,*
> *they shall become like wool.*

Huareo sat naked with his legs crossed, the clothes the guard had given him strewn on the dirt floor of the prison cell. He reminded the friar of Cotubanamá, Cacique of Higüey, who had also been tall and muscular with a bearing of authority. Huareo was robust despite his advancing years and the harsh beatings endured in prison.

Huareo's stare remained fixed and absent when the friar

entered the cell.

"I have never spoken with you, Huareo. I met you with don Juan de Esquivel, I know your son and I have seen you in battle, but never exchanged words." The friar was proud of his mastery of the Taíno language. "I came to ask if you want to prepare your soul for eternal life." He sat on the floor opposite the cacique, beneath a high window with iron bars.

Huareo clenched his fists and remained silent.

It was a small building of thick, stone walls, situated a couple hundred feet from the governor's residence. The room reeked of urine and human waste, and cockroaches scurried about the mud floor scavenging for stale food discarded by the prisoner.

"Why do you think I would want to talk to you about eternal life?" Huareo's eyes flashed red in the dim light.

"They are preparing for your execution, and since you have lived a rich life here on earth, I believe you will want to do the same in the next kingdom."

"I do not want to go to your heaven." The prisoner spat at him.

Fray Antonio wiped spittle from his feet and from the hem of his tunic. "You insult me, Huareo."

"Your people kill and rape us and you say I insult you?"

"We are all born of the same Father, Huareo."

"Then why do you kill my brothers?"

"Our King wants nothing more than the salvation of your souls."

"You have done nothing to bring us salvation."

"Yes, some of us did wrong before God, but your people are also to blame."

"Why are we to blame?"

"You did not listen."

"I want you to leave me now."

"I will take my leave if that is what you want, but before I go, I have a message from your son."

"I do not want you to speak his name. He is no longer my son. You are worse than excrement; you captured his soul and taught him the ways of your people."

"I pray for him and for you, Huareo. Only God will be our Judge on the last day."

"Then tell your governor that he cannot be my judge."

"His mind is made up. You fought against him and he will kill you for it."

"So be it. I will die, but the spirit of my people will live on."

The friar stretched his cramped legs and stood to leave. The smell and heat of the prison stifled him. "Your son wants your mercy and love, Huareo."

"I cannot forgive him for what he has done."

The friar made the sign of the cross. "I ask the heavenly Father to have mercy upon your soul, Huareo, and bring you to everlasting life. We are all descendants of Adam and deserving of God's forgiveness."

"I do not want to hear your prayers and I do not want your friendship. I want you to leave." The Indian dug his fists into the dirt floor.

"I bid you farewell."

"Our people will not surrender, we will continue to fight. Even if you put me to death, my spirit will live, and others will follow in my footsteps to lead my people. The prophecy of our ancestors came true; the bearded ones came to Yamaye to kill us, but we will not submit to them. You can tell your governor this: I am still Cacique Huareo and the spirit of the Taíno still lives in the land."

"I admire your bravery, Huareo." Fray Antonio was

confused by the pride of this Indian. The friar felt nauseous, reeling from the taste of his own bile.

"I know my people will survive your cruelty. We will force you from this place, we will burn your village to ashes. I taught my son what I know so he would become a cacique, but you stole him and tore him from my heart."

The friar fingered the beads of the rosary that fell loosely from the white belt of his tunic.

"You gave him idols to worship, you tricked his soul to believe in one truth, you told him that his father and his people were followers of the devil. Your God will judge you too when that day comes." Huareo opened his legs, stretching the thick chains that bound his ankles with a padlock.

The friar prayed silently to the Holy Spirit to give him wisdom and understanding, counsel and might. He looked within the Indian's eyes and there he saw a common humanity. "May God have mercy upon us both, Huareo." Fray Antonio reached into his pocket and placed the padlock key on the floor next to the prisoner.

He left the Indian sitting in the stench of the cell and slammed the prison door behind him without latching the bolt or turning the key.

Chapter Thirty-five

Huareo was an iguana climbing the steep cliff, sticking to the limestone rock on all fours. The chiefdom of Maima was no more. Smouldering wood and thatch were scattered about the *batey* and the centre poles of the *bohío* stood charred and naked, haunting reminders of his fellow Taíno.

Spirits of the dead traversed the land, driven from their dwelling places in the hollows of the *ceiba*. Ancestral trees had been cut and stripped by the strangers for their houses and ships. In place of the forest, horses and cattle roamed the open ground.

Warriors from other *cacicazgo* greeted him as he wandered through the forest to reach the Guayguata River. They welcomed him to their new homes, ancient caves within the hills that stretched from Maima to Aguacadiba. They paid him homage worthy of a cacique, adorned him with feathers and fed him *casabe*, roasted iguana and turtle, and fruits of *guayaba* and *yayama*.

His own *cacicazgo*, including villages in the land surrounding Aguacadiba, were also burned to the ground. Bodies of men, women and children, who had resisted the enemy, rotted where they were slaughtered. A tall wooden cross, planted as a sign of supremacy, stood in the middle of the *batey*, the ceremonial ground of the Taíno.

He saw the Spanish town of Melilla sprawled out below. Stone houses spread along the shore and rooftops blotched the island forest with blobs of red. The *hacienda* had a stone house for the man in charge and for the workers, wooden huts that replaced the *bohío*. At daybreak, he saw hundreds of Taíno working under the whip of their new masters.

Huareo paddled a *cayuco*, struggling against the rapids of the Guayguata. The early morning mist wrapped itself around the trees of the dark green forest, nourished by spirits of the river. They gave him power and strength to fight the rushing waters, to move the *cayuco* in between the enormous boulders, up the mighty river.

His wives, his eldest daughter, Aquiana, and his *guaribono* greeted him. *Naboría* bore a litter on their shoulders to carry him to Otoao, the place of the high mountain, where his people had made their home. Along a narrow path through the forest, young virgins welcomed him in song, covering the ground with hibiscus petals and broad leaves of the *yarey*, the thatch palm of Yamaye.

Ten *bohío* formed a circle on a flat enclosed by a forest of the sacred *ceiba* deep within the recesses of Otoao. There were gardens of *yuca* and *batata*, peanut and lima bean vines sprawled over the *conuco*. There was fruit that bore in abundance, the guava, avocado, soursop, naseberry and pineapple and closer to the village, men had built pens to capture the *jutía* and iguana.

"Were you held prisoner?" Yari washed his back with warm water and dabbed the sap of the maguey on his wounds.

Huareo lay prostrate with his head on her lap. She gently pressed her fingers to his back, allowing the balm to soothe his cuts and bruises.

"Yes, they held me in their stinking house." He felt the healing pain as the sap seeped into his wounds.

"How did you escape?"

"It was the will of the Great One." He broadened his shoulders and raised himself on his elbows. "I missed you, Yari."

She rubbed his head. "It is good you are here."

"I have not seen Guababo."

Yari looked away. "He is sick, Huareo."

"Where is he?"

"Yabey is attending to him in the forest. Many have a strange illness, and their caregivers have taken it also into their own bodies.

"How is the rest of the family?"

"Your wives and children are safe although we heard that your father Ameyro died."

"I loved him, Yari, even though he sent me away when I was a boy."

"You would not have inherited the *cacicazgo* of Majagua or been my husband." She smiled with him.

Huareo changed the topic. "Are the *cemí* safe?"

"Yes. Yabey guards them in a cave and Aquiana is faithful in her duty towards them."

"Aquiana looks well."

"Since her return from war with the strangers, she has brought your people together, formed a council of *nitaíno* and observed the *areíto* in honour of those who came before us."

"She is a woman now."

"And in need of a husband." She laughed.

"And you, Yari?"

"I have my husband back." She kissed him. "I missed you, Huareo. I still have the pearl of the conch you found in the coral."

"Guard it as your special charm. Have you kept the *guanín* in a safe place?"

"Yes. You should wear it now that you have returned."

"Yari, I am sad for our people."

"You have not failed them, *Guami* Huareo. The strangers have a power we do not understand."

"I should have been more forceful and decisive, acted earlier to send them away."

"They would have slaughtered us all, Huareo. You have not lost and I know you will not surrender."

He sat up and pulled her to him, her legs about his waist.

"It is Huareo," he said, holding his hand over his mouth and nose.

"Cousin, is it you? You must not come near." Guababo's voice trembled.

"I am sorry to see you with sickness, Guababo."

"Please do not stay. I am ugly now." He turned his face and vomited over the side of the *jamaca*. Open sores ranged across his lips and red bumps formed a spotted mask over the rest of his body.

Huareo waved his hands before him but his cousin did not flinch. "Does the *bejique* have no cure?" Huareo asked.

Guababo did not answer.

Jamaca hung from the *majó* trees of the forest. Orange blossoms covered the earthen floor beneath them, the only sign of beauty amidst the emaciated bodies abandoned there to die and rot.

"Can you see me, Guababo?"

His cousin winced from the pain of his sickness. "I am blind, Huareo. The *arijuana* has cursed me with his foulness, poisoned me with his breath." He screamed as he turned in the *jamaca*. "No, the *bejique* has no cure."

"Do not speak, cousin."

"The stranger does not need his sword any more."

"Guababo, always remember that you are *manicato*, a man of good heart."

"I served my cacique with honour but I did my father wrong." Guababo coughed up blood onto his chest.

"I always thought I could have saved you from your father's wrath."

"There was nothing you could have done."

"I was weak, Guababo. You told me a secret and I did nothing to help you."

"We were just boys. I was the foolish one. Damned be the spirit of Macú," Guababo cursed. "I often wondered whether my father had given Hacona his wager for the *batey*."

"It was for your execution."

"How do you know this?"

"Hacona told me."

"Well, blessed be my brother and damned be Majagua."

"Your life was spared and you were my honourable *nitaíno*. I have loved you, cousin and friend, since we were young."

"Do your friend one last favour."

"I will do whatever you ask."

"Fetch me the *naiboa* to drink."

"Yes, I will do it for you. There is no sickness in Coaybey, no strangers there. You will sing and dance with your sister, Caona, and be at peace with your spirit. When you meet her, ask her to tell you her secret."

"What secret?"

"It is hers to tell."

He fetched Guababo the drink and bade his last farewell.

Huareo, the *jíbaro*, man of the mountains, would teach his people the way of the bush. They would seek revenge on the strangers, raid and burn their villages, and kill them. Huareo knew that Yari was right. He would not surrender.

Chapter Thirty-six

Fray Antonio stood with the governor and Pedro de Mazuelo on the roof of the newly expanded Castle Fort to admire the construction of Sevilla la Nueva. It was called *La Nueva* because the governor had sought permission to relocate the town by moving it out of the swamps. The new homes were built of stone mined from the quarry, with roofs of *tejas*, tiles now manufactured on the Island of Santiago.

The governor shook his head. "The natives show little resistance to smallpox. It has spread rapidly from La Española. I estimate that more than one-third of the Indian population has succumbed to the disease."

"It is devastating, Governor." Fray Antonio had ministered to thousands of victims.

"No wonder I had to make provisions for workers to operate the sugar mill that I so ingeniously built for Sevilla la Nueva. Even if the Indians were not dying by the hundreds, they would be useless, too weak for the rigorous work." The governor coughed into his handkerchief. "This island would generate more profit by selling the Indians as slaves to Cuba than to have them work for us."

The governor anxiously awaited the arrival of three hundred African slaves for which a licence had been approved in 1518. Petitions for importing slaves to the New World originated from the Dominican friar, Bartolomé de las Casas, who made a case to the sovereigns that African labour would alleviate the hardships of Indians, who were dying in increasing numbers.

Fray Antonio continued in his efforts to evangelize the natives, to baptize as many as he could and to administer the sacrament of Extreme Unction to the sick and dying.

He felt gratified that he brought solace to their lives amidst harsh living conditions. The island was now completely subdued. Ranches were established where chiefdoms once existed, and Indian villages, except for those in remote areas, had been burned and destroyed. *Encomenderos* were in charge of production, ruling over land formerly occupied by caciques, who had been either killed or deposed. The few natives who remained were subjected to forced labour to operate the farms.

"Dear gentlemen, here is good news." Francisco de Garay drew a letter from his pocket and read it aloud:

> *I approve of and thank you for the care you have taken that the caciques and Indians of the island are instructed and indoctrinated in the ways of our Holy Catholic Faith and subdued and removed from the rites and bad habits and sins in which you say they were accustomed to be living and being.*

"Congratulations, Governor." Pedro de Mazuelo feigned a smile. "I assume the letter is from the King."

Garay caressed his beard, like a cat preening its fur. "Yes, from our very young King of Spain. He praises me for the increase of production in Santiago, the export of bread, cassava, corn, pigs, salted beef and bacon to *Terra Firme*. We have indeed become a prosperous little colony. We have five hundred souls registered including women and children. Antonio, I commend you for your work. The King especially mentions our efforts to instruct the Indians in the Sacrament of Matrimony."

"Thank you, Governor."

Garay stuffed the letter back into his waistcoat pocket. "We must shift our attention to more important matters that concern my own explorations. I have news that Álvarez de Pineda, whom I sent on an expedition to the mainland, was brutally murdered by Indians."

"This is a terrible loss, Governor," said Fray Antonio. "He was a brave *conquistador*."

Garay ignored the friar's remarks. "I am afraid that if we do not act in haste, Hernán Cortés, who has already sailed from Cuba, will claim conquest of La Nueva España. I am seeking a royal patent to outfit my own expedition, ten or eleven ships, I am hoping."

"The colony needs you at this time, Governor. In whose hands will you leave your mill and the King's estates?" The friar glanced over at Mazuelo.

"My son will manage the estates and be heir to my fortunes," the governor stated emphatically.

"Pardon me, sir, if I sound uncivil," said Mazuelo, "but I was never convinced that you would remain here long. When you arrived, your ships were already outfitted for exploration."

"Señor Mazuelo, I brought to Jamaica skilled labour and supplies from which we have all benefited. Some of us, sir, do act honourably in the service of our King. You should know, don Pedro, that His Majesty has requested an official audit of your accounts."

"Your insinuations of wrongdoing are preposterous, Governor. It appears someone has made false reports to the Crown without my knowledge." The treasurer spoke in a high-pitched voice.

"Would you excuse us, Mazuelo? I wish to have a private conference with the friar. Good day, Señor Mazuelo."

"Let us retire to my living room, Friar," said Garay, shaking his head as he watched Mazuelo leave. "That man will be the undoing of this colony."

Fray Antonio turned to face the fresh ocean breeze "This was a blessed land before we came, sir."

"One may think you seditious for making that statement, good Friar." They descended the stairs to enter the thick stone entrance of the new Castillo.

"I speak what is in my heart, Governor."

"Antonio," Garay softened his tone, "you will need to be vigilant when I am absent."

"This is not for me to do, sir. You need to put the government in the hands of a trustworthy *alcalde*, one of your friends, Diego Sánchez de Espinosa or Alonso de Vargas."

"They are busy exploring the south coast of the island for me. Antonio, I want you to stay in touch with my son. I trust him with my life but he is naive to the ways of the world. Mazuelo, on the other hand, is wily and astute in all matters of civil administration and commerce. He has acquired personal wealth from the King's *haciendas* and is using labour from Sevilla la Nueva to develop a mill on the south coast."

"This is all the more reason for you to stay, Governor, for he will be ruthless to the Indians."

"We have found such little gold here, Antonio, that I must take my search elsewhere. Lands richer than Ophir, from which Solomon built his temples, lie waiting to be discovered."

"There is still work to be done here, sir."

"The colony is in fine condition. We have satisfied the King's two most urgent wishes, an increase in production to feed *Terra Firme* and the salvation of the souls of the savages."

"They are not savages, Governor."

Garay stared out through the window and swallowed the Portuguese wine in one gulp. "I often wonder what it would be like to deprive myself of the material pleasures of life. Have you never aspired to be a knight-errant, my dear Antonio, a *caballero andante*?" Garay dipped his fingers in a tray of finely chopped tobacco. "Have you tried this plant of the Indies, Friar?"

"No, sir, I would prefer not to."

The governor gently inhaled the pinch of snuff. "Ah, yes, the aroma is sweet. You should try it, Friar."

"No thank you, Governor."

Francisco de Garay lifted his eyes as if he were in a trance. "I shall discover new lands and find gold for the Spanish Crown. Which Spaniard does not aspire to greatness? Do you know your scriptures well, Friar?"

"Which verses in particular, sir?"

"My dear Antonio, Psalm 12, verse 6:

> *And the words of the Lord are flawless,*
> *like silver purified in a crucible,*
> *like gold refined seven times.*

"All things, even gold, shall pass, Governor."

"Yes, but in this life, the precious metal brings us closer to the purity and goodness of God. Our wise Almirante, don Cristóbal Colón once wrote to the Christian and mighty sovereigns that *gold is the most precious of commodities; gold constitutes treasure, and he who possesses it has all he needs in the world, as also the means of rescuing souls from purgatory, and restoring them to the enjoyment of paradise.*"

"Be assured, don Francisco, the precious metal will not bring you salvation. But I suspect the spirit of adventure courses strongly through your veins, for you are a Basque, sir."

"You look tired, Friar. Have you thought of returning to Spain?"

"Yes, I have considered this of late."

"Do you wish me to make arrangements? I can appoint one of my gentlemen, Alonso de Vargas, to keep watch over Mazuelo." His words were sincere.

"Thank you, but I want to serve a few more years. My job is not yet done. Diego Amayao, the Indian I admire so much, shows an interest in joining the order of mendicants."

"Is this the young sculptor?"

"Yes. His Christian name is Diego del Castillo."

"Is his father not the mad Indian who escaped from us, the one who instigates raids across the island?"

"Huareo."

The governor paused for a moment. "Did we ever discover who unlocked the jailhouse door?"

"No, Governor. It is one of God's mysteries," the friar lied.

"I would rather call it a crime of high treason."

"Good may come of it, Governor. One day father and son may be reconciled."

"That will not happen, Antonio. One is savage, the other Christian."

"Miracles do happen, sir. The holy man, Fray Deule, once told me he had a vision."

"A bright light from the sky?" The governor's voice had a mocking edge.

"In truth, Governor, he did see a shining light, an apparition of the Blessed Mother."

"I am afraid, Antonio, my soul is too spotted and soiled to believe in visions."

"Our Redeemer forgives us all, Governor."

"I am not sure about that. I have bored you long enough. You should go to attend to your priestly matters. I shall leave Santiago sooner than later, before Hernán Cortés gains dominion of La Nueva España."

"You already have all the good fortune you need here in Santiago."

"Yes, but I seek glory, Antonio, more than you could ever imagine."

Chapter Thirty-seven

In the middle of the night, two bands of warriors crawled out of their hiding places in the Blue Mountains. Cacique Huareo led one group and Adofo, an escaped African slave, the other. With spears in hand, keeping low to the ground, they crept down the crooked path to the river.

Huareo bore the *cemí* of Guabancex about his neck, and his body was rubbed with palm oils and painted with the black of the *genipa*. He was at one with the spirits of the land and water, of Yaya and His mother, Atabey.

The strangers feared Adofo and his African followers because they had been warriors in their former land. They were so wild that the white men found no easy way to bridle them, and so clever that the owners could not prevent them from escaping.

"When we approach, we will cover our bodies with branches," Adofo spoke in the words of the Taíno. "We will surprise them in their beds and strike terror into their hearts."

The African was a head taller than Huareo, with broader shoulders and a bulkier body. A scar stretched the length of his left arm and another marked the right side of his face. His fiery eyes were sunken deep below his forehead, which was not flat like that of the Taíno, but bulging from his face. He wore a *nagua*, a cloth about his groin and carried a Spanish sword strung on a cord about his waist.

"We seize their weapons, which we then use to kill them." Adofo wrapped his big arm around Huareo's shoulder. "The Taíno are not bloodthirsty, but you, Huareo, are brave and noble, capable of killing the enemy."

Aquiana climbed into the *cayuco* to sit beside her father who faced Adofo on the opposite seat. The darkness of her skin and hair shone lustrous in the beauty of the night.

"We should have two separate bands of warriors. Aquiana may come with me, if she wishes." Adofo's voice was seductive when he spoke Aquiana's name.

The *cayuco* slipped through the rapids of the Guayguata to reach the flat waters by the sea.

The African pulled an *abeng* from his belt to show Aquiana. She reached for the horn with her hands. It was curved on both ends, longer and thinner than the *guamó*, with a small hole at the tip and a slit on the side. "I will show you how to use it," Adofo said. "I will sound it tonight so the Africans will know we are making an attack."

They moved in two groups of twenty, their shadows dancing in the night. A large cloud glowed in the sky in the shape of a crocodile. That meant the rains were ended and the skies cleared, a time when the *conuco* were full, when the seas calm and the fish plentiful. Huareo wondered if the Taíno would ever again farm and hunt freely in the land.

They climbed the fences of the *hacienda*, quietly so as not to awaken the Spanish dogs. Hugging the ground in the starlight, they stole across the field. Adofo and Aquiana parted from their group and crept to the back of the master's big house. Huareo and the rest entered the workers' huts, which were grouped to one side of the owner's stone building, where they found hundreds of Taíno men, women and children crowded into the rooms. When the surprise visitors nudged them awake, they quickly gathered their possessions and leapt through the doors to freedom.

Suddenly, the vicious dogs broke the silence, bounding out from the direction of the strangers' house into the clearing.

Adofo and Aquiana reappeared to join the others. They quickly lit torches, set the slave houses ablaze and took flight across the field, following those who were scampering to leave the *hacienda*.

Dogs rushed in the direction of the burning houses, but then suddenly stopped and lifted their massive heads and howled at the raging fire. A white man flailing his arms and screaming emerged from the big house, his weapon boomed and spat fire into the field.

Huareo saw five of his *guaribono* fall, their bodies blown up and splattered on the earth from the explosions. The rest danced through the field to dodge the shots that went astray and they climbed the fence to freedom.

"We slaughtered them in their beds," Adofo said to Huareo when they reached the forest. "We thought we killed them all, but one escaped."

"Our men did not die in vain, Adofo, we freed hundreds of our people. *The cemí* were with us tonight." Huareo embraced his daughter as they trekked back to the shores of the Guayguata River.

Chapter Thirty-eight

Fray Antonio sat in the mason's workshop with the Taíno student, Diego Amayao, and the sculptor, Juan de Mendigorría, recently arrived from La Española. Mendigorría was a personal friend of the newly appointed Abbot of Jamaica, Pedro Mártir de Anglería, who had received a royal edict to build a church of stone and tiles in Sevilla La Nueva. The artisan brought with him stone masons trained by architect Alonso Rodríguez, who was commissioned to build a cathedral in Santo Domingo and later in La Nueva España.

"It will be magnificent, Antonio." Mendigorría walked about the shop, inspecting immense stone slabs mined from the nearby quarry.

"It is an answer to prayer, don Juan. I have been worshipping and preaching in a *bohío* for sixteen years." Fray Antonio smiled at Diego Amayao.

"My dear Friar, you will soon have a house of God that rivals any in the New World." Mendigorría bent to inspect the stone the Taíno was chipping. "Our student seems to be skilled with the divine gift of sculpture."

"Yes, your artisans have taught him well, don Juan," the friar remarked. "He has taken as naturally to the artistry of sculpture as he did to the mastery of *La Gramática*."

"*También yo he aprendido el arte de la escultura de mi propia gente,*" Diego said in perfect Spanish.

"I have no doubt you learned some of this art from your people." Turning to Fray Antonio, Mendigorría added, "His mastery of the Spanish language is impressive, Fray Antonio."

"He is an intelligent man."

Mendigorría continued, "The slab's shape is perfect for what we want. It is over six feet high and four feet thick. First, we chop off those pieces we do not need."

"How do we know what to discard?" Diego inquired.

"Here." Mendigorría took the chisel and hammer from the young man to even the edges of the stone. "We make the block as square as we can by cutting off irregular shapes."

"And if the stone is cracked?" Diego ran his fingers over the stone's surface.

"We make sure to check for flaws. Test it with the chisel to see if it is soft or brittle."

Diego rubbed the block of stone as if he were bathing it.

"What are you doing?" Mendigorría inquired.

"I am looking for cracks."

"You appear enamoured as if the stone were your wife." Mendigorría laughed.

"In this way, I can release its spirit." Diego moved his hands over the stone's surface in long, broad strokes.

"My dear Fray Antonio, you need to work harder to evangelize the natives." Mendigorría chuckled in a gentle, teasing way. He was a man of forty years with a corpulent physique, eccentric manners and a reputation for indulgence in the pleasures of wine and women. "The odd behaviour of your Taíno reminds me of my good friend Pedro Mártir, Reverend Bishop of Jamaica. He has never seen this land, yet he is so much in love that he writes ballads to woo her, *La Isla de Jamaica*, as if the island were his mistress."

Fray Antonio laughed. "Jamaica is beautiful, indeed."

"I am sure I can train local artisans to create the beauty the Abbot desires. He calls it not his church, but his *templo*. Be assured that we will build the grandeur of which he dreams in the style of Gothic architecture with rows of thick columns to support naves and buttresses, with an inner chapel for the sanctuary and a grand portal of the most magnificent carvings to form the west gate."

"I am also confident, don Juan, that with proper tutelage, the Taíno will be capable of accomplishing this work. Our challenge now is Governor Mazuelo, who takes our labourers for his sugar mills and fortifications."

"Surely there must be enough Indians on the island."

"The numbers have dwindled, don Juan. We have been fortunate to find the best artisans and masons to build the church."

"I shall make an appeal for don Pedro to observe the Royal Orders." Mendigorría moved to the back of the masons' workshop to examine one of the friezes. "What do we have here?" His voice was alarmed.

"I carved those, sir," Diego said proudly.

"Should these not have angels above the candelabra?"

"Yes, don Juan."

"Did I not show you what I wanted?"

"You did, don Juan."

"But these are not angels, Diego, they are little monsters, a naked Taíno boy and girl. And what are these? Sea shells?" Mendigorría's expression changed from utter shock to amusement. "Antonio, I told you, you have work to do to Christianize these men." His laughter was unrestrained. "Clever, indeed, Diego. Maybe the good Lord will look down favourably on the pagan images within His sanctuary. I take my leave, Fray Antonio, to supervise the building of bricks and mortar for your holy temple."

"God be with you, don Juan."

"Keep good watch over our Indian sculptors, Friar." Don Juan left the workshop, humming a Gregorian chant.

Diego returned to chiselling pieces off the rough slab of stone. "Do you think I am ready, Fray Antonio?"

"For what, my son?"

"To study for the priesthood, Fray Antonio. I feel I have a calling to serve God."

"Only God can tell you this. If you pray to hear His voice, you will know if He is calling you to be His disciple."

"I miss my family, Fray Antonio."

"That is part of the sacrifice, my son. Jesus asked his disciples to leave everything behind in order to follow Him."

"I want to see my father again. Do you think he will forgive me?"

"He needs to repent for having banished you, Diego."

Diego smashed the hammer into one corner of the slab, causing a piece of stone to break free.

"I am not sure that being angry is going to help you."

"St Thomas Aquinas says anger is a passion, not a sin, Friar. I want to tell my story, Fray Antonio."

"What story?"

"My father's story and yours." Diego threw the chisel and hammer down on the ground.

"What will your story tell?"

"Your people in España need to know how you changed life for the Taíno in Jamaica. I need to understand why God would have willed it this way."

"Do you mean you want to show how people as different as you and I could come to live together in the same land?" The friar was sympathetic.

"Our two peoples do not understand each other, Fray Antonio. We are enemies. We want to kill each other." Diego stacked his masonry tools in a corner of the shop. "Yet we both believe in one Spirit, one Father, who has no beginning and no end."

"Yes, but we are different. Your people believe in the existence of many gods, many spirits, but the Christian does not."

"The powers of the *cemí* are real. My father used to tell me of a wicked man named Macú who lived in our village. He once removed the *cemí* of Yocajú from the earth and the Taíno suffered tribulation for a long time until the *cemí* was recovered."

"We do not have *cemíes* in our religion, Diego."

"But you have little statues and *relicarios*."

"Yes, but these are different."

"I am not sure, Fray Antonio. Do you not kneel before them and pray for protection?"

"We do, but *cemíes* are little demons."

"The Taíno believe in Yaya, the Spirit of Spirits, Friar, and just as Christians cannot see their God, so too is He invisible to the Taíno. They learn to commune through the *cemí* for they cannot see Yaya, the Great Spirit."

"We will not solve God's mysteries here, Diego. I will help you tell your story, from that first day I arrived in Jamaica. Let us pray together now for the salvation of both our peoples."

"You believe you are the chosen ones and my people, the Taíno, know that we are all children of the Spirit, no one more special or higher than another. How can this be?"

Before returning to the monastery, Antonio Díaz del Castillo and Diego Amayao knelt together in the masonry shop and recited the Lord's Prayer, first in Latin, then in Taíno:

> *Pater noster*
> *Qui es in caelis*
> *Santificetur nomen tuum...*

> Guakia Baba
> turey toka
> Guami-ke-ni...

Chapter Thirty-nine

Yabey and Cuayaoya held the Spaniard firmly on either side. He stood naked before Huareo. His skin was darkish, his arms and legs skinny without the strength and thickness of a Taíno man.

"Remove his blindfold," the cacique instructed the men, "and let his arms go free."

The stranger reached to cover his genitals. "Huareo, your men dishonour me by stripping off my clothes."

"Your body looks weak." The cacique recognized him to be the man who had freed him from prison. "You are not dishonoured. There is no shame in being without clothes." Huareo turned to Yabey. "Where did you find this man?"

"In a *canoa* on the river, Cacique."

"Were you looking for me?" Huareo asked the stranger.

"I come at the request of the governor. You know who I am. My name is Antonio." His shoulders drooped and his arms were crossed below his navel. "I humbly beg you to return my clothes. I come as your friend, Huareo."

"I know who you are. If you were another stranger, I would have you murdered and thrown in the bush. How did you know I was here?"

"I did not know of your exact hiding place, but we had reports that your men paddled *canoas* up the Guayguata River."

"You are a brave man."

"Governor Mazuelo wants to meet with you."

"Yabey, give him his clothes. He is shivering from the cold of the mountain."

The *bejique* handed the man the long piece of clothing with a belt and beads.

"What does the governor want to talk to me about?" Huareo asked him.

"He wants you to stop your attacks on the Spanish settlements."

"You can tell your governor that I will continue until he sets my people free."

The stranger finished dressing. "Huareo, he will guarantee your freedom and give you rights to own land if you agree to stop."

Huareo shouted, "I already have my freedom and do not need his permission to live on the land. You can also tell your governor that I am still Cacique of Yamaye, Chief of our chiefdoms, and that he has no right to steal our wives and daughters. He is not Cacique, he does not make the rules."

"We need peace in the land, Huareo."

"Your people did not find what they came for, so they made war." Huareo gave Cuayaoya the signal to blindfold the stranger and bind his hands with cord.

The man struggled but was too weak to resist the strength of the Taíno. He panicked. "Let me free, Huareo. I am not your prisoner."

"You are my enemy."

"Do you have any words for your son?"

"Tell him that he betrayed his people."

"I will not tell him that. He asks if he may come to visit you."

"Be gone, stranger *bejique*." Huareo butted the head of the *macana* against Fray Antonio's chest. The Spaniard tripped and lost his balance. "Are you not afraid to be here?"

"Please let me go now." He scrambled to his feet.

"Tell your governor, Antonio, that his men will never find what they came for because the Taíno gave it to the spirits of the river. When you travel the Guayguata, if the sun is bright and the river still, I want you to look down into the water, and after you return to your village, tell your governor what you saw glistening in its depths."

Huareo's men led the stranger from the house of the cacique. When they reached the path, they kicked the blindfolded man in the rear and pushed him down to the river.

Huareo removed the *guanín* from around his neck and placed it on the floor next to his daughter. She had brought his sacred *cemí* from the prayer house to meet with him. The dark wood of the *dujo* felt cold, reminding him of the time he first sat on it as a boy in Majagua's house. He rubbed the face of the *cemí* and felt the shapes of the wide eyes that gleamed in the dark house. He felt the smooth stone belt with the dual carvings of the headless fish and the *tona*, the frog-like figure of Atabey. He reached to place on his lap the three-pointed *cemí* of Yocajú Bagua Maórocoti, the one he had sculpted for his children. He hugged the naked statue of Boinayel, the rain giver, and wiped the tears that streamed down the face of the *cemí*. For a moment, he felt a slight trembling in his legs, but quickly tightened his muscles to regain his strength.

He turned to his daughter. "The spirits are with us, Aquiana, the *cemí* will soon be yours. I am tired and have travelled long and far."

"The *cemí* will help us survive." Her voice was vibrant.

"My wise uncle Guayacán once told me that the spiritual warrior may weaken but is never broken. I want you to have many children, Aquiana, and tell them what you know of the Taíno." Huareo lifted the ceremonial belt. "Here, feel the etchings of the *tona*."

She ran her fingers over the shape of the frog. "It is perfectly carved. I will have many children like the *tona*, Baba." She laughed.

"Attabeira is in the shape of the *tona*. Honour her always, she is Mother of us all."

"My children will be hers, Baba, and I will teach them the ways of the Taíno." She touched her father on his forehead.

"None of our ancestors ever met *arijuana* like the bearded ones, so their spirits have not helped us."

"We will learn and those from Africa will help us." She held his hand.

"Yaya blessed me the day you were born. I have one wish, Aquiana, the same one your mother asked of me."

"I will grant you anything."

"When I die, place my body whole in the grave."

"I will order it, Baba."

"Set me on a *dujo* and tie the belt your mother made around my waist."

"What was she like, Baba?"

"You have her spirit, Aquiana."

"I wonder about her."

"I will be with her again." He lifted himself from the *dujo* and climbed into the *jamaca* to rest. My spirit is troubled, Aquiana."

"I understand. Our people have suffered."

"Yes, and I atone for this daily. But I speak of your brother, Amayao. I once loved him dearly."

"He must want your love and forgiveness, Baba."

"I taught him to honour the *cemí*, I taught him to carve their images and to respect the ways of our people. But he is a stranger, he speaks another language and breathes a different spirit."

"He will want to see you again before you die, Baba. You must speak with him."

"Even if I had bathed him in *digo*, the sacred herb, if I had painted him with the dyes of the *bija* and of the *jagua*, if I had fasted and prayed to Attabeira, I would not have cured him."

"Then you cannot blame yourself, Baba."

"I travelled the dark places of my soul, I came face to face with anger, fear and betrayal, but I still have too much thunder in my voice, and too little lightning in my hand or spirit." He fought his tears. "I promised your mother I would look after you both. I tell you now words of a song I want you to remember:

> They would be our friends,
>   they came to take away the land,
>   make it theirs.
> It does not belong to them or us,
>   the earth does not belong to man,
>   man belongs to the earth.
> We came from the earth,
>   we return to it when we die.
> We cannot take with us
> what we think we own,
>   the only riches
>   are those of the spirit.
>
> We lived free before they came,
>   they were born to be free,
>   we were born to be free.
> They believed they owned us,
>   used us as slaves,
>   killed us for sport.
> They will become slaves,
>   prisoners of power and greed.

They thought us fools,
we have wisdom,
knowledge of our ancestors,
ashes of the earth of Yamaye.
They are the fools,
not us,
they are the cursed ones,
not us.

They told the Taíno,
fear their god.
Their god is no better than ours,
no more powerful, no more knowing.
We do not fear him,
we do not fear death.
They told us
we would be damned,
we sinned against their god.
Our hearts are pure,
our spirit, good and noble.

We are not alone,
we share life
with the *cemí*,
we are one
with the sweetness of life.
Yaya is one spirit,
we are one in His life,
even the bearded strangers
would be His sons.
They angered Him,
they killed the Taíno
soiled the land,
they must perish.

When the Taíno speak
the tongue of the strangers,
say their prayers,
we befoul the rivers and forests,
displease our spirits,
make the Great One angry.

We did not heed the words,
Cacibaquel, Cacique of Haití,
those who remained alive
after his death
would enjoy dominion
for but a brief time,
a clothed people
would come to the land
to overcome and kill us,
we would die of hunger.

The Taíno will not die,
our spirit will live on,
long after Huareo,
his children's children
pass to the land of Coaybey.

Teach the words
of this song
to our people,
Aquiana,
hear them echo
across the blue hills,
valleys of Yamaye,
sing praise to Attabeira,

Mother of all Waters,
Sing praise to Yaya,
Spirit of spirits,
Yocajú Bagua Maórocoti.

And so be it,
Jan, jan katú.

Epilogue
1535

They believe there is a place the dead go, which is called Coaybey and it is located on one side of the island, which is called Soraya.

Fray Ramón Pané

Most Sacred, Catholic Majesty of the Holy Roman Empire,

I hope that having read my story, you have learned of the ways of our Taíno people, of the sufferings they endured, and the heroism with which they resisted the invasion of a new and strange people.

Born on the Island of Jamaica, named Santiago, my Christian name is Diego del Castillo, baptized by the holy Franciscan friar, Antonio Díaz del Castillo, who, God rest his soul, went wandering and was never found despite repeated search parties sent by then Governor don Pedro de Mazuelo. It is owing to the good friar's guidance and teachings that I made my way to La Española to enter the Monasterio de San Francisco to study for Holy Orders.

Everything worsened in Santiago after the departure of Governor Francisco de Garay. Pedro de Mazuelo and the Auditor, Torralba, made plans to acquire the governor's properties that included two sugar mills and hundreds of Indians who had been under his care. They made use of and profited by them as their own private property, selling Indians, slaves, horses, beasts of burden, cattle, bread and birds, and making cargoes thereof. They drove terror into the hearts of the natives, who left the haciendas to escape the cruelty of their masters. The runaways were forced to live in the mountainous regions of the island, where they now enjoy freedom from their oppressors.

With the skills my father taught me, and with the teachings of an Italian sculptor, whom the late Abbot of Jamaica, Pedro Mártir de Anglería, sent to Jamaica, I helped with the construction of the Catholic Church for which you sent money. We used a masonry workshop in Sevilla la Nueva to produce friezes that were designed to decorate portals of the new house of God, but this work came to naught. The town of Sevilla la Nueva is now in ruins, abandoned by the Spaniards, pillaged and burned by the Taínos. Your subjects live in the town, Santiago de la Vega, where don Pedro de Mazuelo built his sugar mills on the south coast of the island.

I should like to inform your Majesty, that eight hundred gold pesos given to Sevilla la Nueva by the late Pedro Mártir and equivalent amounts given by your Royal Majesties were never used for building the church, according to the wishes of your Majesty. The perpetrator of these crimes, Pedro de Mazuelo, still resides in Jamaica.

My father was Cacique Haureo whom the Spaniards called, el Loquillo. *He fought valiantly to free his people and for this, his legacy will remain with Jamaicans forever. He died a rebel leader in the Blue Mountains, where his spirit lives in the woods and waters of his land of birth. My heart is heavy with the burden of shame for having betrayed him, but I praise God for the blessing of the opportunity I had to meet with him before he died.*

My sister, Aquiana, is now cacique of the Taíno. Africans joined her communities and together they have become the fierce cimarrones *whom the Spaniards fear so terribly.*

Your officials, my Lord, and oftentimes your clergy, did your Majesty a terrible disservice in the way that they settled the colony. Tens of thousands of Taíno died at their hands and from the onslaught of la viruela, *the disease that ravaged them without mercy.*

Your countrymen believe the Taíno are savages who worship idols, that they are impure for they wear no clothes, they eat spiders, lizards and serpents, and are guilty of every capital sin known to man. Los españoles *think the Taíno are lazy, that they cannot govern themselves and that they look like the devil with their painted bodies. Your Royal Majesty, this could not be further from the truth. They are an innocent people before God. Before your countrymen came, they governed their lives according to the laws of nature and reason. They believe in one God who is father of us all.*

I write as your humble servant to beseech your Majesty to order officials of Jamaica to find a means to bring a peaceful end to hostilities that beset the island. A peace treaty with the cimarrones *will not only help to protect the rights of the Taíno, but will also prevent more deaths from occurring among the Spaniards who live in terror of the mountain people.*

I am a Christian, but Taíno blood runs deep within my veins.

I implore you, as I know that you want nothing more than for your officials to take care always that the Indians do not receive ill-treatment, to consider the words of a lowly friar to be worthy of your Majesty's attention, so that the Taíno, the Good and Noble Ones of las Indias, be given the rights of freedom and equality.

> *Your humble servant,*
> *Fray Diego del Castillo,*
> *Who kisses your royal feet.*
>
> *Monasterio de San Francisco*
> *Santo Domingo*
> *Anno Domini, 1535.*

Afterword by the Author

At the beginning of the sixteenth century, Huareo was one of ten paramount Taíno chiefs of the island of Jamaica, which was estimated to have had a population of between 60,000 and 75,000 inhabitants. His name first appeared in the journals of Diego Méndez and Hernando Colón, who were marooned in Jamaica on Columbus's fourth voyage, 1503 to 1504.

Huareo and those who opposed colonization by the Spaniards became Jamaica's first ancestral heroes. They struggled valiantly, yet tragically to protect the lives and identity of their people against the invasion of a new and strange culture.

The historical narrative of *Huareo* is set in Jamaica, between 1490, two years before Christopher Columbus reached the Bahamian islands, and 1535, twenty-six years following the occupation of Jamaica by the Spaniards in 1509. For six hundred years prior to this, the Taíno and their immediate ancestors of the Ostionoid period lived throughout the Bahamas, the Virgin Islands, parts of the Leeward Islands and the four large islands of what now comprise the Greater Antilles, Cuba, La Española, Puerto Rico and Jamaica. They developed a sophisticated way of life, which included the establishment of *socio-political chiefdoms* and the emergence of a common language. They evolved over centuries through the blending of the cultures of migrants who had come from Central and South America to settle the archipelago of the Caribbean. Their language and culture, Arawakan in origin like that of the Island Caribs, developed over time to take on characteristics distinct from these other ethnic groups.

This work of historical fiction recreates the daily lives of Jamaica's early inhabitants by using carefully researched historical data of the period. I gathered information by visiting Taíno sites in the Caribbean islands, by studying primary and secondary sources in Spanish and by consulting historians and archaeologists. These inquiries taught me that the structure of Taíno society in Jamaica was similar to, and in most respects, as advanced as that of other islands. Jamaicans were known by the Spaniards to be *expert artisans and people of the quickest wytte, with the largest and most beautiful canoes they had ever seen.* Today, we have evidence of the sophisticated artistry of Jamaican Taíno artefacts housed in the British Museum and the National Gallery of Jamaica. Today, we also have over three hundred identified land sites with an abundance of relics of a pre-Columbian period.

This novel only tells part of the story. Much more needs to be discovered, through archaeology, history and literature, about the interconnectedness and relationship of early Jamaican communities to others in the Caribbean. Archaeologists, Robyn Woodward (2010), Phillip Allsworth-Jones (2008), Lesley-Gail Atkinson (2006) and Dr Ivor Conolley (2011), and the Archaeology Division of the Jamaica Heritage Trust have taken huge strides in giving Jamaican pre-history international recognition.

Although hundreds of thousands of Taíno people lost their lives in Jamaica, Cuba, Hispaniola, Puerto Rico and The Bahamas in the first thirty years of Spanish rule, their culture remains very much alive in the Caribbean region today. Their bloodline lives on in their descendants in Maroon communities and in general populations of Jamaica and other islands. Their language and culture have survived over centuries in the places, plants, foods and customs of the Caribbean.

The Taíno are our forebears, people who helped to name and shape the early course of Caribbean history. The historical novel, *Huareo*, is about the heroism of one of these, a Taíno cacique who led his people with bravery and nobility. It is the story of how one man fought for the survival of his culture, for his chiefdom not to be deposed by the stranger king. It is a celebration of one of the early heroes of our past, written in tribute to all the good and noble people who once inhabited Yamaye, the land of many springs, the isle Columbus said was the fairest of them all.

We who are gathered here before you all,
You all are seeing us, I know.
You all are not here with us now,
But I know your spirits are here with us.
Leyland Klentkian

Acknowledgements

I thank **Georgianne Kennedy**, my wife and lifelong friend, the person to whom the novel is dedicated, for her love and support throughout the project, for being the best companion on field research, and for her expert editing skills, without which I would not have been able to publish the novel.

Amanda, Sarah and Julia, my three beautiful daughters, I thank for their ongoing encouragement and love, to Sarah, for her precious artwork and valuable critique of the manuscript.

Ruth Walker, author and professional editor, I thank for her detailed editing of the work and encouragement in the early stages of the project.

Dr Lynne Guitar, Resident Director of Council on International Educational Exchange, Santiago, Dominican Republic, an outstanding scholar of Amerindian studies, I thank for her expertise in editing, her detailed notes and changes to the manuscript. Lynne has an in-depth knowledge of Taíno culture. I am grateful for her friendship, generosity and attention to my work. Abrazos!

Roberto Múcaro Borrero, President of the United Confederation of the Taíno People, I thank for his painstakingly thorough analysis of the manuscript, for cultural insights he brought to the text, amendments, editorial comments and challenges he posed to my sometimes Judaeo-Christian biases. I am truly grateful.

Dr Robyn Woodward, Archaeologist, Simon Fraser University, I give thanks for her critique and editorial comments, expert knowledge of the New Seville archaeological site in Jamaica, and for her permission to publish a copyrighted photograph of the Neptune Stone, Frieze of the Spanish Church at Sevilla la Nueva.

Dr Ivor Conolley, Archaeologist, University of the West Indies, I offer gratitude for his feedback, knowledge and great interest in Jamaican archaeology, and for organizing visits to Taíno sites in the Parish of Trelawny, Jamaica.

Dr Aleric Josephs, Lecturer of History and Archaeology, University of the West Indies, Mona, needs thanking for her thorough and insightful critique of the manuscript.

Valerie Facey, art historian and publisher, who showed a keen interest in the project by generously sharing her knowledge of Jamaican Taíno culture, deserves my appreciation. She gave copyright permission for the publication of photographs of Taíno artefacts housed in the National Gallery, Jamaica.

Dr Swithin Wilmot, Dean, Faculty of Humanities and Education, University of the West Indies, Mona, I offer thanks for his ongoing support and friendship, his extensive knowledge of Caribbean history and assistance with research.

Rachel Manley, award winning author and poet, I thank for her friendship, interest in the project and generosity in sharing resources.

Kamau Edward Brathwaite, Poet and Professor of Comparative Literature, NYU, I am indebted to for his encouragement and permission to use an excerpt from his poem, "Colombe".

Dr James Near, my son-in-law, I thank for his assistance with research while at Oxford University.

Pearl Beckford, Discovery Bay, Jamaica, I thank for her extensive knowledge of Jamaican folklore.

Elsa Green, Bamboo, St Ann, I thank for her help in sourcing fruit and foods native to Jamaica, and for explanations of how these are used and prepared.

Sean Ascott, Discovery Bay, Jamaica, I appreciate for his first-hand experience and knowledge of fishing and boating.

Glen Pawelski of Mappingspecialists Ltd., I offer gratitude for expertise in mapmaking.

Robbi Siegel of Art Resource Inc and **Daisy Njoku** of the Smithsonian Institution deserve much gratitude for their assistance.

Jorge Estevez, Research Assistant, Smithsonian Institution, Office of Latin America, I thank for reading the manuscript and for his encouragement and advice.

Christine Randle and her team at Ian Randle Publishers, I thank you for publishing my work.

Notes & References

Title Page

Huareo...Cacique of Jamaica at the time of the arrival of Columbus. Mentioned by Oviedo, Hernando Colón and Diego Méndez as a 'Great Cacique' residing in an area called Melilla (present-day, Port Maria), thirteen leagues to the east of Santa Gloria, (present-day St Ann's Bay).

Page vi

Those who remain alive...and they will die of hunger...Quoted and adapted from Fray Ramon Pané (1999, 31).

Page vii

Jamaica, it is the fairest island that eyes have beheld; mountainous and the land seems to touch the sky... Hernando Colón quotes his father, Christopher Columbus (2008, 134).

Page vii

"But did his vision....the whips uncurled desire?"... Excerpt from "Colombe", quoted with permission by Kamau Brathwaite (1992, 17).

Page x

He is in heaven and is immortal, and no one can see Him, and He has a mother. But He has no beginning, His name is Yocajú Bagua Maórocoti. Quoted and adapted from Pané (1999, 3–4).

Page 1

Image of *tona*... created by Sarah Kennedy based on actual pictographs in Jamaican caves. *Tona* is the generic name for frog. The most common tree frog endemic to Jamaica is the laughing frog, *Osteopilus ocellatus*. The *coquí* is a different species, endemic to Puerto Rico.

Page 2

The Island of Yamaye with Names of Taíno Chiefdoms <1509...
Data gathered from (Padrón, 2003, 160), (Bennett and Sherlock 1998), Buisseret (1996), Allsworth-Jones (2008) and Atkinson (2006). Names and locations of chiefdoms are actual, not fictional.

Yamaye...Name for the island of Jamaica given by the Taíno to Columbus on his first voyage. The term Yamaye first occurred in Christopher Columbus (1892, 135). It can also be found in G.A. Aarons (1994).

Chapter One

Page 4

the short legs of the *cemí*, the spirit of Majagua's ancestors...
(Stevens-Arroyo 2006, 220–21) suggests that *cemíes* are spirits, 'intermediaries in Taíno religion between the high god and the world of human action.'

Page 6

Caribe...The Taíno used the term to refer to a separate tribe of people who dwelled in the smaller islands and with whom they often had hostile encounters. The Spaniards believed the Caribs of the Lesser Antilles to be a fierce and cannibalistic people.

Page 6

finely cut leaves of green tobacco...*powdered tobacco – the green tobacco that the Taíno used for cojoba is a special kind that stays green even when dry and is so strong that no one uses it today, although some is still grown in Higuey for medicinal purposes.* (Editorial comment by Lynne Guitar)

Page 8

Next to the *cojoba* stand of Boinayel was another image of the rain spirit... A magnificent carving found in 1792 along with two other artefacts in the Carpenter Mountains in the Parish of Vere (present-day St Catherine, Jamaica). They are housed in the British Museum (Allsworth-Jones 2008, 8).

Page 9

Opiyelguobirán... *The zemi Opiyelguobirán has four feet, like a dog, they say, and is made of wood, and often at night he leaves the house and goes into the jungle. They went to look for him there, and when they brought him home, they would tie him up with rope, but he would return to the jungle.* Pané (1999, 28–29), Arrom (1975, 101) and others make parallels to Cerberus in Greek Mythology.

Page 10

"I have word that a cacique and his son, Hatuey, are coming..." Hatuey was a legendary Taíno cacique who fled Haití to Cuba in the early sixteenth century to escape persecution by Spaniards. He is Cuba's first National Hero. (See note, Chapter 30, "*I do not want to go where Christians go.*") He is presented as a character in the novel, but there is no historical evidence that he visited Jamaica.

Page 11

white-crowned pigeons... *Patagioenas leucocephala*, commonly called baldpate in Jamaica.

Page 13

drinking *ajiaco*, the pepperpot stew... Pots of stew were often kept on the fire for weeks. The *ajiaco* contained game, seafood, vegetables stock, peppers and pimento.

Chapter Two

Page 16

fishing nets... Christopher Columbus (1960, 64–65) notes that the Taíno used nets for fishing, sometimes referred to as *nasa*. In Puerto Rico, the Taíno word means fish trap.

Page 17

They rubbed the white cotton lines through the slits of the wood... The practice of darkening and strengthening cotton fishing lines by using red dye of the mangrove has been passed down through generations of Jamaican fishermen.

Page 17

One group, a set of small suns resembling a one-legged man...
Refers to Orion's Belt from William F. Keegan and Lisabeth A.
Carlson, *Talking Taíno: Caribbean Natural History from a Native
Perspectives* (2008, 189). It is claimed that the Taíno associated
the constellation Orion with the myth of Anacacuya. Fish
were most abundant when Orion appeared in the night sky
from December to March (Stevens-Arroyo 2006, 181).

Page 17

Huareo remembered the story of his ancestor, Guahayona...
(Pané 1999, 11).

Page 18

A cold breeze had descended from the Blue Mountains... There
is no evidence to suggest that the Taíno used the term, 'Blue
Mountains.' The name for a place of the high mountains was
Otoao.

Page 19

corrals... Bartolomé de las Casas notes that 'the Taíno kept large
groupers in fish corrals and harvested them as needed'
(Keagan and Carlson 2008, 51).

Page 19

Anamaquique... Diego Méndez, who was marooned in Jamaica
with Columbus in 1504, mentioned the name of this chiefdom
in his journal. He described it as the village of Cacique
Ameyro, in the most eastern end of the island.

Page 20

as strong as the spirit that sings in the wind... adapted from
quotation by Phil Gottfredson, *this is to possess the spirit that
sings in the wind.* http://www.blackhawkproductions.com/
poetrynative.htm

Page 21

At the beginning of each growing season... Ángel Rodríguez
Álvarez, *Astronomía en la Prehistoria del Caribe Insular:*

Arqueoastronomía de las Plazas Megalíticas Antillanas (2006, 258–60) suggests that the Taíno would have planted yuca twice within a ten-month period, ideally at the end of each dry season. The *yuca* would take up to twelve months to mature and could be stored in the ground for two or more years.

Chapter Three

Page 25

yuke, **the heavy stone belt**...Also known as *coa*. Smaller, lighter weight stone belts and perhaps elbow stones may have been worn for purpose of playing the game to help in the deflection of the ball. The large belts, conceivably too heavy to be used when playing, may have been more ornamental (Rouse 1992, 115). Lynne Guitar comments: *It was believed for a long time that the Taíno wore these stone belts while playing batey, but recent discoveries of ancient rubber resin that was found in the Bahamas indicate what is much more logical – these heavy stone belts were moulds upon which the Taíno put raw rubber to cure in the sun. They carefully cut them around the inside, turned them inside out (so the designs were on the outside of the rubber), and wore these rubber belts around their waists to play the game.* (Editorial comment by Lynne Guitar)

Page 25

Baibrama, the *cemí* who helped the *yuca* to grow... According to Taíno belief, the *cemí* of Baibrama was burned and blackened during a war. Afterwards, people washed him with the juice of the *yuca*. *And his eyes reappeared and his body grew...And they washed him with water and the aforesaid juice so that he would be large; and they affirm that he brought diseases to those who had made that cemí because they had not taken him yuca to eat* (Pané 1999, 27).

Page 26

Busicá guakia para yucubia... Adapted from *Diccionario Taíno Ilustrado* (2002, 37).

Roberto Borrero in his editorial comments suggests that *Maboya* literally means, 'without sweetness.' The Taíno conceived of the bad spirit as a trickster, someone who deceives and leads others away from the truth. The Spanish introduced a different notion of 'evil', which had connotations of damnation, the devil and punishment. In Taíno spirituality, all energies emanate from the same source, The Spirit of Spirits.

Page 30

You know what the people will do... If a male was thought to be possessed with the *maboya* spirit, it was the custom to dig out his eyes and crush his scrotum using a *manaya*, an axe made of stone, fastened to a wooden handle.

Chapter Four

Page 34

They greeted by touching each other's foreheads... Lynne Guitar comments: *In Las Casas' final book about the Taíno, he indicates that they greeted each other "by touching each other's foreheads." This makes a lot of sense, for they wore carved images of their favourite cemí on cotton and gold cords on their foreheads. They believed the cemí lived inside people's heads. Thus, touching foreheads would be greeting both the living person and the cemí.*

Page 34

batú... The ball was made from a combination of cotton, roots of trees and a resin taken from the *cupey* tree (*clusia rosea, rose apple*). Moulds in museums in Dominican Republic show that the ball was a little smaller than the modern day baseball.

Page 36

Yayael, the son of Yaya... According to Taíno belief, the son of Yaya was sent into exile for wanting to kill his father as described in "How they say the sea was made" (Pané 1999, 13).

Chapter Five

Page 40

Attabeira...The Mother of the Great Spirit had many names, Atabey, Yermao, Guacar, Apito and Zumicao (Pané 1999, 4).

Chapter Six

Page 42

to seek permission for sacrifice...*Through the Garden Ceremony we admit our guilt to the invisible masters of these trees and ask them for their favour. The song cleanses us of that guilt.* David M. Guss (1989, 36) in *To Weave and Sing*, quoting Giménez (1981, 40), who describes the practices of the Yekuana people in the Upper Orinoco. Bartolomé de las Casas in *La Historia de las Indias* also gives descriptions of these rituals in Chapter CXX.

Page 43

I have fasted... Bartolomé de las Casas in *Historia de las Indias*, Chapter CLXVII, describes the fasts kept by the Taínos.

Page 44

"would enjoy their dominion for but a brief time because a clothed people would come to their land who would overcome them and kill them, and they would die of hunger... Quoted from Pané (1999, 31). Bartolomé de las Casas, Peter Martyr D'Anghera (1457–1526) and other chroniclers documented that the Taínos had prophesied the coming of the Europeans.

Page 45

"I have a buyón... Duerden (1897, 258) documents evidence of an abundance of flint found in the middens of Jamaica.

Chapter Seven

Page 48

"I was born in the island of Guanahaní in the Lucayos... Guanahaní is the Taíno name for present-day island of San Salvador, recognized by most scholars as the site of the first landfall of Christopher Columbus in the New World, October 12, 1492. Discussion of debate regarding the exact location can be found in *Hispaniola: Caribbean Chiefdoms in the Age of Columbus* (Wilson 1990, 43–45).

Lucayos is the Taíno name for the Bahamian islands. Bartolomé de las Casas in *La Historia de las Indias* claims that, even though many dialects were spoken in The Bahamas, Cuba, Jamaica, Haití and Boriquén, Taínos were able to communicate using a common language.

Page 49

The boats are mountains floating on the water... Aztecs used similar words to describe the first sightings of the Spanish ships. *Cantares Mexicanos: Songs of the Aztecs* (1985).

Page 50

cacicazgo **of Sagua...**Columbus's ships, Santa Maria, Pinta and Niña sailed to the chiefdoms of Sagua, Baracoa and Maisí of the island of Caobana (Cuba) before leaving for Haití, which the Spaniards re-named La Española. See Map of Taíno chiefdoms in *Art and Archaeology of Pre-Columbian Cuba*, 26.

Chapter Eight

Page 57

The true warrior is the one who goes into the dark places within himself to find the truth... Quoted from 'The Spiritual Warrior' by Phil Gottfredson: http://www.blackhawkproductions. com/poetrynative.htm.

Page 57

Yes, and it came to pass that one day Yaya... Paraphrased from Taíno Myth, *How They Say the Sea was Made* (Pané 1999, 13).

Page 58

He is in heaven and he is immortal and no one can see him... (Pané 1999, 3).

Page 59

juice of the *digo***...** Las Casas, Chapter 167, makes reference to the juice of this herb that is similar to *coca* in Peru. Stevens-Arroyo (2006, 145–6) discusses significance of the Taíno rite of washing with a special herb. He claims that *digo* may refer to a ritual rather than to the name of a plant. The word is used frequently in the myths told by Pané (1999, 6–7; 31).

Page 59

You will learn that every tree has its own spirit…lead your people to sickness and death. Reference for ideas expressed here is Guss (1989). It is an excellent source for understanding the Amerindian cultures of South America.

Chapter Nine

Page 61

"The stranger cacique returned to his own land and left forty men to build homes in Haiti." This refers to the failed mission of La Navidad, a fort built by the Spanish in 1492 in La Española. Columbus returned in 1493 to find all 39 men dead.

Page 62

"He believes you dig gold from the rivers of Yamaye to make jewellery… *The Journal of Christopher Columbus*, 58. The Spaniards understood, as did the Taíno, the difference between gold and guanín. The Spaniards were in search of gold and did not understand why the Taíno treasured the more imperfect metal, *guanín*. They soon discovered it was an alloy of gold, silver and copper. The Taíno did not smelt gold, but obtained the jewellery by way of trade with natives of Yucatán.

Page 62

"Hundreds of the bearded ones have arrived to settle and build their own village."…

This is a reference to La Isabela. Columbus returned to La Española in 1493 with 17 ships and a thousand men.

Page 62

Guacanagarí is their friend…Cacique Guacanagarí helped Columbus to salvage the wreckage of Santa Maria in 1492 and to build the fort at La Navidad in La Española.

Page 63

Behecchio...one of five principal caciques of Haití. He controlled over half the island together with Cacique Caonabó. Behecchio was able to establish control of his own *cacicazgo* named Xaraguá by marriage to 30 women from villages in the area (Keegan 2007, 122).

Chapter Ten

Page 66

our mothers and fathers were born from the cave of Cacibajagua... "Concerning the place from which the Indians have come and in what manner" in Pané (1999, 5–6).

Page 66

"Leave your husbands...Quoted and adapted from Pané (1999, 7–8).

Page 66

And let us take much *güeyo*...Pané (1999, 23). This note refers to a hallucinogen, a mixture of tobacco and ashes of a species of the aquatic plant, *mourera fluviatilis*. It may also be similar to the substance, *digo*.

Page 67

"My father told me a story once... of the day men went to bathe in the river..." Pané (1999, 11–12).

Page 70

sipped the *cusubi*, the fermented juice of the *yuca*...There is no evidence that the Taíno used an alcoholic beverage. However, there is nothing to suggest that they did not. In Amerindian cultures of South America, fermented beverages were made from a variety of sources include maize and cassava. (Editorial comment by Lynne Guitar)

Page 71

BIBI ATABEY   MOTHER ATABEY...Adapted from an excerpt of a prayer by Caracoli. http://tainonaborias.ning.com/

group/thewayofthecemi/forum/topics/bibi-atabey-taino-
prayer-for

Page 71

Hundreds of dancers and musicians... For descriptions of Taíno
musical instruments and dance, see Lynne Guitar (2006).

Chapter Eleven

Page 73

**a time when the one-legged man was nowhere to be seen in the
sky**... This is a reference to the month of May. See Stevens-
Arroyo (2006, 179–81). See also note, Chapter Two: *a set of
small suns.*

Page 73

appearing as peaks of mountains... The Aztecs used this image to
describe the first sightings of Spanish ships.

Page 73

Three boats rose up out of the sea... The Niña, the San Juan and
the Cardera, with approximately 54 men and boys on board,
approached the shores of Jamaica on the afternoon of May 5,
1494. See Morison, *Admiral of the Open Sea.*

Page 74

They were as long as the largest *canoa*...The caravels Columbus
sailed to Jamaica were not as large as the Santa Maria, the
flagship used on his first voyage. *San Juan* was the biggest
of the three with a tonnage of 70 tons. *La Niña* was smaller,
50–60 tons with 50 feet of deck length. Columbus reports in
his journals that some Jamaican canoes belonging to caciques
were longer than this.

Page 74

from the bowels of the boat, a sound louder than thunder...
The Aztecs described cannon fire as a large ball that looked
like stone firing from the bowels of the Spanish ships. In
describing Columbus's first sightings of Jamaica, Andrés
Bernáldez in *Memorias del Reinado de los Reyes Católicos* (1962,

451) reports that Columbus's ships fired a "blank salvo from the lombards."

Page 75

They dropped heavy anchors... Prevented by the natives from going ashore, Columbus anchored his ships on the night of May 5, 1494 outside the bay that he named Santa Gloria (present-day St Ann's Bay).

Page 75

The first bay the strangers tried to enter was shaped like a bohío... Columbus named this bay Puerto Seco (present-day Discovery Bay). He was again prevented by the natives from going ashore (Colón 2008, 134).

Page 76

The three giants entered the bay which was open to the sea without the protection of a coral reef... This refers to present-day Río Bueno, presumably named because Columbus found an ample supply of water there.

Page 76

The bows were similar to those of the Caribe... The Caribs were known to use bows and arrows as did the Taíno of Haití. No archaeological evidence exists to suggest the Taíno of Jamaica used them, but with frequent travel between the islands, it is highly unlikely they would not have known or seen them.

Page 78

A man, dressed in long, brown clothing... Reportedly on board one of Columbus's ships was a "pious abbot" of Lucerne (Thomas 2003, 164–5).

Page 78

Santiago, Santiago... Battle cry of the Spanish commonly used in the conquest of America. Sometimes, the expression used was *Santiago y cierra, España*, meaning "St James and attack, Spain." The *conquistadores* called upon the patron saint of Spain, St James, for victory in battle.

Chapter Twelve

Page 79

two caciques from beyond the mountains... Columbus sailed from Puerto Bueno, on May 9, departing Jamaica, May 14, 1494 from *Golfo de Buen Tiempo* (Montego Bay). He returned to sail the south coast, leaving Cuba on July 22, "being denied a fair wind for Hispaniola (Colón, 142). Padrón (2003) quotes from Bernáldez (1870), cap. CXXXI, paints a vivid description of Columbus' visit to *Bahía de la Vaca,* (Portland Bight, St Catherine).

Page 82

his most prized virgins for song and dance... For description of *areíto*, see Martyr, Vol. II, 644, quoted by Guitar (2006).

Chapter Fourteen

Page 92

They capture our caciques and kill them... In 1494, Caonabó, Cacique of Maguana in Haití, was captured. The Spaniards blamed him for decapitating 20 of their men in La Navidad. Battles ensued in which thousands of Taíno were killed. In March 1495, Cacique Guatiguaná was defeated and captured; in May 1496, Bartolomé Colón, brother of the Admiral, captured 14 caciques, among them another principal cacique, Guarionex.

Page 93

...served in *canarí*, clay bowls... Lesley-Gail Atkinson (2006, 148) provides detailed descriptions of pottery forms unique to Jamaica. Two basic shapes were common, round and oval (boat-shaped), the latter being more common. "These vessels usually have both ends elevated and often terminate in cylindrical or flat handles that flare at the tips." Artefacts of Jamaican pottery are part of Institute of Jamaica's collections.

Chapter Fifteen

Page 94

Caona cried out from the *jamaca*... Not much is known of disease prior to the coming of Columbus. Evidence exists to show that there was a form of tuberculosis. *The Columbian Exchange: http://www.learnnc.org/lp/pages/1866.*

Chapter Sixteen

Page 99

The people of Haití tried to appease them... our powers cannot tame them or make them human."... Ideas sourced from Guss (1989).

Chapter Seventeen

Page 104

Bright feathers of the red-tailed hawk ...The *bejique* traditionally wore feathers of a bird of prey on his upper body and head to enable him to fly to the next world. See *Pre-Columbian Art and Culture from the Caribbean* (1997, 141). He also used *cemíes* with carvings of the owl and bat to symbolize his flight into the region of the dead from which he would return the patient's soul captured by the evil spirit (96). Feathers of the red-tailed hawk, endemic to Jamaica, would likely have been used. The Taíno name was *guaraguao. In these instances, the bejique may also have used the feathers of the woodpecker and owl.* (Editorial comment by Roberto Borrero).

Page 104

He unwrapped the herb of the *güeyo*... Pané (1999, 21–22) describes in detail how the *bejique* cured the sick.

Page 104

the leaves of the wild onion...Whereas most species of onion the Spaniards knew were cultivated, the "New World" had indigenous varieties of wild *allium*.

Page 104

in rhythm to the sound of the *maraca*... *The bejique's maraca was made from one branch of a tree, carved from its innermost core, carefully and meticulously hollowed out. Musicians' maracas were made from hollowed gourds filled with small stones, with a stick for a handle, just like today.* (Editorial comment by Lynne Guitar)

Page 105

they would have beaten him, broken his arms and legs with the *macana*... Pané (1999, 24).

Page 106

Maquetaurie Guayaba, the Spirit of the Dead... Descriptions are adapted from Stevens-Arroyo (2006, 228).

Page 106

When he thought he held his Caona in his arms, he felt nothing ... Adapted from "Concerning the shape they say the dead have" in Pané (1999, 19).

Chapter Eighteen

Page 107

Two *navíos* sat squat, rammed fast into the sandy shore of the bay... Columbus and 116 of his crew beached the wrecked caravels, *Capitana* and *Santiago* on June 25, 1503 in a bay the Spanish had named *Santa Gloria* (today known as St Ann's Bay) on Columbus's first voyage.

Columbus's son, aged 14, was marooned in Jamaica in 1503 and wrote an account of his father's fourth voyage in *The Life of the Admiral Christopher Columbus by his son, Ferdinand*. Diego Méndez, a loyal friend of the Admiral, also provided an eyewitness account included as part of his will, in *Select Letters of Christopher Columbus*, 204–34.

Page 109

My name is Diego Méndez... Diego Méndez de Escobar served under Columbus on his fourth voyage, perhaps earlier. He distinguished himself through acts of bravery and loyalty, and was promoted to be the principal *escribano* or scribe of the expedition. He later captained one of Columbus's ships. He would have been 28 years old in 1503 when he first met Cacique Huareo. He died in 1536 in Spain.

Chapter Nineteen

Page 113

"I am Diego Méndez and my companion is Bartolomeo."... In his journal, Méndez writes of his encounter with the "great Cacique Huareo" in the place the Spaniards later called "La Melilla" (present-day Port Maria). Bartolomeo Fieschi was a nobleman and captain of one of Columbus' ships on his fourth voyage.

Page 116

the new governor and our *almirante* are not friends... Nicolás de Ovando y Cáceres was Governor of Hispaniola, 1502–09, known for his extreme cruelty to the Taíno.

Page 116

It pleased God...with hearty good will...Words of Diego Méndez quoted from his Will, published in *Select Letters of Christopher Columbus With Other Original Documents Relating To His Four Voyages To The New World*, 215.

Page 117

The strangers wanted to visit the extreme end of the island... In his Journal, Méndez records that he exchanged names and friendship with Cacique Ameyro. He acquired a canoe and gained passage back to Santa Gloria with six Taíno by offering the cacique a brass helmet, coat and shirt.

Chapter Twenty

Page 120

I have been confined for months in this place, *lodged on the open decks of our ships*... Italics in this passage are quoted from a letter, thought to have been written by Christopher Columbus while he was marooned in Jamaica, 1504. This was published in *The New York Times*, October 12, 1893.

Page 121

He will cover the light of the moon... Columbus was able to predict from his almanac the exact date of a full eclipse of the moon, March 1, 1504.

Page 121

Not long after, a *navío* came to the Bay of Maima.... A small caravel, chartered by Diego Méndez, arrived in Jamaica on June 29, 1504.

Chapter Twenty-one

Page 125

Bibi Atabey...Huareo... Poem edited and contributed by Roberto Borrero.

Part Three

Page 152

Map of Sevilla la Nueva 1509–35. The map was created by Mapping Specialists Inc., based on data gathered from Aarons (1984; 1983); Cotter (1970); and Woodward (2010).

Chapter Twenty-four

Page 154

Benedictus Deus/Benedictum Nomen Sanctum eius.... Catholic prayer, *The Divine Praises*, Blessed be God, Blessed be His Holy Name.

Page 154

Don Juan de Esquivel, Captain and first Governor of the Island of Jamaica.... On November 1509, Juan de Esquivel and 80 men arrived at Sevilla la Nueva (present-day St Ann's Bay) with royal instructions to colonize the island of Jamaica in the name of King Ferdinand of Spain.

Page 154

Pánfilo de Narváez.... Castillian, 1478–1528. He assisted in the conquest of Cuba and later ran an expedition to Mexico and Florida. Bartolomé de las Casas was eye witness to Pánfilo de Narváez's rampages in Eastern Cuba. Bartolomé de las Casas, *Historia de las Indias* (1951), p. 525.

Page 155

Fray Juan de la Deule, the friar's religious companion... Franciscan, Fray Juan de la Deule accompanied Christopher Columbus on his second voyage (1493) along with Ramón Pané, the hieronymite friar whom Columbus had instructed to live among the Taínos in La Española to learn their language and record their customs (Macdonald 2010, 5).

Page 155

Gloria Patri, et Filio, et Spiritui Sancto/Sicut erat in principio, et nunc, et semper/et in saecula saeculorum.... Catholic prayer in Latin, Glory be to the Father, and to the Son, and to the Holy Spirit/As it was in the beginning, is now, and always/and to ages of ages.

Page 157

Remember, Antonio, you are subordinate to civil administration.... In July 1508, King Ferdinand signed a decree from Rome that placed all ecclesiastical matters and property under the direct patronage and supervision of the monarchy.

Chapter Twenty-five
Page 164

it is necessary for this purpose.... Quoted from "Instructions for the Comendador Ovando, 1501, Colección de Documentos... de Indias 42 vols (Madrid, 1864-1884), 13–25; 31. This reference was cited by Parry and Keith (1984, 255). Documents published as early as 1493, "Royal Orders Concerning Indians" (Gibson 1968, 41) state that the "Indians be treated very well and lovingly, without any injury, seeking to maintain much communication and familiarity between them."

Chapter Twenty-six

Page 172

kegs of wine.... Wine was stored in *arrobas* (Parry and Keith, 108).

Page 172

quintal.... A unit of weight equal to 100 kilograms.

Page 172

casks.... Olive oil was stored in casks called *pipas*.

Page 172

nine hundred bushels.... The Spanish used the word *cahiz* to mean a unit of measure for volumes of dry commodities. Nine hundred bushels would be equivalent to 50 *cahizes*.

Page 173

using a design with the church and plaza as the central focus.... Dr Lynne Guitar's editorial comment: *The prototype designed by Nicolás de Ovando and implemented in Santo Domingo would become a typical Spanish design. It was so efficient and showed so well the power of the monarchy that King Ferdinand decreed it to be the model for all further Spanish settlements in the Americas.*

Chapter Twenty-seven

Page 180

They work our men day and night to find gold.... Letter of King to Diego Colon stated his intention for don Juan de Esquivel and Christians in Jamaica to find gold and that they must "be very careful to make the Indians grow as much food as possible" (Cundall, 1).

Page 182

If you walk in the night and are fearful.... Peter Martyr D'Anghera, Volume 1, 172.

Page 182

"He will guard us against sickness...." "He (Baibrama) brought sickness to those who had made that zemi because they had not taken him yucca to eat" (Pané 1999, 27).

Page 183

if you do not keep watch.... Antonio Stevens-Arroyo (2006, 139–40) makes reference to petrification as a form of punishment. See also, Pané (1999, 5–6).

Page 184

When the strangers come to our land, Opiyelguobirán will walk off into the night, and we shall not find him.... *Opiyelguobirán, the cemí whom they tied with a rope so that he would not get loose, disappeared one night after the strangers came to their land. The bejique followed his tracks to the edge of a lagoon, but they could not find him, and he did not return after that* (Pané (1999, 28–29).

Chapter Twenty-eight

Page 185

Milady.... Letter inspired by *Letters and People of the Spanish Indies Sixteenth Century*, ed. James Lockhart and Enrique Otte (Cambridge: Cambridge University Press, 1976).

Page 186

it does not seem to harm them...."Costumbres" in Francisco Lopez de Gómara, *Historia General de las Indias*, XXVIII, 65. Even though Gómara is criticized for his inaccuracies, (he never visited the Americas but drew his information from conquistadores on their returns to Spain), his writings provide a fascinating portrayal of the times.

Page 186

maravedí.... A copper coin, first minted in Spain for use in the New World at the start of the sixteenth century. A governor's salary was approximately 20,000 maravedís. One peso, one-pound weight of "good gold" was worth about 450 maravedís in coin.

Page 187

Ave María gratia plena, Dominus tecum.... Latin for Catholic prayer, Hail Mary, full of grace, the Lord is with thee.

Page 188

He pointed to a dark brown water jug.... Lesley-Gail Atkinson (2006, 170–71) describes distinctive characteristics of New Seville ware, a type of colonoware pottery found in the Cotter collection.

Page 189

bloodshed we saw in the capture of Cotubanamá.... Bartolomé de las Casas, Book 2, Chapters 17–18.

Page 189

the natives are malicious beings, incapable of natural judgment... (Thomas 2003, 422).

Page 189

Our monarchs charged us with the duty of benign subjugation... Navarrete (4:38) 1, 410, p. 189.

Page 189

"There are reports of finds..." Reports vary. Primary sources indicate that some gold was smelted in Jamaica in the early period, but nothing in comparison to Cuba and Hispaniola.

Page 191

I hear your companion, Fray Deule, is not well.... Juan de la Deule arrived in Jamaica from La Española in 1509 with the first group of colonists and died within the first few years of residence there (Tibesar 1957, 384).

Page 191

He was reminded of the Founder of his Order, St Francis of Assisi.... Reference: **http://www.piercedhearts.org/ theology_heart/life_saints/francis_assisi_life.htm**

Page 192

Credo in unum Deum, Patrem omnipotentem, factorem caeli et terrae, visibilium omnium et invisibilium... Opening words of Nicene Creed, Catholic prayer in Latin, *I believe in one God, the Father Almighty, Maker of heaven and earth, and of all things visible and invisible.*

Page 194

La Gramática Castellana... . A grammar of the Castilian language, written by Antonio de Lebrija (1441–1522).

Page 194

the sacrament of penance and confession.... The Spanish translation is *el sacramento de la penitencia y confesión.*

Page 194

because they offend God...to sin no more. Paraphrased from the Catholic prayer, The Act of Contrition.

Chapter Twenty-nine

Page 198

poisoned with the juice of the *tibey* and the manchineel.... The Taíno may have used a deadly poison derived from the apple-like fruit of The Manchineel tree, *Hippomane mancinella.* Spanish named the fruit *manzanilla de la muerte,* apple of death. Manchioneal, Portland derives its name from the Taíno word. *Tibey* is a weed with a poisonous sap.

Page 199

the earth suddenly shook beneath their feet.... Descriptions are based on the Aztecs' account of hearing the cannon fire (León-Portillaed 1992, 30).

Page 200

We stripped him of his clothes to see if he had a navel and then carried him to the middle of the river, where it is deep.... Based on a factual account of Cacique Urayoán of Haití ordering his men to hold a Spaniard under water to see if he

would survive drowning. The Spaniard's name was Diego
Salcedo.

Chapter Thirty

Page 203

"I do not want to go any place where Christians go."... The
conversation between Fray Antonio Díaz del Castillo and
two Taínos condemned to death is inspired by the account
of Hatuey by Bartolomé de las Casas. Hatuey fled Haití to
organize a rebellion in Cuba to prevent the Spaniards from
settling there. His efforts failed and he was captured and
executed on February 2, 1512 (de las Casas 1992, 27–29).

Page 204

**A messenger summoned Fray Antonio to the governor's stone
fortress....** By 1512, Esquivel had erected a substantial
structure that could be described as a fortified house or
fortress, and he governed with the assistance of two alcaldes
and a council (Aarons 1983, 41).

Page 204

**"You have been generous in assigning Indians to Rodrigo and
other nobles..."** As many as 1500 *encomendados* worked the
estates of the admiral and his lieutenant. Wright (1921, 72).
Esquivel did not have royal authority to set up the *encomienda*
system. The earliest documents concerning such allotments
are *cédulas* dated September 1514, ordering Indians to be
given to Rodrigo de Villareal, Alonso de Buiga, Anton Serrano
de Cardona (Arch. de Ind. 41, 6, 1/24, fo. 13' seqq; Deagan
(2002), p.105. See note, Chapter Thirty-four for explanation
of *La Encomienda*.

Page 204

**He believes we are negligent in the conversion and pacification
of the Indians...** King Ferdinand registered complaints in a
letter dated December 12, 1512, to Diego Colón (Cundall and
Pietersz 1919, 2).

Page 205

His Majesty has paid heed to malicious rumours... The King showed suspicion of Esquivel in a letter to Diego Colon, February 1512. "Although I consider Juan de Esquivel a good man from what you have written me about him, yet it might be that he has some leaning that way" (Cundall (1919, 2).

Page 205

He has given orders to have *la residencia* imposed on me... Residencia is a judicial review made at termination of office. It was first conducted in 1501 in La Española when Nicolás de Ovando reviewed the administration of his predecessor, Governor Francisco de Bobadilla. Encyclopaedia Britannica http://www.britannica.com/EBchecked/topic/499152/residencia)

Page 205

thirty of our best crossbowmen who have received permission to join Velázquez... (Cundall (1919, 2).

Page 205

"Perhaps this is the reason for the King's suspicion... Juan de Esquivel was a *converso*, a Spaniard who converted from the Jewish faith to escape persecution by Queen Isabella and King Ferdinand who expelled Jews from Spain in 1492 (Tibesar 1957, 378).

Page 206

but remember not to take your devotion as seriously as our Dominican friends... Dominican Fray Antonio Montesinos in his famous sermon of December 4, 1511, Santo Domingo, condemned to hell all the colonists who were keeping Taínos in bondage as *encomendados*. See note, Chapter 34, *I do not want a repeat of what happened in Santo Domingo.*

Page 206

"make sure my wife and children are cared for... Juan de Esquivel left a widow, Leonor de Guevara and daughters (Wright 1921, 73).

Part Four

Page 207

Guayguata... Present-day Wagwater River.

Page 208

The Island of Santiago, called Jamaica, 1525... Map created by Mapping Specialists Inc. from data gathered from Osborne (1977); Buisseret (1996); Sherlock (1998); Padrón (2003). For a more detailed map of Spanish Jamaica, see Cundall (1915, 7).

Chapter Thirty-one

Page 209

Reflections in this chapter were inspired by readings of *Cantares Mexicanos*.

Page 212

Buibá maboya....Jan, jan katú... Adapted from Solá, Edwin Miner (2002, 37).

Chapter Thirty-two

Page 213

Pedro de Mazuelo... By 1514, a new administration was in place for Jamaica. Juan de Esquivel died that year (exact date unknown) in Jamaica, reportedly of natural causes. On November 28, 1514, King Ferdinand addressed Francisco de Garay as "Our Colonizer of the Island of Jamaica. Pedro de Mazuelo was sent out as *tesorero*, arriving in November 1514, six months prior to Garay who did not reach Jamaica until May 1515 to take up his position as second Spanish Governor of Jamaica.

Page 213

Juan de Medina... A Taíno cacique, baptized Juan de Medina, and members of his family worked as skilled masons and artisans building the governor's fort and stone church (Sherlock and Bennett 1998) and (Osborne 1977).

Page 214

An African walked with the *tesorero*... *As early as June 1513, permission was given to Esquivel, or his wife, or daughters, to import to Jamaica three slaves, who had, however, to be Christians* (Cundall 1919, 1). This marked the first arrival of Africans to Jamaica. As early as the 1440s, Portuguese traders had brought slaves to the Iberian Peninsula from regions of Africa, present-day Nigeria and Mauritania.

Page 215

We are the new Israelites... *Suma de Geografía* by Martín Fernández de Enciso (1519, 32).

Page 215

Marismeño... A breed of *horse* indigenous to the marshes of the Guadalquivir River in Spain. Columbus may have introduced this breed to the Americas because of their rugged nature and ability to survive extreme temperatures.

Page 215

Laws of Burgos... Laws of Burgos were promulgated on December 27, 1512. The document was an official code from the King of Spain to guide settlers in the treatment of natives. It introduced the use of the *encomienda* system. See note, Chapter Thirty-four. See also (Gibson, 1968, 61–82).

Chapter Thirty-three

Page 219

Let us give praise... Prayer adapted from "Bibi Atabey"

http://tainonaborias.ning.com/group/thewayofthecemi/forum/topics/bibi-atabey-taino-prayer-for

Page 222

That you acknowledge the Church...and shall make slaves of them... Quoted from the text of the *Requirimiento* (Gibson 1968, 59–60). The *Requerimiento* was a written declaration of sovereignty and war, read by Spanish military forces to assert their dominion over the Americas (Wikipedia). The document was first used in practice in La Española on June 14, 1514.

Page 222

Tómalo... Attack command meaning, "Get him." Bartolomeo de las Casas uses term to describe a dog attack on a cacique of the Island of Saona, La Española.

Chapter Thirty-four

Page 225

don Francisco de Garay... He was of Basque origin. He sailed with Columbus in 1493 to settle La Española. He found riches there, became the *Aguacil Mayor* of the island before his appointment by the King in 1514 as Governor of Jamaica.

Page 225

Pablo de la Rentería... He was a good friend and business partner of Bartolomé de las Casas in Cuba and visited his brother Salvador in Jamaica in 1514. He spent the Lenten season in the Franciscan monastery in Sevilla and arranged for a shipment of provisions to be sent to Cuba for las Casas (Winter 1984).

Page 225

the Encomienda system... The Crown 'commended' Indians to the Spaniards who, in turn, became their *encomenderos*. They had rights to exact labour or tribute from the Indians (their *encomendados*). In return for this labour, the *encomenderos* were required to protect the Indians and provide religious instruction for them (Hanke 1949).

Page 226

neither *Capitán* Perea nor Camargo could control the local population... (Padrón 2003, 54).

Page 227

I know you are in favour with don Diego Colón... Francisco de Garay was related to King Fernando el Cátolico through marriage to María de Toledo, wife of Diego Colon.

Page 227

I do not want a repeat of what happened in Santo Domingo...
Bartolomé de las Casas quotes from Montesinos's sermon based on Matthew 3:3: *I am a voice crying in the wilderness.* *"Tell me, by what right or by what interpretation of justice do you keep these Indians in such a cruel and horrible servitude? By what authority have you waged such detestable wars against people who were once living so quietly and peacefully in their own land?"*

Page 227

"the humble friar de la Deule whom we both knew well..."
Both Francsico de Garay and Fray Juan de la Deule sailed to La Española with Columbus on his second voyage in 1493.

Page 228

"Records show the royal revenue is short..." *He (Garay) reported in June 1515 that Mazuelo had taken over the King's properties (haciendas). He asked that all business of the island should be entrusted to him (Garay), as Mazuelo was a man of no experience* (Cundall 1919, 3).

Page 228

Santiago... The name of the island, Jamaica, appears as Santiago in official documents of the King from 1515 onwards (Cundall 1919, 3).

Page 228

I also intend to build a sugar mill.... A sugar mill is referred to as *ingenio* in Spanish. Francisco de Garay had a sugar mill built in 1516 less than a quarter mile away from the swamps. Woodward, in *Xaymaca* (2009), describes mill excavations in Sevilla la Nueva, 2001/2002. It produced 125 tons of sugar cane annually (Aarons 1983, 42).

Page 232

wisdom and understanding, counsel and might... Isaiah 11:2

Chapter Thirty-five

Page 235

Many have a strange illness... Smallpox, referred to in the literature as the pestilence or *la viruela*, spread in La Española in December 1518 to infect the native population that had little or no resistance to the disease. The epidemic spread to Puerto Rico, Jamaica and Cuba in 1519 and to the mainland, Yucatán, in 1520. Estimates of casualties from the pandemic vary from one third to one half of the native populations infected, resulting in hundreds of thousands of deaths. Crosby (2003) gives explicit descriptions of the sickness and its impact on the native people of the Americas.

Chapter Thirty-six

Page 238

Sevilla la Nueva... Garay removed the settlement of Sevilla from its first site to build a second town of which the Crown appointed him warden on June 19, 1519 with a salary of 20,000 maravedís a year (Wright 1921, 74). Aarons (1983, 96) situates Sevilla la Nueva to be bordered to the east by present-day Church River and to the west by Parson's Gully, at an elevation of 15 feet above sea level (45), 300-400 feet south of the castle site. By September 1519, it was estimated that 500 Spanish colonists were on the island (42).

Page 238

arrival of three hundred African slaves... in *El Indio Antillano* (400–401), Caballos notes in "Licencias de Escalvos Negros a las Antillas (1504–1518)" that Lorenzo de Gorrevod received a licence to import 4,000 African slaves to the "Antillas." Two shipments of these to Jamaica: 20 slaves on August 02, 1515 in the name of Gómez Mexía de Figueroa, and 300 slaves on August 16, 1518 in the name of Lorenzo de Gorrevod.

Page 239

I approve of and thank you... they were accustomed to be living and being... Translated from a letter by Charles V to the Governor of Santiago, dated August 29, 1519. The original source is from *Archivo General de Indias*, quoted by Wright (1921, 94).

Page 239

I assume this letter is from the King... Ferdinand's grandson, Charles, declared himself King of Spain (Castile, León and Aregón) in March 1516. His daughter, Joanna, was not fit to govern.

Page 239

"Yes, from our very young King of Spain..." Charles, born February 24, 1500.

Page 239

"He praises me for the increase of production..." Cundall (1919, 4) cites examples from the King's letter to Garay, dated August 29, 1519.

Page 239

"We must shift our attention to more important matters..." In 1518, Garay outfitted three ships and appointed cosmographer Alonso Álvarez de Pineda to command the fleet with the intention of discovering a passage to India. On his second voyage in 1519, he was captured and killed by Aztecs.

Page 240

Hernán Cortés... He set sail from Cuba in 1519 to the mainland and by 1521 conquered the Aztec empire.

Page 240

La Nueva España... Mexico

Page 240

Some of us, sir, do act honourably in the service of our King... "July 1519, the King gave instructions for Juan Lopez de Torralba, when appointed *Contador* of the Island of Santiago, called Jamaica, that he was to audit the accounts of Pedro de Mazuelo" (Cundall 1919, 3–4).

Page 241

Diego Sánchez de Espinosa and Alonso de Vargas... Padrón (2003, 26) makes reference to Diego Sánchez de Espinosa, Alonso de Vargas and Martin Vazquez who accompanied Garay to the south coast of Jamaica where they discovered *llanos*, flat lands, fertile for growing crops and developing farms.

Page 242

"gold is the most precious of commodities... restoring them to the enjoyment of paradise." Quoted from "Fourth Voyage of Christopher Columbus: A Letter Written by Don Christopher Columbus" in R.H. Major (2007, 196).

Page 243

"I shall leave Santiago sooner than later..." In a letter to officials of the Island of Santiago in January 1522, the King made mention of the absence of Francisco de Garay (Cundall 1919, 5). He ran an expedition in June 1523 to Panuco with "11 ships transporting 144 cavalry, 300 bowmen on foot, 200 harquebusiers and 200 swordsmen." He came into conflict with Cortés who had already claimed rights to that part of Mexico (Padrón 2003, 60).

Page 243

"I seek glory..." Garay died in Mexico, December 27, 1523, *poor and far from home, having been once rich, because he had not been satisfied with the good fortune he had achieved in Jamaica* (Herrera y Tordesillas 1973).

Chapter Thirty-seven

Page 244

the white men found no easy way to bridle them... *bozales* was a term used in Spanish America to refer to African born slaves. It is derived from the word meaning bridle (noun) or wild, not broken in (adjective).

Page 245

abeng ... An instrument made from the horn of a cow, originally used in time of war by Africans to communicate messages. It is still in use today in the Maroon communities of Jamaica (Dunham 1946, 53–54).

Page 245

The crocodile... The Taíno saw the Milky Way in the shape of a crocodile

Chapter Thirty-eight

Page 247

Fray Antonio sat in the mason's workshop... Woodward provides evidence from New Seville excavations circa 2002 of the existence of masonry workshops, *filled with partially finished limestone architectural decoration and sculpture,* located just north east of the Spanish mill. "Sevilla la Nueva" in Xaymaca (2009), p. 42.

Page 247

Juan de Mendigorría... Mendigorría was a personal friend and relative of the newly appointed Abbot of Jamaica, Peter Martyr, who received funding from King Charles V to build a church in Sevilla la Nueva. He sailed from Spain to Las Antillas on April 26, 1525 with an *armada* of 24 ships and arrived in Jamaica to supervise the building of the church (Iñiguez 1946, 32).

Editorial comment and quotation by Robyn Woodward: *They (the Seville sculptures) were done by a very competent artist who had sufficient talent to be entrusted with a "Royal Commission". The Seville stones are done in the Plateresque style of first half of the 16th century. This style incorporates Roman grotesques and graceful arabesques. The King provided a considerable amount of funds for this commission, so the work would not have been assigned to a provincial artist. In masons/sculptors workshops – a typical apprenticeship would take a minimum of 7–8 years before a talented apprentice would become a "journeyman" and then would be employed in a workshop of a Master before becoming a master himself. The Seville stones are simply not something the friars were trained to do. The Taíno could have been taught to quarry blocks, cut and finish blocks by the masons working with the Master of the sculpture workshop.* (Contributed by Robyn Woodward through personal correspondence.)

Page 247

Pedro Mártir de Anglería... was appointed Abbot of Jamaica in 1524. He never visited the island but received a royal edict to build a church of tiles and stone in his name (Padrón 2003, 116–18). Construction of the church began at the end of 1525.

Page 247

"También yo he aprendido el arte de la escultura de mi propia gente"... Translation: "I also learned the art of sculpture from my own people."

Page 248

he writes ballads to woo her, la Isla de Jamaica, as if the island were his mistress..." Peter Martyr referred to Jamaica as his wife (Iñiguez 1946, 31).

Page 248

rows of thick columns... Sloane (1660–1753, lxvi–lxvii) and Angulo Iñiguez (1946, 30). The Church was exceptional by Caribbean standards (Padrón 2003, 118). The site was just east of the new piazza of Sevilla la Nueva, about 400 yards south of the Governor's Castle, on the grounds of present-day Catholic Church in St Ann's Bay. The foundation measured 84 x 64 feet (Aarons 1983, 45–46).

Page 249

Governor Mazuelo... Despite suspicions of fraud, Pedro de Mazuelo succeeded Francisco de Garay as Governor in 1523.

Page 251

Guakia Baba, turey toka, Guami-ke-ni... http://www.taino-tribe.org/taino-prayer.htm

Chapter Thirty-nine

Page 252

He stood naked before Huareo... This scene was inspired by the true story of Enriquillo, Cacique, rebel leader and Taíno hero of La Española (Guitar 2007).

Page 253

Taíno gave it to the spirits of the river... Part of Jamaican folklore today is the story of the golden table hidden within the rivers. See "The Tale of the Golden Table" in *Jamaican Folk Tales and Oral Histories*, 50.

Page 254

the spiritual warrior may weaken but is never broken... Quoted from "The Spiritual Warrior" by Phil Gottfredson: http://www.blackhawkproductions.com/poetrynative.htm.

Page 256

I still have too much thunder in my voice, and too little lightning in my hand or spirit... Adapted from an Apache proverb, quoted by Phil Gottfredson in "The Spiritual Warrior": http://www.blackhawkproductions.com/poetrynative.htm.

Epilogue

Page 261

They believe there is a place the dead go, which is called Coaybey and it is located on one side of the island, which is called Soraya... (Pané 1999, 17–18).

Page 263

Pedro de Mazuelo and the Auditor, Torralba, made plans to acquire the governor's properties... (Padrón 2003, 56).

Page 263

as their own private property... and making cargoes thereof... Quoted from Cundall (1919, 8).

Page 264

The perpetrator of these crimes, Pedro de Mazuelo, still resides in Jamaica... ÁREA DE IDENTIFICACIÓN Top of Form Código de Referencia:ES.41091.AGI/1.16403.2.1131// SANTO_DOMINGO,1121,L.1,F.135R-

Page 264

Cimarrones... This term was originally used to mean domestic cattle that escaped into the mountains. Later, colonizers applied the name to Indians who escaped from the *encomiendas*. By 1530, the word was used to refer also to fugitive African slaves. It is believed that the word, maroon, may have derived from this.

Page 264

la viruela... smallpox; see note Chapter Thirty-five: *Many are sick with an illness we do not know.*

Page 265

that the Indians do not receive ill-treatment... quoted by Cundall (1919, 4) from a letter dated August 1519, written by Carlos V to Garay.

Afterword

Page 267

estimated to have had a population of between 60,000 and 75,000 inhabitants... These figures vary widely. Early chroniclers reported 10 times this number in Puerto Rico and Jamaica (Rouse 1992, 7).

Page 267

Ostionoid period... Rouse's classification (1992, 52–53) identifies this period in Caribbean pre-history, 600–1500 AD, claiming that the Ostionans may have been Jamaica's *original settlers* (96). Name is derived from identification of redware pottery, characteristic of Ostiones, Puerto Rico (Rouse 1992, 92–96).

Page 267

Socio-political chiefdoms... quoted from Allsworth-Jones (2008, 45).

Page 268

structure of Taíno society in Jamaica was similar to, and in most respects, as advanced as that of other islands... Despite Rouse's classification of Taínos (Western, Classic and Eastern) (2008, 8), he admits that *the class system of the Classic Taínos may have extended into Jamaica* (p. 18; 7), based on the fact that the *chroniclers indicate that the native Jamaicans had the greatest variety of ornaments among the Western Taínos* (18). Ivor Conolley (2011) supports this claim *that Jamaica does not fit neatly into the Western Taíno classification* (37).

Page 269

stranger king... (Keegan 2007, 1–3).

Page 269

We who are gathered here... But I know your spirits are with us... George Anthony Aarons (1994, 3), quoting Leyland Klentkian, a Lokono Arawak of Guyana, on occasion of The Candlelight Vigil, June 1–3, 1992, Nassau, Bahamas.

Glossary
of Taíno Words with English Meanings

A note on orthography: I have used the standard spelling rules of Spanish (including accents) to approximate the sounds of Taíno words. The variations that may cause confusion to the speaker of English are the silent **h** in Spanish, and the letter **j** that is pronounced like **h** in English. I have indicated English spellings in Glossary, where appropriate.

Taíno	English
aguacate	Avocado pear; equivalent word in Spanish
ají	Hot pepper; equivalent word in Spanish for pepper. English pronunciation, *ahí*
ajiaco	Pepperpot stew. English pronunciation, *ahiaco*.
areíto	Central religious ceremony of the Taíno, celebrated for various cultural reasons including, harvest, marriages, funerals, war etc. They lasted hours, sometimes days.
arijuana	Stranger. English pronunciation, *arihuana*.
aruna	Brown pelican.
Atabey, Attabeira	Mother of all Waters; Mother of The Great One.
aura	*Cathartes aura*; the turkey buzzard, known in Jamaica today as the John crow.
baba	Father.
Bagua	Sea.
Baibrama	*Cemí*, patron spirit of harvest.
batata	Sweet potato.
batey	Ceremonial ground, ball court; name of ball game.
batú	Ball used in ceremonial ball game.

bejique	A doctor and spiritual advisor with many functions: curing the sick, communing with spirits, preparing for ceremonies. Pronounced *behike* in English.
bibi	Mother.
bija	The fruit of the achiote tree (*bixa orellana*), commonly known as annatto; seed was used to create a red dye. English pronunciation, *biha*.
bohío	Home, house, circular in shape; also, the island of Haiti, the homeland of the Taíno.
Boinayel	The son of **Boina**, the serpent; the spirit who brings rain.
Boriquén	Island of Puerto Rico; Land of the Valiant One.
buibá	You be gone.
burén	Flat clay griddle used for cooking the bread of the *yuca*.
buyón	Knife; refers also to parrot fish.
cachicata	Fish commonly known as the grunt in Jamaica.
caguará	Clamshell used for grating cassava and other tubers.
cacicazgo	Chiefdom.
cacique	Chief; word adopted into both English and Spanish languages. Sometimes spelled in English, *kasike*.
caimán	Crocodile.
canarí	clay bowl
caney	Rectangular shaped home of the cacique.
canica	Excrement.
canoa	Canoe; reportedly the first Taíno word to be officially incorporated into the Spanish lexicon, 1495.

caoba	Mahogany tree.
Caobana	Cuba; the big island.
Caona	A person's name meaning Golden One.
Caribe	Carib people.
cayuco	Small canoe used to navigate rivers.
Cauta	Ancestral mountain in Haití with two caves.
casabe	Bread in the form of a tortilla, prepared from the flour of the *yuca*; word adopted into the Spanish language.
ceiba	Silk cotton tree.
cemí	Sculpture inhabited by deity; ancestral spirit.
cigua	Whelk, sea snail, *cittarium pica*.
coa	Wood stick for digging, ploughing fields.
cobo	Conch, *strombus gigas*.
cojoba	An hallucinogen of crushed tobacco and ash and herbs; act of communing with spirits while smoking the substance. The plant was known as **cojóbana**: *Anadenanthera peregrine*, known as *Acacia peregrina* in Jamaica. Pronounced *cohoba* in English.
conuco	Mounds of raised beds used for planting.
coaybey	Heaven.
curujey	*Bromelia* plant.
cusubi	Liquor prepared from the juice of the *yuca*.
d'aniki	My heart.
dajao	The Jamaican mountain mullet; *agonostomus monticola*. Pronounced in English, dahao.
digo	A herb; see note Chapter Eight.
dujo	Ceremonial seat of the cacique; usually of wood with four legs and head with intricate carvings in form of an animal. Pronounced *duho* in English.

genipa	Tree, *Genipa americana*; black dye was extracted from crushed seed.
goiesa	Spirit of the living.
Guabancex	Spirit of winds and storms, hurricanes.
guacamayo	Name for various species of parrots of tropical America, in Spanish, *papagayo*.
Guahayona	Cacique hero of Taíno mythology.
guaísa	Mask.
Guajeri	Title of distinction, equivalent of "Sir" or "Your Grace", "*Señor*" or "*Vuestra merced*" in Spanish.
guajey	Musical instrument; shaker made from the gourd of the pumpkin, *cucurbita argyrosperma*.
Guami	Title of respect indicating nobility or equivalent to English concept of Lord.
Guamikeni	Chief or Great One of the land and sea; term used to address supreme chiefs as well as Spaniards at the beginning of the conquest.
guamó	Conch shell cut in the shape of a trumpet.
guanábano; annona	Fruit, soursop; also name of fish, *diodon hystrix*, commonly known in Jamaica as porcupine or soursop fish.
guanín	Golden disc worn by caciques as symbol of their authority; alloy of gold, silver and copper.
guaribo/ guaribono	Brave, valiant man, warrior; *guaribono* (plural form).
guasábara	War cry used by warriors; war or battle.
guataca	Gourd of the calabash.
guatiao	Friend, person with whom name is exchanged in bond of friendship.
guatú	Fire.
guayaba	Guava; word derived from Taíno; equivalent word in Spanish, *guayaba*.

Guayaba	Spirit, *cemí* of the dead.
guayabón	*Coccoloba diversifolia,* same family as the sea grape, sometimes called pigeon plum.
guayacán	*Lignum vitae* tree; also, a person's name. Spanish called it, *el palo santo,* known to cure many illnesses.
guaymen	Fish commonly known as the yellow jack.
guayo	Stone grater.
güeyo	Mixture of herbs, tobacco leaves, ash, and a species of aquatic plants used as emetic.
güëy	Sun.
güira	Musical instrument; shaker made from the gourd of the pumpkin, *cucurbita argyrosperma.*
Haití	Mountainous land; present-day Island of Hispaniola.
inrirí	Woodpecker.
jagua	Fruit tree, *genipa americana,* seed contains black dye used for colouring cotton and for body paint. Pronounced in English, *hagua.*
jamaca	Hammock, pronounced *hamaca* in English. Spanish word, *hamaca,* also derived from Taíno.
jataca	Bowl made from the calabash. Pronounced in English, *hataca.*
jiba	Forest. Pronounced in English, *hiba.*
jíbaro	Man of the mountain. Pronounced in English, *híbaro.*
jiguero	Calabash. Pronounced in English, *higuero.*
jobo	Hog plum, *spandias mombin. Hobo* (English)
juey	Blue land crab; *Cardisoma guanhumi. Huey* (English)
jutía	*Capromys pilorides,* a rodent, part of diet of the Taíno. Pronounced in English, hutía.

Lucayos; Lukku-Cairi	The Bahamas; the people of the islands.
maboya	Bad spirit; trickster.
macana	Thick club made of wood, used as a weapon during battle; macaná, Taíno word meaning, to kill.
Macocael	*Cemí* with no eyelids; keeps watch over ancestral caves.
Macú	Person's name; *maku* means without eyes.
macuto	Deep basket made from woody vines.
magüey	The agave plant, of genus *Furcraea*, in particular, the century plant.
maisí	Liquor made from corn.
majá	Large snake.
Majagua	Person's name; *ma* means large; *jagua*, sacred fruit of the Taíno.
majó	Blue Mahoe, Jamaica's national tree.
mamey	Mammee apple; *Mammea Americana.*
manaca	Royal palm.
manicato	Person of good spirit.
manatí	Manatee; seacow. English word derived from Taíno; equivalent word in Spanish.
manaya	Stone axe with wooden handle.
maraca	Musical instrument made from gourd of the calabash, with stones or beads inside; equivalent word in Spanish.
Márohu	Twin spirit of weather that is dry.
matuco	Wooden staff, also used as walking stick.

mayohuacán	Wooden drum; musical instrument. *It was made out of the trunk of a tree and could be "as thick as a man. Most of the mayohuacanes had an oval, an open slit, or an "H" shape carved into the top to allow the sound to come out* (Guitar 2006). Aquino (1977) spells it *mayohavau*.
naboría	Persons in the community with specific responsibilities; equivalent of today's middle or 'working' class. Aquino (1977) refers to them as servant class (*sirviente o criado*).
nagua	Short skirt, loincloth worn by married women.
naiboa	Poisonous juice of the *yuca*.
naje	Oar.
nati	Breasts.
nitaíno, nitayno	Equivalent of nobility in Taíno society; close advisors of the cacique. *Nombre de caballero o señor principal* (Bartolomé de las Casas); a gentleman or important person in the community.
opía	Spirit of the dead.
Opiyelguobirán	The Guardian of the Dead.
otoao	Place of the high mountains.
pargo	Fish, the red snapper.
sarobey	*Gossypium barbadense*; sea island cotton that the Taíno used to make hammocks, belts, loin cloths etc.
sibucán	Cloth sieve for straining pulp of grated cassava.

Taíno	Distinct cultural group of people of Amerindian origin; Good and Noble ones; a distinct language of Arawakan origin they spoke in common. They inhabited the Bahamas, Eastern Cuba, Jamaica, Hispaniola, Puerto Rico and Virgin Islands.
tibes	River stones.
tibey	*Hippobroma longiflora*, Star of Bethlehem; a weed endemic to the Caribbean, with white flower and poisonous sap.
tiburón	Shark; equivalent word in Spanish.
toa	Several meanings: large river; sound baby makes for woman's breast; the sound the frog makes.
tobacú	Thin tubes of inhalator, made from hollowed sticks or branches, used to smoke pulverized herbs. The use of the word may be debatable. *Cachimba* is used in Puerto Rico, but this may be African in origin.
tona	Frog; in other Amerindian languages, means "water".
túbano	Rolled tobacco in form of cigar; Reference: http://taino-facts.blogspot.ca/2012_12_01_archive.html and Aquino (1977).
turey	Sky.
tuyra	Person of bad spirit, used to describe the Spaniards.
yaguasa	West Indian whistling duck.
Yamaye	Land of Springs, Land of Wood and Water, the Island of Jamaica.
yarey	Palm, *sabal jamaicensis*, native to Caribbean, used along with other thatch palms to roof houses.
Yari	Female name meaning good place or jewel.

Yaya	Supreme One, Spirit of Spirits, invisible.
Yayael	Son of Yaya.
yayama	Pineapple.
Yocajú Bagua Maórocoti	Spirit of the *yuca*, sea and land. Pronounced *Yokahú* in English.
yuca	Cassava.
yucayeque	Village.
yuke	Ceremonial stone belt; also known as *coa* or sacred *coa*.

Sources: Aquino. 1977. *Diccionario de Voces Indígenas de Puerto Rico*

Sola. 2002. *Diccionario Taíno Ilustrado*

'Diccionario de Voces Taínas'. 2002. UCTP: http://www.uctp.comoj.com/VocesIndigena.html

Pané. 1999. *An Account of the Antiquities of the Indians*

Keegan, William F. and Lisabeth A. Carlson. 2008. *Talking Taíno: Caribbean Natural History from a Native Perspective.*

Muñiz. 2004. *Mi Pueblo Taíno.*

Glossary of Spanish Words with English Meanings

Spanish	English
alcalde	Appointed official of government of Spanish colonies, usually involved serving in judicial capacity as member of local council.
almirante	Admiral, title given to Christopher Columbus and later, to his son, Diego.
blanca	Copper coin containing trace of silver; worth less than a *maravedí*.
bonete	Hat, cap.
caballero andante	Knight errant
caballo	Horse. The Taíno were reportedly terrified of the horse, an animal they would not have known.
cañon	Cannon.
capitanes	Captains.
casa fuerte	Strong house, name given to Columbus's house in La Isabela, Hispaniola, 1493.
cascabel	Small bell attached to a hawk's leg dating back to practices of falconry in medieval times.
castillo	Small castle, name given to Columbus's house in Isabella, Hispaniola, 1493.
converso	Jews or Moslems and their descendants who converted to Catholicism during the 15th Century to avoid persecution.
demonio	Devil.
diós mío	My God.
discípulos	Disciples.

el fuego de la sangre	Fire in the blood; fiery nature.
escudero	Swordsman.
espada	Sword. Spanish sword was sharpened on both sides, two-edged, "de dos filos".
espejo; espejillo	Mirror; small mirror.
gobernador	Governor.
hábito	Religious habit or tunic; Franciscan habit, a full-length robe, originally of handspun wool tied at waist with white cord.
hacienda	Large landed estate; many owned by royalty in Spain.
hato	Herd, but commonly used in Spanish Jamaica to refer to a cattle ranch.
hijo de puta	Son of a whore.
huracán	Hurricane.
la Santa Fé	The Holy Faith.
las Indias	The Indies; terminology derived from Columbus's belief that he had sailed to India.
lazo	Hilt of a sword.
levántate	Get up.
loquillo	Madman.
maíz	Corn (Taíno in origin).
maravedí	Spanish, bronze coin, first minted in 1505 in Seville, Spain for use in La Española.
monasterio	Monastery.
navío	Generic name used in literature for caravels, ships used in 16th century.
Nuesto Señor	Our Lord.

perro de presa canario	Canarian bloodhound.
relicario	Relic.
rey, reyes	King(s); sovereigns.
tapia	Wall made with wooden frame and of rammed mud, limestone and aggregates, common building material used in 15th century Sevilla, Spain.
tejas	Tiles for roofing or flooring.
templo	Temple.
tesorero	Treasurer, appointed by the Crown, to administer fiscal affairs of the colony.
vecindades	Communities; neighbourhoods.
vecino	Member of community in colonial Spanish America.
vidrio	Glass.
viruela	Smallpox disease.

Bibliography

Aarons, G.A. "Sevilla la Nueva: Microcosm of Spain in Jamaica Part I: The Historical Background." *Jamaica Journal* 16, no. 4 (1983): 37–46.

——. "Sevilla la Nueva: Microcosm of Spain in Jamaica Part II: Unearthing the Past." *Jamaica Journal* 17, no. 1 (1984): 28–37.

——. "The Taíno of Yamaye: The Ancestral Jamaicans." Unpublished manuscript, with permission of author, 1994.

Allsworth-Jones, Philip. *Pre-Columbian Jamaica.* Tuscaloosa, Alabama: The University of Alabama Press, 2008.

Allsworth-Jones, Philip and Kit Wesler. "The Jamaican Taíno Project." http://www.greencastletropicalstudycenter.org/Jamaican_Taíno_project.pdf.

Álvarez, Ángel Rodríguez . *Astronomía en la Prehistoria del Caribe Insular: Arqueoastronomía de las plazas megalíticas antillanas.* Puerto Rico: Editorial Nuevo Mundo, 2006.

Arrom, José Juan. *Mitología y artes prehispánicas de las Antillas.* México, D.F.: SigloXXI, 1975.

Atkinson, Lesley-Gail, ed. *The Earliest Inhabitants: The Dynamics of the Jamaican Taíno.* Kingston, Jamaica: University of the West Indies Press, 2006.

——. "Taíno Influence on Jamaican Folk Traditions" http://www.jnht.com/download/influence.pdf , 2010.

Aquino, Luis Hernández. *Diccionario de Voces Indígenas de Puerto Rico.* Río Piedras, Puerto Rico: Editorial Cultural, 1977.

Bennassar, Bartolomé. *The Spanish Character: Attitudes and Mentalities from the Sixteenth to the Nineteenth Century.* Berkley, CA: University of California Press, 1975.

Bercht, Fatima et al., eds. *Taíno: Pre-Columbian Art and Culture from the Caribbean.* New York, New York: The Monacelli Press Inc. and El Museo del Barrio, 1975.

Bernáldez, Andrés. *Historia de los Reyes Católicos don Fernando y doña Isabel,* Sevilla. 2 volumes. 1870.

——. *Memorias del Reinado de los Reyes Católicos.* Madrid: Blass, S. A.: Tipográfica, 1962.

Bierhorst, John, trans. *Cantares Mexicanos: Songs of the Aztecs*. Translated from the Nahuatl. Stanford, CA: Stanford University Press, 1985.

Brathwaite, Kamau. *Middle Passages*. Newcastle upon Tyne, UK: Bloodaxe Books Ltd, 1992.

Brown, Dee. *Bury My Heart at Wounded Knee: An Indian History of the American West*. New York: Henry Holt and Company, 1970.

Buisseret, David. *Historic Jamaica from the Air*. Kingston, Jamaica: Ian Randle Publishers, 1996.

Byne, Arthur and Mildred Stapley. *Spanish Architecture of the Sixteenth Century: General View of the Plateresque and Herrera Styles*. New York and London: G.P. Putnam's Sons, 1917.

Caballos, Esteban Mira. *El Indio Antillano: Repartimiento, Encomienda, y Esclavitud (1492–1541)*. Bogotá, Colombia: Ediciones ALFIL LTDA, 1997.

——. *Las Antillas Mayores: 1492–1550. Ensayos y Documentos*. Madrid, España: Iberoamerican, 2000.

Campbell, Keron C. St. E. *Endemic Trees of Jamaica*. Kingston, Jamaica: Institute of Jamaica, 2010.

Cassidy, Frederic G., and R.B. Le Page, eds. *A Dictionary of Jamaican English*. Kingston, Jamaica: University of the West Indies, 2002.

Coke, Thomas. *A History of the West Indies Containing the Natural, Civil, and Ecclesiastical History of Each Island with an Account of the Missions. Vol. 1*. Great Britain: Frank Cass & Co. Ltd, 1971.

Colón, Hernando. *Historia del Almirante Don Cristóbal Colón*. Barcelona: Linkgua ediciones S.L., 2008.

——. *The Life of the Admiral Christopher Columbus by his son, Ferdinand*, translated and edited by Benjamin Keen. New Brunswick, NJ: Rutgers University Press, 1992.

Columbus, Christopher. *El Descubrimiento de América,* translated from French by D. Luis Navarro y Calvo, Tomo II. Madrid: Librería de la Viuda de Hernando y C, 1892. http://archive.org/details/eldescubrimiento02humbrich.

——. *The Journal of Christopher Columbus*. Trans Cecil Jane. New York: Clarkson N. Potter, Inc, 1960.

——. *Select Letters of Christopher Columbus With Other Original Documents Relating to His Four Voyages To The New World.* Translated and edited by R.H. Major. USA: Kessinger Publishing, 2007.

Conolley, Ivor Courtney. "Montego Bay Pottery and Culture in Western Jamaica: Significance and Implications for Jamaican Taíno Pre-history." Unpublished doctoral thesis for the Degree of Philosophy and Archaeology, University of the West Indies: Mona, Jamaica, 2011.

Cotter, C.S. "The Discovery of the Spanish Carvings at Seville." *The Jamaican Historical Review* 1, no. 3 (1948): 227–33.

——. "Sevilla Nueva: The Story of an Excavation." *Jamaica Journal* 4, no. 2 (1970): 15–22.

Crosby, Alfred W. Jr. *The Columbian Exchange: Biological and Cultural Consequences of 1492.* Westport, CT: Praeger, 2003.

Cundall, Frank. *Columbus and the Discovery of Jamaica.* Kingston, Jamaica: The Institute of Jamaica, 1894.

——. *Historic Jamaica.* London: The West India Committee for The Institute of Jamaica, 1915.

Cundall, Frank and Joseph L. Pietersz, eds. *Jamaica Under the Spaniards: Abstracted from the Archives of Seville.* Kingston, Jamaica: Institute of Jamaica, 1919.

D'Anghera, Peter Martyr. *De Orbo Novo: The Eight Decades of Peter Martyr D'Anghera.* Translated from the Latin with Notes and Introduction by Francis Augustus MacNutt. Volumes One and Two. New York: The Knickerbocker Press, 1912.

de Benavente, Toribio. *Historia de los Indios de la Nueva España.* Ediciones de Claudio Esteva Fabregat. Madrid, España: Dastin Historia, 2001.

de las Casas, Bartolomé. *A Short Account of the Destruction of the Indies.* Edited and translated by Nigel Griffin. London, England: Penguin Books Ltd, 1992.

——. *Apologética Historia Sumaria.* 3rd ed. 2 vols. Edited by Edmundo O'Gorman. Mexico City: UNAM, 1976.

——. *Historia de las Indias.* Edición de Agustín Carlo y estudio preliminar de Lewis Hanke. México: Fondo de Cultura Económica, 1951.

———. *History of the Indies*. Translated and edited by Andrée M. Collard. New York, Evanston, and London: Harper and Row, Publishers, 1971.

———. *In Defense of the Indians*. Translated and edited by Stafford Poole, C.M. DeKalb, IL: Northern Illinois University Press, 1992.

Deagan, Kathleen and José María Cruxent. *Columbus's Outpost among the Taínos: Spain and America at La Isabela, 1493–1498*. New Haven and London: Yale University Press, 2002.

Dictionary of the Taíno Language. http://members.dandy.net/~orocobix/terms1.htm

Duerden, J.E. "Aboriginal Indian Remains in Jamaica." *Journal of the Institute of Jamaica*. II, no. 4, July 1897.

Dugard, Martin. *The Last Voyage of Columbus*. New York, NY: Little, Brown and Company, 2005.

Dunham, Katherine. *Katherine Dunham's Journey to Accompong*. New York: Henry Holt and Company, Inc, 1946.

Elliott, J.H. *Imperial Spain: 1469–1716*. London: Edward Arnold Publishers Ltd, 1963.

Fernández de Oviedo y Valdés, Gonzalo. *Sumario de la Natural Historia de las Indias*. Las Rozas, Madrid, España: Dastin, 2002.

Fundación Fernando Ortiz. *Catauro: Revista Cubana de Antropología*. Año 5, No. 8, julio-diciembre de 2003. El Vedado, Ciudad de la Habana, Cuba: Publicación semestral de la Fundación Fernando Ortiz, 2003.

Gibson, Charles, ed. *The Spanish Tradition in America*. New York: Harper Publishers, 1968.

Granberry, Julian and Gary S. Vescelius. *Languages of the Pre-Columbian Antilles*. Tuscaloosa: The University of Alabama Press, 2004.

Guitar, Lynne. "New Notes about Taíno Music and its Influence on Contemporary Dominican Life." *Issues in Caribbean Amerindian Studies* VII, no. 1, December 2006–December 2007.

———. "A Fire in the Land that Will Not Go Out: Sixteenth-century Hispaniola and the First Cimarrones (Maroons) in the Americas." Paper presented at JNBC/Socare Bicentenary Conference, Discourses of Resistance: Culture, Identity, Freedom and Reconciliation, December 5–8, 2007.

Guss, David M. *To Weave and Sing: Art, Symbol, and Narrative in the South American Rain Forest*. Berkeley, CA: University of California Press, 1989.

Hanke, Lewis. *The Spanish Struggle for Justice in the Conquest of America*. Dallas: Southern Methodist University Press, 1949.

———. *Aristotle and the American Indians*. *Chicago*: Henry Regnery Company, 1959.

Herrera y Tordesillas, Antonio de. *General History of the Vast Continent and Islands of America*. Volume I. New York, N.Y.: AMS Press Inc, 1973.

Iñiguez, Diego Angulo. *El Gótico y el Renacimiento en las Antillas: Arquitectura, Escultura, Pintura, Azulejos, Orfebrería*. *Sevilla*: Escuela de Estudios Hispano-Americanos, 1947.

Jacobs, H.P. "The Spanish Period of Jamaican History: An Assessment of the Present State of Knowledge". *The Jamaican Historical Review* III, no. 1–3 (1957).

Keegan, William F. *Earliest Hispanic/Native American Interactions in the Caribbean*. Edited with and introduction by William F. Keegan. New York and London: Garland Publishing, Inc, 1991.

———. *The People who discovered Columbus: The Prehistory of the Bahamas*. Gainsville, FL: University Press of Florida, 1992.

———. *Taíno Myth and Practice: The Arrival of the Stranger King*. Gainesville: University Press of Florida, 2007.

Keegan, William F. and Lisabeth A. Carlson. *Talking Taíno: Caribbean Natural History from a Native Perspsective*. Tuscaloosa: The University of Alabama Press, 2008.

Keller, John E., ed. *Amadis of Gaul, Books I and II: A Novel of Chivalry of the 14th Century Presumably First Written in Spanish*. Revised and re-worked by Garci Rodríguez de Montalvo, prior to 1505, Translated from the Putative Princeps of Saragossa, 1508 by Edwin B. Place and Herbert C. Behm. Lexington, Kentucky: The University Press of Kentucky, 1974.

Kinney, Angela M., ed. *The Vulgate Bible: Volume IV: The Major Prophetical Works*. Translated by Douay-Rheims. Cambridge, MA: Harvard University Press, 2012.

León-Portilla, Miguel, ed. *The Broken Spears: The Aztec Account of the Conquest of Mexico*. Boston: Beacon Press, 1992.

Lockhart, James and Enrique Otte, eds. *Letters and People of the Spanish Indies Sixteenth Century*. Cambridge, UK: Cambridge University Press, 1976.

López de Gómara, Francisco. *Historia General de las Indias*. Barcelona: Linkgua ediciones, 2008.

Lovén, Sven. *Origins of the Tainan Culture, West Indies*. Göteborg, Sweden: Elanders Bokfryckeri Akfiebolag, 1935.

Macdonald, Lauren Elaine. "The Heronymites in Hispaniola, 1493–1519." A Thesis presented to the Graduate School of The University of Florida in partial fulfilment of the requirements for the degree of Master of Arts, University of Florida, 2010. http://ufdcimages.uflib.ufl.edu/UF/E0/04/21/73/00001/macdonald_l.pdf

Martínez, Cristian. *Tureiro: Areyto de la Tierra y el Cielo: Mitología Taína*. Santo Domingo, República Dominicana: Publicaciones del Banco Central, 2007.

Miura, Enrique Martínez. *La Música Precolombina: Un Debate Cultural después de 1492*. Barcelona: Ediciones Paidós Ibérica, 2004.

Montás, Onorio. *Arte Taíno*. Dominican Republic: Banco Central de la República Dominicana. Muñiz, Rafael González, 1999.

——. *Mi Pueblo Taíno: Un Recorrido por el Mundo de nuestros Indios Taínos de Borikén*. Colombia: Panamericana Formas e Impresos S.A, 2004.

Morison, Samuel Eliot. *Admiral of the Ocean Sea: A Life of Christopher Columbus*. Boston, MA: Little, Brown and Company, 1992.

Moure, Ramón Dacal and Manuel Rivero de la Calle. *Art and Archaeology of Pre-Columbian Cuba*. Pittsburgh: University of Pittsburgh Press, 1996.

Myers, Kathleen Ann. *Fernández de Oviedo's Chronicle of America: A New History for a New World*. Austin, TX: University of Texas Press, 2007.

Núñez Cabeza de Vaca, Alvar. *Chronicle of the Narváez Expedition*. Translated by Fanny Bandelier. London, England: Penguin Books, 2002.

Oliver, José. *Caciques and Cemí Idols: The Web Spun by Taíno Rulers between Hispaniola and Puerto Rico.* Tuscaloosa, AL: The University of Alabama Press, 2009.

Osborne S.J., Francis J., *History of the Catholic Church in Jamaica.* Aylesbury, Buckinghamshire: Caribbean Universities Press, 1997.

Padrón, Francisco Morales. *Primeras Cartas sobre América (1493–1503).* Sevilla, Spain: Secretariado de Publicaciones, Universidad de Sevilla, 1990.

——. *Spanish Jamaica.* Translated by Patrick E. Bryan. Kingston, Jamaica: Ian Randle Publishers, 2003.

Pagden, Anthony. *Hernán Cortés: Letters from Mexico.* Translated, edited with a new introduction by Anthony Pagden. New Haven: Yale University Press, 1986.

Pané, Fray Ramón. *An Account of the Antiquities of the Indians.* Durham and London: Duke University Press, 1999.

Parry, John H., and Robert G. Keith. *New Iberian World: A Documentary History of the Discovery and Settlement of Latin America to the Early 17th Century in Five Volumes: Volume II: The Caribbean.* New York: The New York Times Book Co., Inc, 1984.

Pérez-Mallaína, Pablo E. *Spain's Men of the Sea: Daily Life on the Indies Fleets in the Sixteenth Century.* Translated by Carla Rahn Phillips. Baltimore and London: The Johns Hopkins University Press, 1988.

Raphael, M. *A Documented History of the Franciscan Order: 1182–1517.* Part 1. Published by the author, Associate Professor of Church History, Catholic University Washington, DC, 1944.

Robinson, James. *Finer than Gold: Saints and Relics in the Middle Ages.* London: The British Museum Press, 2011.

Ross, Denison E. and Eileen Power, eds. *The Travels of Marco Polo.* London: Routledge & Kegan Paul Ltd, 1931.

Rouse, Irving. *The Taínos: Rise and Decline of the People who Greeted Columbus.* New Haven and London: Yale University Press, 1992.

Senior, Olive. *Encyclopaedia of Jamaican Heritage.* St Andrew, Jamaica: Twin Guinep Publishers Ltd, 2003.

Sherlock, Philip M. *The Aborigines of Jamaica*. Kingston: The Institute of Jamaica, 1939.

Sherlock, Philip and Hazel Bennett. *The Story of the Jamaican People*. Kingston: Ian Randle Publishers, 1998.

Sloane, Sir Hans. *A Voyage to the Islands Madera, Barbados, Nieves, S. Christophers and Jamaica, with the Natural History of the Herbs and Trees, Four-footed Beasts, Fishes, Birds, Insects, Reptiles, &c. of the Last of Those Islands*. 2 volumes. London: B.M. [Benjamin Motte] for the Author, 1660–1753.

Solá, Edwin Miner. *Diccionario Taíno Ilustrado*. Serie Puerto Rico Prehistórico Vol. 1. Puerto Rico: Edwin Miner Solá, 2002.

Stevens-Arroyo, Antonio M. *Cave of the Jagua: The Mythological World of the Taínos*. Scranton: University of Scranton Press, 2006.

Tanna, Laura. *Jamaican Folk Tales and Oral Histories*. Miami and Kingston: DLT Associates Inc, 2000.

Thomas, Hugh. *Rivers of Gold: The Rise and Fall of the Spanish Empire*. London, England: Penguin Books, 2003.

Tibesar, Antonine S. "The Franciscan Province of the Holy Cross of Española, 1505–1559." *The Americas* 13, no. 4, (April 1957): 377–89. Catholic University of America Press on behalf of the Academy of American Franciscan History.

Tyler, Lyman S. *Two Worlds: The Indian Encounter with the European, 1492–1509*. Salt Lake City: University of Utah Press, 1988.

Vigneras, Louis, André. "Diego Méndez, Secretary of Christopher Columbus and Aguacil Mayor of Santo Domingo: A Biographical Sketch." *The Hispanic American Historical Review* 58, no. 4 (November 1978): 676–96.

Wilson, Samuel M. *The Archaeology of the Caribbean*. Cambridge: Cambridge University Press, 2007.

——. *Hispaniola: Caribbean Chiefdoms in the Age of Columbus*. Tuscaloosa and London: The University of Alabama Press, 1990.

——. *The Indigenous People of the Caribbean*. Gainesville, FL: University Press of Florida, 1997.

Woodward, Robyn. "Sevilla la Nueva" in *Xaymaca: Life in Spanish Jamaica: 1494–1655*. By Rebecca Tortello and Jonathan Greenland. Kingston, the Institute of Jamaica, 2009.

Wright, I.A. "The Early History of Jamaica (1511–36)." *The English Historical Review* XXXVI, no. CXLI (1921): 70–95.

Wynter, Sylvia. "New Seville and the Conversion Experience of Bartolomé de las Casas." *Jamaica Journal* 17, no. 2 (May 1984): 25–32.

———. "New Seville and the Conversion Experience of Bartolomé de las Casas." *Jamaica Journal* 17, no. 3 (August–October 1984): 46–55.

Yupanqui, Titu Cusi. *An Inca Account of the Conquest of Peru.* Translated by Ralph Bauer. Boulder, Colorado: The University Press of Colorado, 2005.

Illustrations & Photographs

Huareo, copy of acrylic painting by Lloyd George Rodney, copyright © Fred W. Kennedy, used as front cover of book.

Ships of Christopher Columbus at Sea, with copyright permission of Library of Congress, used as back cover of book.

Image of water motif, copyright © Sarah Elise Kennedy, designed from Bird Figure, *cojoba* stand with turtle at base, p. vii. It is used throughout the novel as a section divider within chapters.

Family Tree of Huareo, copyright © Fred W. Kennedy, p. viii.

Image of *tona*, copyright © Sarah Elise Kennedy, p. 1. It is used at start of each of four sections of the novel.

The Island of Yamaye with names of Taíno Chiefdoms <1509, map copyright © Fred W. Kennedy, designed by Mapping Specialists Ltd., p. 2.

Dujo, image copyright © The Trustees of British Museum. Location of artefact: British Museum, London, Great Britain, p. 137.

Boinayel, image copyright © The Trustees of British Museum. Location of artefact: British Museum, London, Great Britain, p. 137.

Boinayel, copyright © The Trustees of the British Museum / Art Resource, NY Wooden figure. Taíno, 1200-1500. Used for the ritual inhalation of a hallucinogenic substance called *cojoba*, was found in a cave in the Carpenter mountains in Jamaica. Wood, 40 x 17 cm. Location: British Museum, London, Great Britain, p. 138.

Yocajú Bagua Maórocoti, image copyright © The Metropolitan Museum of Art. Image source: Art Resource, NY. Three-Cornered Stone with Face. Dominican Republic; Taíno. 13th-15th century. Limestone fossiliferous. Height 6-3/4 in. (17.1 cm). Purchase, Oscar de la Renta Gift, 1997 (1997.35.2).

Location: The Metropolitan Museum of Art, New York, NY, USA, p. 139.

Hatuey, copyright © Sarah Elise Kennedy, drawing based on the historical monument of Hatuey, Baracoa, Cuba. p. 140.

Macocael, photograph of petroglyph, Lluidas Vale Caves, St. Catherine, Jamaica, copyright © J. Pauel, Jamaican Caves Organization. p. 141.

Baibrama, image copyright © The Trustees of the British Museum / Art Resource, NY. Wooden figure. Taíno, 1200-1500, found in a cave in the Carpenter Mountains in Jamaica. Wood, 40 x 17 cm. Inv. Location: British Museum, London, Great Britain, p. 142.

Colour engraving by Theodore de Bry (1528-1598). From *"Americae Tertia IV"*, 1594. Image copyright © The Metropolitan Museum of Art. Image source: Art Resource, NY. p. 143.

Carving of Bird (pelican) with *cojoba* **platform,** copyright © Valerie Facey. Photo credit: Kent Reid. Location of artefact: Jamaican Taíno Culture, Collection: National Gallery of Jamaica, Kingston, Jamaica. p. 144.

The Landing of Columbus at Puerto Bueno, copyright © The Institute of Jamaica. Image appears on p. 29 in *Columbus and the Discovery of Jamaica* by Frank Cundall, The Institute of Jamaica, 1894: Kingston, Jamaica. p. 145.

Cemí **wood carving on staff,** copyright © Valerie Facey. Photo credit: Kent Reid. Location: Jamaican Taíno Culture, Collection: National Gallery of Jamaica, Kingston, Jamaica. p. 146.

Taíno pictographs, image copyright © Fred W. Kennedy. Location: Mountain River Cave, Jamaica, p. 147.

Opiyelguobirán, image copyright © Smithsonian Institution, Washington. Location of Taíno artefact: Smithsonian Institution. p. 148.

Hatuey, copyright © Art Resource, NY. A Carmelite monk attempts to convert Hatuey, Taíno cacique, to Christianity just before his execution by burning at stake on February 2, 1512. Artist: anonymous, 16th century. p. 149.

Neptune Stone, Frieze of Spanish Church at Sevilla la Nueva, image copyright © Robyn Woodward. Unknown artist: 1524–1534. First published, *Xaymaca* (2009), p. 20. Artefact, property of National Heritage Trust. p. 150.

Sevilla la Nueva 1509-1535, map copyright © Fred W. Kennedy. Designed by Mapping Specialists Ltd., p. 152.

The Island of Santiago called Jamaica 1525, map copyright © Fred W. Kennedy. Designed by Mapping Specialists Ltd., p. 208.